Plain Words

Plain Words

A Guide to the Use of English

Ernest Gowers

Revised and updated by Rebecca Gowers

PARTICULAR BOOKS
an imprint of
PENGUIN BOOKS

PARTICULAR BOOKS

Published by the Penguin Group
Penguin Books Ltd, 80 Strand, London WC2R 0RL, England
Penguin Group (USA) Inc., 375 Hudson Street, New York, New York 10014, USA
Penguin Group (Canada), 90 Eglinton Avenue East, Suite 700, Toronto, Ontario,
Canada M4P 2Y3 (a division of Pearson Penguin Canada Inc.)
Penguin Ireland, 25 St Stephen's Green, Dublin 2, Ireland
(a division of Penguin Books Ltd)
Penguin Group (Australia), 707 Collins Street, Melbourne, Victoria 3008, Australia
(a division of Pearson Australia Group Pty Ltd)
Penguin Books India Pvt Ltd, 11 Community Centre,
Panchsheel Park, New Delhi – 110 017, India
Penguin Group (NZ), 67 Apollo Drive, Rosedale, Auckland 0632, New Zealand
(a division of Pearson New Zealand Ltd)
Penguin Books (South Africa) (Pty) Ltd, Block D, Rosebank Office Park,
181 Jan Smuts Avenue, Parktown North, Gauteng 2193, South Africa

Penguin Books Ltd, Registered Offices: 80 Strand, London WC2R 0RL, England

www.penguin.com

First published in Particular Books 2014
001

Text revisions and updates © Rebecca Gowers, 2014

The moral right of the reviser has been asserted

Set in 10.5/13.5pt Adobe Caslon Pro
Typeset by Jouve (UK), Milton Keynes
Printed in Great Britain by Clays Ltd, St Ives plc

A CIP catalogue record for this book is available from the British Library

ISBN: 978-0-141-97553-5

www.greenpenguin.co.uk

MIX
Paper from
responsible sources
FSC
www.fsc.org   FSC® C018179

Penguin Books is committed to a sustainable
future for our business, our readers and our planet.
This book is made from Forest Stewardship
Council™ certified paper.

CONTENTS

PREFACE

Ernest Gowers was born in 1880 into a well-heeled London family. His father, Sir William Gowers, was a celebrated neurologist, one of the founders of the discipline, whose immense body of work on the subject is today described by Oliver Sacks as 'matchless'. But this work—minute, illustrated observations of disorders ranging from syphilis to writer's cramp—was not the only comprehensive record he left behind. He also kept delightful accounts of all the larks and entertainments that he provided for Ernest and his siblings. They went to the river for steamer rides, to Lord's for the cricket, to the Zoo to see Jumbo the Elephant, and to the Egyptian Hall for performances by the amazing automaton artist, Zoe. They took in magic displays where people's heads were cut off, ladies disappeared and electric storms ripped round the room. They even visited the famous Wild West show, where Annie Oakley shot glass balls out of the air while Buffalo Bill commanded massed ranks of rough riders.

But these pleasures were hard earned. William Gowers's own upbringing had been impoverished by comparison. His father, a Hackney bootmaker, died when William was only eleven, catapulting the boy into a world marked by graveyards, gun shops and gelatine factories. This misfortune for the child, compounded by the death of all his siblings, seems to have led him to seize almost with desperation on whatever chances came his way. There is scant record of his early education, but he started his career in medicine aged sixteen as the apprentice of a country doctor, at the same time studying by correspondence for the London University matriculation. Diaries he kept at the time show him to have been exhausted and sometimes harrowed by this existence, one requiring an effort of will on his part of a kind we now associate with the young Charles Dickens. And it is therefore perhaps little surprise that when the time came—beyond the cowboys and elephants and other jollifications—Dr Gowers would take great care over the formal education of his sons.

Ernest Gowers was sent to Rugby in 1895. He went on to read Classics at Cambridge, and in 1903 passed what was by then a genuinely competitive exam for the Home Civil Service. Though he also soon afterwards qualified as a barrister, he did not take up law. Instead, he remained in the Civil Service, advancing rapidly, until in 1911 he was appointed Principal Private Secretary to Lloyd George, then Chancellor of the Exchequer.

This was, as Gowers would later recall, a stormy period in which to take up post. Lloyd George was attempting against the odds to usher a 'socialist' National Insurance Bill through Parliament: he faced virulent public opposition, not least from the British Medical Association and the Northcliffe Press. And getting the Bill passed was merely the start. In short order, Gowers found himself one of a crack team of young civil servants charged with the immense task of making the resulting Act work. These young men were nicknamed the 'loan collection' because they had been drawn from across several departments, but Gowers called them a 'desperate remedy'. Not only were they being asked to implement from scratch an entire system of health and unemployment insurance, and somehow to explain its complexities clearly to the public, but they were also being required to do so in a matter of months. Difficult as this task was, however, those to whom it had fallen would soon view it as having been good preparation for the yet greater challenges that came with the outbreak of war.

In 1914 most members of the loan collection were reassigned.

Though Gowers continued to work at Wellington House, the building where the National Insurance Commission was based, this was now a front: 'Wellington House' became the code name for a covert propaganda unit. Gowers started as its General Manager, but within a year had risen to the position of Chief Executive Officer. The job of the unit was to make the case for going to war. Many writers secretly agreed to give their services, among them H. G. Wells, J. M. Barrie, Sir Arthur Conan Doyle, John Buchan, Arnold Bennett, A. C. Benson, Robert Bridges, G. K. Chesterton, John Galsworthy, Sir Arthur Quiller-Couch, Henry James, Hilaire Belloc, Rudyard Kipling and Thomas Hardy. A. S. Watt, the prominent literary agent, was drawn in both as an adviser and as a go-between conducting undercover negotiations with sympathetic publishing houses. It was important to the credibility of the works sponsored by the unit—initially books and pamphlets, in many languages—that its existence should remain unknown. Within nine months 'Wellington House' had more than ninety titles in print, with two and a half million copies of these titles circulating at home and abroad.

When the war ended, Gowers was appointed permanent head of the Department of Mines; his working life between the wars would be almost entirely devoted to coal. He was knighted for these labours, but found the work intensely frustrating. The coal owners left him, he said, in 'despair': he described the 'force of self-interest' among them as 'centrifugal'. He was relieved, therefore, in the aftermath of the General Strike, to be given three years as Chairman of the Board of Inland Revenue. There he began a campaign to ensure that tax officials should seem approachable and should be easy to understand in their letters to taxpayers. But he was soon returned to coal.

Only when the Second World War loomed would Gowers again be diverted, asked to give some of his time to planning for civil defence. Then, very shortly after the war began, he was appointed Senior Regional Commissioner for London. What this meant in practice was that for almost the whole of the war, and the worst of the Blitz, he coordinated the civil defence of the capital.

His base was a bunker beneath the Geological Survey Office at the Natural History Museum. Churchill's instructions to him were daunting: 'If communication with the Government becomes very difficult or impossible, it may be necessary for you to act on behalf of the Government . . . without consultation with ministers.' In this event—particularly if the Government had fled London— it would be Gowers's duty to govern the city directly himself. Its seven million people would be his responsibility, and he could order any emergency measures he thought fit. 'Such action, duly recorded,' explained Churchill, 'will be supported by the Government, and the Government will ask Parliament to give you whatever indemnification may subsequently be found neces- sary.' Gowers speculated in a speech of 1943 that if he were ever forced to assume these powers, the matter would end with him dangling from a lamp post. His bunker was supplied with three separately laid telephone lines, and he could only hope that they would never all be blown up at once.

Gowers wrote after the Blitz, 'Everyone expected that we should infallibly be bombed like hell', but noted that, despite this, when the war actually began, London was 'thoroughly unprepared' because 'what had to be prepared for was unknown'. If it was impossible to work out in advance all the measures that would be needed in any attempt to counter the damage done by the bombing, it was equally impossible to grasp ahead of time the huge administrative challenge of implementing these measures. Gowers was forced to take swift decisions in what he called 'hide- ous' and 'desolating' circumstances with very little useful precedent to guide him; but he would come to be praised for the inspiringly imperturbable way in which he went about his duties as

Commissioner. When he wrote later about his admiration for the Londoners he had served, he said simply this, 'We withstood'.

Gowers, writing in the midst of war, described himself as 'but a transient and embarrassed phantom flitting across the stage of history'. Once the war had ended, his name was added to a Treasury list of those increasingly referred to as 'the Great and the Good', people who were thought suitable for such posts as chairing advisory committees and Royal Commissions. Several of these appointments came his way in quick succession. He chaired the New Town Development Corporation for Harlow, one of the towns built to relieve homelessness among London's bombed-out East Enders. He also chaired a wide array of committees. One investigated allowing women to join the Foreign Service; another, shop opening hours; a third, the preservation of historic houses; a fourth, measures to combat foot-and-mouth disease. Most prominently, though, starting in 1949, he chaired a Royal Commission into Capital Punishment. The Commission was asked to consider whether there were rational arguments for imposing tighter limits on Britain's use of the death penalty, but Gowers controversially breached these terms in the Commission's report, where he raised the idea that the best policy might be—as he found himself passionately believing—to abolish it altogether.

PLAIN WORDS

Gowers undertook his many chairmanships at the same time as doing the work for which he was destined to be best remembered. He had spoken out about baroque official English at least as early as 1929, when he remarked in a speech that he gave on civil servants:

> 'It is said: first, that we thirst for power over our fellow-men and lose no opportunity of sapping the freedom of the public

by extending the tentacles of bureaucracy; secondly, that in our administration we are unimaginative, rigid, cumbrous, and inelastic; and thirdly, that we revel in jargon and obscurity'.

Gowers agreed at least in part with these criticisms, and he returned to the theme in a talk that he gave in 1943 to civil defence workers. There had been a fear, once a lull set in after the Blitz at the start of the war, that the various civil defence services would be unable to keep their members at 'concert pitch' against further aerial bombardment (which was indeed to come). Gowers's talk was one of many designed to entertain these workers and keep them from getting too 'browned off'. He pointed out to his audience with humorous regret that, in the innumerable circulars they all received daily, examples of verbal 'mistiness and grandiloquence' were 'as plentiful as blackberries', and argued for a new style of official writing, both friendly and easy to understand. These comments caught the attention of Whitehall, and three years later the Treasury invited him to produce a training manual for civil servants on the art of writing plain English.

The slim volume that Gowers first produced on the subject was deemed by those who had commissioned it to be a success, so much so that the idea was mooted that it should now be published as a book for general sale. Gowers was offered a flat fee of £500—normal for the time and even generous by Treasury standards. But he demurred, turning for advice to his old friend A. S. Watt, the literary agent with whom he had worked secretly on propaganda during the First World War. With Watt's encouragement, Gowers asked instead for a royalty. The Treasury was enormously displeased by what would come to be characterised as his wish to have a 'flutter'. Letters went back and forth. Acid remarks were scribbled in the margins of file notes. When at last Gowers won the day, the decision was unprecedented. One of those negotiating with him wrote to him in a letter, 'Like you,

I hate arguments about money—although I must admit you do it frightfully well'.

Plain Words was first published in April 1948 by His Majesty's Stationery Office, which crucially had access to paper supplies. By Christmas the book had gone through seven reprints, selling more than 150,000 copies. The Treasury, surprised and encouraged by this, asked Gowers to write a new book, an *ABC of Plain Words*, designed as a reference manual with its entries arranged in alphabetical order. When this work came out in 1951, it too was a success, again taking the Treasury by surprise. Nearly 80,000

H.M. Stationery Office.
Dear Sirs,
    Re your announcement of the 20th ult., I am directed to state that it would be definitely appreciated if you would give active consideration to my recent application of the 15th inst. for the despatch of one copy of the publication "Plain Words."

Taxes, May 1948

copies sold in the first year alone, even as the earlier work continued to sell: by this point Gowers's 'flutter' had netted him roughly ten times the sum the Treasury had first offered. But though the *ABC* did well, Gowers was unhappy with its layout, believing it to be an awkward fit with his more discursive notes on style. The best answer, all agreed, would be to find a way to combine the *ABC* with the original *Plain Words*, creating a new book under the title *The Complete Plain Words*. When this third, definitive version of Gowers's work came out in 1954, it was yet again swiftly a bestseller, rapidly taking the total sale of the 'Plain Words' titles to well over half a million copies. Remarkably, it has remained in print ever since.

In 1951, after an approach from Oxford University Press, Gowers agreed in principle to be 'a sort of ganger' overseeing a party of workers engaged in the monumental task of revising Henry Fowler's idiosyncratic classic, *A Dictionary of Modern English Usage*. After hesitations that lasted half a decade, OUP went further and asked Gowers to be the editor. He accepted this commission at the age of seventy-six and finished the job when he was eighty-five. A year after his edition of Fowler was published, Gowers died of throat cancer caused by a lifetime of smoking. Not long before, however, in an interview with the *New Yorker*, he remarked with typical good humour that although living such a long life was 'all rather deplorable', his recent labours had given him 'rather the sensation'—an agreeable one, he admitted—that he would be going out with 'a bang'.*

---

* This account of the life and work of Ernest Gowers and of his father draws both on a private family archive of documents, and on the writings of Ann Scott in her books *William Richard Gowers 1845–1915: Exploring the Victorian Brain* (Oxford University Press, 2012), written with neurologists Mervyn Eadie and Andrew Lees; and *Ernest Gowers: Plain Words and Forgotten Deeds* (Palgrave Macmillan, 2009).

THE COMPLETE PLAIN WORDS REVISED

Had Gowers survived a little longer after revising Fowler's work, he might have revised his own. He had discussed the idea with his publisher, writing, 'there is quite a lot in the book that I should like to alter'. But with his death, *The Complete Plain Words* languished, and it was several years before another civil servant, Sir Bruce Fraser, was invited to take on the job. In Fraser's preface to the second edition, published in 1973, he called Gowers's work elegant, witty and 'eminently sensible', and explained that he had tried to keep the flavour and spirit of the original. In a line he threw into Gowers's own prologue, Fraser compared 'flat and clear' writing to 'honest bread and butter', and warned against spreading it with either the 'jam' of eloquence, or the 'engine-grease' of obvious toil.

There was no question, two decades on, that the book needed an overhaul, and Fraser had a good go at it, supplying some excellent new jokes ('I have discussed the question of stocking the proposed poultry plant with my colleagues'). But in his cheery assault on the text, he went considerably beyond the bread-and-butter plainness that he himself advocated. He introduced into the book the phrase 'the guerdon of popular usage', spoke of 'flatulent' writing, and described Hemingway's imitators as sounding as though they were 'grunting'. Where Gowers had written about the attraction between certain pairs of words, Fraser wrote of words that 'walk out with other charmers'. He coined the needless term 'pompo-verbosity', only to contrast it (to no understandable effect) with 'verbopomp'; and in order to shoehorn 'verbopomp' into the text, he took out 'Micawberite', a word Gowers had used, not unreasonably, after quoting Mr Micawber.* So it went on. Towards the end of his edition, Fraser threw in a

* See p. 120, footnote.

sentence criticising writing that reminded him of 'an incompetent model flaunting a new dress rather than a sensible woman wearing one'. But he himself was far from a perfect match for his imaginary sensible woman.

The most unfortunate single sentence that Fraser added to the book, one for which there is no evidence Gowers would have felt the slightest sympathy, was this:

> Homosexuals are working their way through our vocabulary at an alarming rate: for some time now we have been unable to describe our more eccentric friends as *queer*, or our more lively ones as *gay*, without risk of misunderstanding, and we have more recently had to give up calling our more nimble ones *light on their feet*.

Fraser first makes the vocabulary of English 'ours' and not 'theirs', then imperiously blames homosexuals for hijacking 'our' vocabulary. Even had this claim to ownership of the language been legitimate, the blame was misconceived: the word *queer* only came to mean 'homosexual' because those whom he calls 'we' made it a derogatory term, while 'light on his feet' was an insult designed to imply that a man was suspiciously good at dancing. For all that, the second edition of *The Complete Plain Words* was a success, and many readers preferred it to what came next.

The third edition, published in 1986, and edited by the linguist Sidney Greenbaum and the lexicographer Janet Whitcut, showed evidence not of Fraser's 'jam' so much as of the 'engine-grease' that he considered equally dangerous. It was Greenbaum and Whitcut's idea of being judicious, for example, to amend Fraser's comment above so that it now began: 'Homosexuals and lesbians are working their way through our vocabulary at an alarming rate ...'. It is hard to imagine one editor making this change, let alone a second agreeing to it. It is even harder to imagine lesbians being grateful for the nod.

Greenbaum and Whitcut revised directly from Fraser; they seem never to have considered reinstating material from the original that Fraser had cut. Among other drawbacks, this led to ever greater confusion in the matter of voice. Fraser had said of Gowers's friendly use of *I* that it 'would clearly be wrong to flatten the tone of his book by depersonalising his views'. Fraser therefore simply threw in his own *I* and lofty *we* as well, roughly indicating in his preface which parts of the second edition were his alone. But Greenbaum and Whitcut found this too much, and in the third edition did systematically depersonalise the writing. Gowers's 'I like to think' becomes their 'it would be pleasing to think', and so on. Elsewhere, they substituted their own *we*.

It is true that there were two of them, but this change had unhappy results. First, they effectively appropriated Gowers's role as author—to show their approval, they explained, of what he had said. Second, with their *we* spread far and wide, they introduced a coercive, patronising tone into the third edition. Gowers himself had sometimes used *we*, but when he did he almost always meant 'you the reader and I the person writing this sentence' (e.g. when he says of certain types of adverbs, 'we have all seen them used on innumerable occasions'). Greenbaum and Whitcut, by contrast, regularly deployed *we* as here: 'We are to prefer, in fact, *conclude* rather than "reach a conclusion" . . .'. The advice may be good, but Gowers would never have dreamed of expressing it this way. The tone of *we are to prefer* is what he called 'chilly' (and fought against: see p. 19). The words *in fact*, as used here, he would have struck out as padding (see pp. 112–18). *We are to prefer X rather than Y* is unidiomatic (see p. 69) and therefore needlessly risks distracting the reader (see p. 36). Gowers would have written of preferring word X *to* phrase Y. And *rather than*, being a longer way of saying *to*, is a waste of paper (see p. 24). In short, Greenbaum and Whitcut were so far immune to the advice of the book they were editing that they managed to violate four of its precepts in half a sentence.

Their other main change to the book's written style may have been a better idea, but it was one they also failed to implement convincingly. Though they kept in the advice that said (in their own wording) 'you may sometimes find it least clumsy to follow the traditional use of *he*, *him* and *his* to include both sexes', they set about removing this use from the text. No doubt they recognised it as fusty. Yet their campaign was erratic. On some pages they substituted indigestible spates of *he or she*; on others, they left *he* to stand, as though the effort of changing it suddenly defeated them. And where they rewrote whole sentences to get round the problem, the results could be leaden. As an example, Gowers had opened with the remark that: 'Writing is an instrument for conveying ideas from one mind to another; the writer's job is to make his reader apprehend his meaning readily and precisely'. Under Greenbaum and Whitcut, this became 'the writers' job is to make the readers apprehend the meaning readily and precisely'.

The second and third editions obscured more than Gowers's authorial voice. When Fraser revised the book in 1973, he also stripped out a great many of the examples Gowers had given of poorly handled English, not because the substitute examples were clearer or more helpful, but because Fraser hoped to do away with the original version's 'dated air'. The effect of this, naturally enough—with brand-new references to Edward Heath and the expanded EEC—was to give the work a 1970s air instead, which it kept through the third edition. It is inevitable that in the twenty-first century this improvement has become the literary equivalent of brown varnish.

THE RELEVANCE OF THE ORIGINAL BOOK TODAY

The first step towards restoring *The Complete Plain Words* has therefore been to do away with all the jam and engine grease. The fourth edition disregards the third and second, and instead directly revises the first. It also reverts to Gowers's preferred title, *Plain Words*: he confessed late in life that he thought adding '*The Complete*' had made it sound 'ridiculous'. Most of his examples of bungled writing are now back in, in the hope that the 1940s world the reader once again glimpses will no longer seem drab and disheartening, but rather will add to the interest of the book. It is not now perhaps so tiresome to come upon references to withdrawn garments, coupons and requisitioning; to German prisoners marrying local girls; to the Trading with the Enemy Act, or the fear inspired by blister-gas bombs. Mention of the stop-me-and-buy-one man selling ice creams from the back of his tricycle may even have a certain charm. What is more, some of the concerns of the original book face us anew. We too have 'our present economic difficulties'. We too wrestle with deficits and the problems of youth unemployment. A debate continues over whether mothers should be 'constrained' to go out to work. And sadly it still strikes home to read of a 'growth of mistrust of intellectual activities that have no immediate utilitarian result'. Even strictures on wasting paper are once again a feature of the times, though in 1954 paper shortages were a continuing consequence of the war.

Many of the quotations chosen by Gowers to demonstrate poor handling of English were drawn from documents he had encountered in his work, and so we read in passing of National Insurance, tax instructions, coal, New Town legislation, and whether or not it is suitable to execute women by hanging. But though there are also numerous references to the Second World War, his own record is only glancingly touched on when, in an entry about the Blitz, he strikes a sudden personal note: 'I used to think during the war when I heard that gas mains had been affected by a raid that it would have been more sensible to say that they had been broken'. Even here, the uninformed reader would have no way of knowing that the author of this stray comment had himself led the organisation responsible for ensuring that those 'affected' gas mains were mended again.

In the *Penguin Dictionary of Troublesome Words* (1984), Bill Bryson draws on *The Complete Plain Words* for an example of misused commas found in a wartime instruction booklet for airmen training in Canada. The booklet's author had argued for learning to use clear English by warning that, 'Pilots, whose minds are dull, do not usually live long'. Bryson caps this with the comment, 'Removing the commas would convert a sweeping insult into sound advice'. Gowers's own comment had been, 'The commas convert a truism into an insult'. The shift from one to the other may seem negligible—Gowers's deadpan 'truism' becomes Bryson's more anodyne 'sound advice'. But this strongly marks a difference of historical perspective: Gowers's barb is that of a man for whom the survival of Allied pilots had very recently been a matter of the greatest importance in the fight to keep German bombers from reaching London.

Nor is Gowers's sardonic reflection on the value of clear English at a time of catastrophic bombing raids on the capital quite as irrelevant today as one might wish. After terrorist outrages in the city in July 2005, the public transport system came to a halt, people were forced to walk for miles, and the city's hospitals were overrun. While the Blitz spirit of its citizens was immediately vaunted in the press, the coroner subsequently charged with investigating the bombings found that there had been delays in caring for some of the victims because those working for the different emergency services had been unable to understand one another's jargon. The coroner's report contains what Gowers would doubt-less also have considered a truism: 'In a life-threatening situation everyone should be able to understand what everyone else is saying'. It is disturbing to discover that the official response to this comment was the promise that a 'best practice' 'Emergency Responder Interoperability Lexicon' with 'additional user-relevant information', though not 'mandated', would nevertheless be 'cascaded' through various training courses.

If that seems impenetrable, what of the English used by the broad range of today's civil servants? Does their language also evince functional non-interoperability, and might they too, therefore, still benefit from a little advice in the spirit of *Plain Words*?

Apparently so. Representatives of the Local Government Association have grown so exasperated by official jargon that they have taken to publishing an annual list of what they optimistically call 'banned' words, ones the LGA would like to see eliminated from all documents put before the public. The list is enormous, and includes *informatics, hereditament, beaconicity, centricity, clienting, disbenefits* and *braindump*. As for the question of written style in the Civil Service, not long ago the *Daily Mail* raged against a government minister who had seen fit to waste time concocting an expensive report for 'mandarins' on how to write a straight-forward letter. This report, according to the *Mail*, was filled with 'excruciatingly pedantic' warnings against, for instance, the use of meaningless adverbs, and of passive fillers such as *it is essential to note that*.

Gowers, in this book, agrees with both suggestions. They conform to what would become his most widely quoted maxim: 'Be short, be simple, be human'. And whatever the *Mail* thinks, this maxim is still quoted today, even where Gowers himself is forgotten. Harrogate Borough Council, for example, prints it uncredited as a tag at the bottom of every page of its guide to using clear English, a booklet with the uncapitalised title *put it plainly*.

Merely printing the tag is not enough, of course. To carry out what it proposes requires thought. This is demonstrated by Harrogate Council's own Corporate Management Team, who declare in what they call an 'endorsement' of the guide, 'Better then to write as if we were speaking to the recipient of our communication'. Though shortish, this sentence is neither simple, with its inflated vocabulary, nor human, with its patronising 'we'. Had the team absorbed Gowers's maxim, which they print thirty-one times in their manual, they might instead have said, 'When you write to someone, use a plain and friendly style'.

In March 1948, in a debate in Parliament on 'Government English', Mr Keeling, representing Twickenham, revealed that important official documents had been discovered to be incomprehensible to the general public. He argued that unless something was done about this, the business of various departments would fall into disrepute. He then welcomed the fact that *Plain Words* was about to be published, and hoped that it would help. Mr Pritt, Hammersmith North, could not resist a cutting response: 'I have often wondered what the Tory party were interested in. They are not interested in getting anything done. But when we are talking about words their attendance is doubled—there are about seven of them'.

It may surprise the modern reader that Gowers soon found himself criticised for being too liberal in his advice: he discovered for himself, what he would later be told by one of the OUP 'scrutineers' who helped him to revise Fowler, that he would have to 'mediate between the old hatters and the mad hatters'. The old hatters were disgruntled by his willingness in *Plain Words* to break what they considered 'the rules', even as the mad hatters interpreted his advice to write plainly as an example of 'the snobbishness of the educated'. Meanwhile in odd corners of

Whitehall much was made of the impropriety of encouraging junior civil servants to be plain with their superiors.

Though Gowers wrote about 'rules', he made it clear that he understood them as conventions. His view in sum was this: 'Public opinion decides all these questions in the long run. There is little individuals can do about them. Our national vocabulary is a democratic institution, and what is generally accepted will ultimately be correct'. How long a given rule might stand was anybody's guess. He therefore advised civil servants, who must write comprehensible English for unknown readers, that they should neither 'perpetuate what is obsolescent' nor 'give currency to what is novel', but should 'follow what is generally regarded . . . as the best practice for the time being'.

BRINGING *PLAIN WORDS* UP TO DATE

That is all very well, but who can say what current 'best practice' is? Old hatters and mad hatters continue to broadcast their views. Some believe that Good English, bounded by antique superstitions, is their birthright, to be fought for with the ardour of the Light Brigade at Balaclava. Others dismiss so-called 'good' so-called 'English' as a risible manifestation of elitism. It is daunting to have to pick a path between these two camps, yet a fresh revision of *Plain Words* must do just that. Gowers once remarked that if a person were forced to choose, 'it would be better to be ungrammatical and intelligible than grammatical and unintelligible', only to add, 'But we do not have to choose between the two'. Perhaps this new edition of his book is best thought of as being for those who instinctively agree, but who seek guidance on the prevailing conventions—so far as they can be discovered—of clear, formal prose.

When Gowers's work first came out, he was praised by *The Times* for his 'sweetly reasonable' advice, and by the *Daily Telegraph*

News Chronicle, 14 April 1948

for a prose style that was 'itself a model of how plain words should be used'. After sixty years, it has of course been necessary here and there to modernise both his advice and his writing, and I have attempted to do so, but lightly. There are instances in the original where Gowers's style no longer stands. He starts sentences with the word *nay*, says the trouble *about* X, and that a railway clerk telephoned *to* him. He writes of a subject that *has not* a true antecedent, and of a person's need to make sure he knows *what are* his rights of appeal. None of this sounds quite right any more, and so I have made small changes—what the managers of the London Underground call 'upgrade works'. Habits of punctuation and spelling have also altered over the decades. Gowers's *to-day*, *jig-saw*, *mother-tongue* and *danger-signal* become *today*, *jigsaw*, *mother tongue* and *danger signal*; *acknowledgment* and *connexion* become *acknowledgement* and *connection*, etc. His fondness for semicolons, which was striking when he wrote, is even more striking today. Though I am fond of them too, and have left many in place, I have removed about a hundred from the book. There are various misquotations in the original that I have attempted to correct, and I have also very slightly reordered the contents where this makes the line of argument clearer.

Then there is the matter, mentioned earlier, of the use of *he*, *him* and *his* to stand for everyone. In the line referred to above, 'make sure he knows what are his rights of appeal', Gowers happened to be invoking the taxpayer; and in 1954 (though of course women also paid taxes) it was standard to use an indeterminate *he* to do so. There are those who still use this 'makeshift expedient', as it is called later in these pages, but there are others who would never think of it, and yet others who reject it on purpose. (Anyone who vaguely assumed of the London coroner mentioned above that she was a man, or who wrongly imagined likewise of the government minister excoriated by the *Daily Mail* that she was a man, must concede that supposedly neutral terms are not necessarily neutral in practice.) In 1965 Gowers admitted that he had spent 'an awfully long time' worrying over how to revise what he considered Fowler's old-fashioned pronouncements in this area. Half a century on, opinions have moved further still. The indeterminate masculine pronoun, which Gowers eventually settled on calling a 'risk', is now so widely taken to be in breach of the very friendliness that he so keenly advocated, that I have removed all examples of the use from his writing.

Few revisers faced with decisions of this kind can be so lucky as to have a manifesto by the original author to draw on, but Gowers's preface to his revisions of Fowler provided me with just such a guide. OUP had instructed him to keep as much of Fowler's original work as possible, but asked him to remove any false predictions, and to make sure that no dead horses were being flogged. Gowers wrote in his preface: 'I have been chary of making any substantial alterations except for the purpose of bringing him up to date'. And this has been my approach too.

The saddest instance of a false assumption made by Gowers is found in a defence he gave of the word *ideology*. He believed it to be a useful alternative to *creed*, 'now that people no longer care enough about religion to fight, massacre and enslave one another to secure the forms of its observance'. A few remarks of this kind, and the odd digression that is no longer apropos, I have quietly edited out of the text. I have also removed examples of obsolete advice, such as that a *casualty* is properly an accident and not the accident's victim. But though it was easy to class various small points of this kind as dead horses, where I could not feel sure, I chose to be cautious.

If I have left advice in the book that strikes readers as superfluous, I hope they will feel pleased that they did not need to be told rather than cross that they were. And if some of the current abuses that I mention go rapidly out of date, hurrah for that too. Many people who argue that 'correctness' is not of the utmost or even 'upmost' importance will still flinch at 'organisationalised suboptimalism', and agree that it is worth resisting new words of the type that Gowers called 'repulsive etymologically'.

In this edition of *Plain Words*, I, other than in these few paragraphs of the Preface, is always Ernest Gowers's authorial voice. Any interjection of mine, designed to bring a subject up to date, is clearly marked as a 'Note', or is a footnote, and finishes with a tilde glyph: ~.

Of course a person revising a usage guide lives in fear of being caught out and found wanting. In his private letters, Gowers wrote anxiously of captious, zestful critics waiting to pick out

errors in his work.* I have had scrutineers of my own attempting
to save me from this fate, to whom I am extremely grateful, but
all flaws of revision in these pages remain my responsibility alone.
I do not doubt that I will be thought of by today's old hatters as
a mad hatter, and by today's mad hatters as an old hatter, and by
both, probably, as a bad hatter: because I dared to tinker with a
much loved work, because I bothered to do so, because I did not
tinker with it enough. And there is no way to proof oneself against
all these objections at once. But what I can say is that in revising
a book known over decades for making people smile, my greatest
wish was that it should continue to do so a little longer.

For the sheer hard work on this project by many of them, and
the encouragement given to me by all, I would like to thank Ann
Scott, Patrick and Caroline Gowers, Timothy Gowers and Julie
Barrau, Katharine Gowers, Tanglewest Douglas, Raymond
Douglas, Helen Small, Mark Kilfoyle, Derek Johns, Bryan Garner,
Rebecca Lee and Marina Kemp.

Rebecca Gowers
October 2013

---

*Harold Nicolson, reviewing *Plain Words* for the *Spectator* in 1948, mocked
Gowers for writing in the second sentence of his book that to 'some officials'
it might seem 'a work of supererogation'. In *The Complete Plain Words*, rather
than make plain 'a work of supererogation' (one that goes beyond the call of
duty), Gowers rewrote his opening to say that he suspected his book would be
received, not now by 'some' but by 'many' officials, 'without any marked
enthusiasm or gratitude'.

Plain Words

I

PROLOGUE

Do but take care to express your self in a plain easy manner, in well-chosen, significant and decent Terms, and to give an harmonious and easy Turn to your Periods. Study to explain your Thoughts, and set them in the truest Light, labouring, as much as possible, not to leave 'em dark nor intricate, but clear and intelligible.

CERVANTES, quoted in MAYANS Y SISCAR's *Life*,
trans. John Ozell, 1738

The final cause of speech is to get an idea as exactly as possible out of one mind into another. Its formal cause therefore is such choice and disposition of words as will achieve this end most economically.

G. M. YOUNG, *Last Essays*, 1950

The purpose of this book is to help officials in their use of written English as a tool of their trade. I suspect that this project may be received by many of them without any marked enthusiasm or gratitude. 'Even now,' they may say, 'it is all we can do to keep our heads above water, turning out at top speed writing in which we say what we mean after our own fashion. Not one in a thousand of the people who will read our work knows the difference between good English and bad, so what is the use of all this highbrow stuff? It will only prevent us from getting on with the job.'

But what is this job that must be got on with? Writing is an instrument for conveying ideas from one mind to another; your job as a writer is to make the reader grasp your meaning readily and precisely. Do you always say just what you mean? Do you yourself always know just what you mean? Even when you know what you mean, and say it in a way that is clear to you, will it always be equally clear to your reader? If not, you have not been getting on with the job. 'The difficulty of literature', said Robert Louis Stevenson in *Virginibus Puerisque*, 'is not to write, but to write what you mean; not to affect your reader, but to affect him precisely as you wish.' Let us take one or two examples given later in this book to illustrate particular faults, and, applying this test to them, ask ourselves whether the reader is likely to catch at once the meaning of

> Prices are basis prices per ton for the representative-basis-pricing specification and size and quantity.

or of

> Where particulars of a partnership are disclosed to the Executive Council the remuneration of the individual partner for superannuation purposes will be deemed to be such proportion of the total remuneration of such practitioners as the proportion of his share in partnership profits bears to the total proportion of the shares of such practitioner in those profits.

or of

> The treatment of this loan interest from the date of the first payment has been correct—i.e. tax charged at full standard rate on Mr X and treated in your hands as liability fully satisfied before receipt.

or of

> The programme must be on the basis of the present head of
> labour ceiling allocation overall.

or, to take an example from America, so as to show that ours is
not the only country in which writers sometimes forget that what
has meaning for them may have none for their readers, of

> The non-compensable evaluation heretofore assigned to you
> for your service-connected disability is confirmed and con-
> tinued.   (Quoted in *Time*, 1947)

All these were written for ordinary readers, not for experts.
What will the ordinary reader make of them? The recipients of
the last three may, painfully and dubiously, have reached the right
conclusions—the particular taxpayer that no more money was
wanted from him, the builder that no further labour was likely
to be allocated to the job in question, and the veteran that he was
still denied a disability pension. But no one receiving the first
example could unlock the secret of its jargon without a key, and
what the recipient of the second can have made of the explanation
given is anyone's guess. Yet in all these examples the writers may
be presumed to have known exactly what they meant. The obscurity was not in their thoughts but in their way of expressing
themselves. The fault of writing like this is not that it is unschol-
arly but that it is inefficient. It wastes time: readers are left
puzzling over what should be plain, and a writer who bungles
the job may have to write again to explain further.

Professional writers realise that they cannot hope to affect a
reader precisely as they wish without care and practice in the
proper use of words. The need for the official to take pains is
even greater. If what a professional writer has written is wearisome
and obscure, the reader can toss the book aside and read no more.

But only at their peril can members of the public ignore what an official has tried to tell them. By 'proper use' I do not mean grammatically proper. It is true that there are rules of grammar and syntax, just as in music there are rules of harmony and counterpoint. But one can no more write good English than one can compose good music merely by keeping the rules. On the whole the governing norms of English grammar are aids to writing intelligibly; they distil successful experiments made by writers of English through the centuries in how best to handle words so as to make the intended meaning plain. Some rules, it is true, are arbitrary. One or two actually increase the difficulty of clear expression. But even these should be respected, because lapses from what for the time being is regarded as correct irritate readers educated to notice errors, distract their attention, and so make them less likely to be affected precisely as you wish. Nevertheless, I shall not have too much to say about textbook rules because they are mostly well known and well observed in official writing.

The golden rule is not a rule of grammar or syntax. It concerns less the arrangement of words than the choice of them. 'After all,' said Lord Macaulay, 'the first law of writing, that law to which all other laws are subordinate, is this,—that the words employed shall be such as to convey to the reader the meaning of the writer' (*Edinburgh Review*, 1833). The golden rule is to pick out those words and to use them and them only. Arrangement is of course important, but if the right words alone are used, they generally have a happy knack of arranging themselves. Matthew Arnold was reported by George Russell, his 'grateful disciple', to have said, 'People think that I can teach them style. What stuff it all is! Have something to say and say it as clearly as you can. That is the only secret of style'. That was no doubt said partly for effect, but there is much truth in it, especially in relation to the sort of writing we are now concerned with, in which emotional appeal plays no part.

This golden rule applies to all prose, whatever its purpose, and indeed to poetry too. Illustrations could be found throughout the gamut of purposes for which the written word is used. At the one end of it we can turn to Shakespeare, and from the innumerable examples that offer themselves choose the lines from Sonnet 33,

> Kissing with golden face the meadows green,
> Gilding pale streams with heavenly alchemy . . .

which, as a description of what the rising sun does to meadows and rivers on a 'glorious morning', must be as effective a use of thirteen words as could be found in all English literature. At the other end we can turn (for the golden rule can be illustrated from official writing in its observance as well as its breach) to the unknown member of staff of the General Post Office who by composing the notice that used to be displayed in every post office

> Postmasters are neither bound to give change nor authorised
> to demand it

used twelve words hardly less efficiently to warn customers of what must have been a singularly intractable dilemma. At first sight there seems little in common between the two. Their purposes are very different, one being descriptive and emotional, the other instructional and objective. But each serves its purpose perfectly, and it is the same quality in both that makes them do so. Every word is exactly right; no other word would do as well; each is pulling its weight; none could be dispensed with. As was said of Milton's choice of words in the quotation that heads Chapter VI, 'Fewer would not have Serv'd the Turn, and More would have been Superfluous'.

It is sometimes said that the principle of plain words can be overdone. That depends on a writer's purpose. If what you want is to use words to conceal your thoughts, and to leave a blurred impression on the minds of your readers, then of course plainness will not do. And there may be occasions when prudence prompts this course. Even those who do want to express their thoughts sometimes prefer not to do so too plainly. C. E. Montague, that rare artist in words, once amused himself by tilting against exaggerated lucidity. He said:

> Even in his most explicit moments a courteous writer will stop short of rubbing into our minds the last item of all that he means. He will, in a moderate sense of the term, have his non-lucid intervals. At times he will make us wrestle a little with him, in the dark, before he yields his full meaning . . .
>
> (*A Writer's Notes on his Trade*, 1930)

But the writers for whom this book is intended have the whole adult population as their readers. The things an official has to say are in the main concerned with telling people what they may or may not do, and what they are or are not entitled to: there is no room here for experiments with hints and nuances. No doubt officials do in fact sometimes make us wrestle with them in the dark before yielding their full meaning—sometimes indeed no amount of wrestling will make them yield it. But it is charitable to suppose that this is by accident, not by design.

Just as those servants of the Crown whose weapon is the sword have had to abandon the gay trappings of regimental uniforms and assume the dull monotony of battledress, so those who wield the pen must submit to a similar change. The serviceable is now more needed than the ornamental. A report by a departmental committee on the teaching of English draws the same conclusion. Its authors write that the fact that 'the hurry of modern life has put both the florid and the polished styles out of fashion, except for very special audiences, is not to be deplored if this leads to a more general appreciation of the capacity of the plain style'. And

'By "plain"', they add, 'we do not mean bald but simple and neat' (HM Stationery Office, 1921).

Although your first requisite as a writer is to know what meaning you wish to convey, you need to choose the right words in order that you may make your meaning clear not only to your reader but also to yourself. As the same departmental report notes, 'English is not merely the medium of our thought; it is the very stuff and process of it'. Moreover the less one makes a habit of thinking, the less one is able to think: the power of thinking atrophies if it is not used. George Orwell wrote this about politicians, but it is true of all of us:

> A scrupulous writer, in every sentence that he writes, will ask himself . . . What am I trying to say? What words will express it? . . . And he will probably ask himself . . . Could I put it more shortly? Have I said anything that is avoidably ugly? But you are not obliged to go to all this trouble. You can shirk it by simply throwing open your mind and letting the ready-made phrases come crowding in. They will construct your sentences for you— even think your thoughts for you, to a certain extent—and at need they will perform the important service of partially concealing your meaning even from yourself.
>
> ('Politics and the English Language', *Horizon*, 1946)

'Go to all this trouble' is not an overstatement. Few common things are more difficult than to find the right word, and many people are too lazy to try.

This form of indolence sometimes betrays itself by a copious use of inverted commas. 'I know this is not quite the right word', the inverted commas seem to say, 'but I can't be bothered to think of one that is better'; or, 'please note that I am using this word facetiously'; or, 'don't think I don't know that this is a cliché'. If the word is the right one, do not be ashamed of it. If it is the wrong one, do not use it. The same implied apology is often made in conversation by interposing *shall I say?* or *you know*, or by ending every sentence with a phrase like *and so on* or *sort of thing*. Officials cannot do that, but they betray their own indolence by their unwillingness to venture outside a small vocabulary of shapeless bundles of uncertain content—words like *position, arise, involve, in connection with, issue, consideration* and *factor*—a disposition, for instance, to 'admit with regret the position which has arisen in connection with' rather than make the effort to tell the reader specifically what is admitted with regret. Clear thinking is hard work, but loose thinking is bound to produce loose writing. And although clear thinking takes time, the time that has to be given to a job to avoid making a mess of it not only cannot be time wasted but may in the end be time saved.

It is wise therefore not to begin to write until you are quite certain what you want to say. That sounds elementary, but the elementary things are often the most neglected. Some people, it is true, can never be sure of clarifying their thoughts except by trying to put them on paper. If you are one of these, never be content with your first draft; always revise it. Within the Civil Service, authoritative advice has varied in its emphasis on the need for revision. In the Foreign Office a memorandum on draft-writing, after recommending simplicity, continued:

> It is a commonplace that this simplicity does not always come in a first draft even to the greatest stylists. Redrafting takes time, and I know that members of departments have little enough time to spend on it these days. But it is up to them, for heads of departments and under-secretaries have still less time to spare ...

The Ministry of Health ended a similar memorandum:

> I do not expect our letters to be models of the best English prose, and I do not want time taken in answering letters (which

is already too long) to be increased still further by unnecessary
labour in the preparing, and, still less, the polishing of drafts . . .
But it is clear that there are ways of saying what is meant in
shorter, plainer and better English.

These pieces of advice are not irreconcilable. They relate to
rather different types of communication, and both are no doubt
wise. But I am sure that you should fear more the danger of putting out slipshod work by omitting to revise it than that of
delaying public business by excessive polishing. Very few can
write what they mean and affect their readers precisely as they
wish without revising their first attempt. There is a happy mean
between being content with the first thing that comes into your
head, and the craving for perfection that makes a Flaubert spend
hours or even days on getting a single sentence to his satisfaction.
The article you are paid to produce need not be polished but it
must be workmanlike.

The official must use the written word for many different purposes. In Parliamentary Bills, Statutory Orders and other legal
documents, precision is so important that these constitute a class
apart with which this book is not concerned: the next chapter
forms a brief digression to explain more fully why. But there
are many other classes of official document—despatches to Her
Majesty's representatives abroad, reports of commissions and
committees, circulars to local authorities and similar bodies,
departmental instructions, minutes, and correspondence with
other departments and with the public, as well as documents
explaining the law to the millions for whom, beyond ordering
their daily lives in countless ways, it now creates complicated
personal rights and obligations—and when writing any of these
the object of the official must be the same: to make the reader
understand what is meant as readily and precisely as possible.

II

A DIGRESSION ON LEGAL ENGLISH

> Even when the counsel in chambers is merely 'advising on a case,' or drawing up a conveyance of property, he is really thinking of what view the court and its judges will take of his advice or his draftsmanship if any dispute arises upon them . . . The supreme test in every case is: 'Will this stand the scrutiny of the court?'
>
> *Stephen's Commentaries on the Laws of England*, 17th edition (1922)

The obtrusive gracelessness of legal English arises from the necessity of being unambiguous, and that is by no means the same as being readily intelligible. On the contrary, the nearer you get to the one the further you are likely to get from the other.

The reason why certainty of meaning must be the paramount aim in legal drafting is clear enough. Legal documents impose obligations and confer rights, and neither the parties to them nor those who draft the documents have the last word in deciding exactly what those rights and obligations are. That can only be settled in a Court of Law on the words of the document; but words, with their penumbra of meaning, are an imperfect instrument for expressing complicated concepts with certainty. It is the duty of all who draft these authoritative texts to try to imagine every possible combination of circumstances to which their words might apply and every conceivable misinterpretation that might be put upon them, and to take precautions accordingly. When drafting, they must limit by definition words with a penumbra dangerously large, and amplify with a string of near-synonyms words with a penumbra dangerously small. They must eschew all pronouns when their antecedents might possibly be open to dispute, and circumvent every potential grammatical ambiguity. They must avoid all graces, and not be afraid of repetitions, while all the time keeping an eye on the rules of legal interpretation, and on the case law that concerns the meaning of particular words. No one can expect pretty writing from anyone thus burdened.

The peculiarities of legal English are often used as a stick to beat the official with. An example of this is the following, by an evening-paper gossip-writer, about a Bill just introduced in Parliament:

> It is written in that abominable civil service jargon, which is as stiff, heavy, lumbering and ungraceful as a wheelbarrow being pushed through sodden clay ... It would be a Herculean task to teach the Civil Service to write its own language creditably.

That the style of Bills, Statutory Orders and other such documents has peculiarities cannot be denied, but if it is jargon*—an arguable question—its species is the legal not the official. It is written by lawyers, not by civil servants (in the sense in which the critics use the term), and its peculiarities arise from causes exactly opposite to those of the peculiarities alleged against ordinary officials.

---

* The proper meaning of *jargon* is writing that employs technical words not commonly intelligible. *Catachresis*, for instance, is grammarians' jargon for using a wrong word in a wrong sense. When grammarians call writing jargon merely because it is verbose, circumlocutory and flabby, they themselves commit the sin of catachresis that they denounce in others.

Those of the one come from a desire to convey a precise meaning; those of the other—so it is said—come too often from a reluctance to convey any meaning at all.

I do not mean to imply that there is no room for improvement in the drafting of statutory documents; but such writing is prudently left to a specialised branch of the Civil Service, and therefore falls outside the scope of this book. It is more a science than an art; it lies in the province of mathematics rather than of literature, and its practice needs long apprenticeship.*

The only concern of ordinary officials is to learn to understand legal English, to be able to act as interpreters of legal English to ordinary people, and to be careful not to let it taint their own style of writing, a subject to which we will return.

* Though in 1948 Gowers put legal English outside the scope of *Plain Words* for the reasons given above, in doing so he made the argument that legal writing could not be elegant and still serve its purpose. He was immediately accused by critics of having a 'blind spot' and of being 'too indulgent to legal draftsmen'. Gowers was not markedly contrite in reply, but other authors have since dedicated whole books to battling 'legalese': they continue even now to hold him accountable in their work for having exaggerated the difficulty of making legal English simpler. For anyone who is curious about this debate, Gowers's argument is given in more detail in the Appendix on p. 274. ~

This then is Style ... essentially it resembles good manners. It comes of endeavouring to understand others, of thinking for them rather than yourself—of thinking, that is, with the heart as well as the head ... So, says Fénelon ... 'your words will be fewer and more effectual; and while you make less ado, what you do will be more profitable'.

QUILLER-COUCH, *On the Art of Writing*, 1916

Having thus cleared the decks, we can return to the various other purposes for which official writing has to be used. In the past it consisted mostly of departmental minutes and instructions, inter-departmental correspondence, and despatches to governors and ambassadors. These things still have their places, but in volume they must have been left far behind by the vast output now neces-sary for explaining the law to the public. An immense quantity of modern social legislation and innumerable statutory controls have been necessitated by the war and its consequences. Yet mem-bers of the public are still supposed to know the law without being told, and ignorance is no excuse for breaking it. That was all very well in the days when ordinary citizens had little more concern with the law than an obligation to avoid committing the crimes prohibited by the Ten Commandments; no niceties needed explaining to them then. Today, however, our daily lives are con-ditioned by an infinity of statutory rights and obligations. Even if the laws that define them were short, simple and intelligible, the number of these laws alone would prevent most people from discovering by their own study what they all were.

The official must be the interpreter. Now this is a task as delicate as it is difficult. An official interpreting the law is looked on with suspicion. It is for the legislature to make the laws, for the executive to administer them, and for the judiciary to interpret them. The official must avoid all appearance of encroaching on the province of the Courts. For this reason it used to be a rule in the Civil Service that when laws were brought to the notice of those affected by them the actual words of the statute must be used. In no other way could officials be sure of escaping all imputation of putting their own interpretation on the law. Here, then, we have a dilemma. If the official is tied to the words of the law, and if, as we have seen, the words of the law in order to be precise are less than readily intelligible, how is the ordinary person to be helped to understand it?

No doubt much can be done by selection and arrangement, even though the words used are those of the Act. But the official finds it more and more difficult to give helpful explanations other than by departing from them. And something even more than that is needed to carry out the exhortation given by a President of the Board of Trade to his staff: 'Let us get away entirely from the chilly formalities of the old-style correspondence which seemed to come from some granite monolith rather than from another human being'. The old rule is indeed yielding to the pressure of events. A new technique is being developed for those pamphlets and leaflets that are necessary to explain the law to the public in such matters as PAYE and National Insurance. Its guiding principles are to use the simplest language and avoid technical terms, to employ the second person freely, not to try to give all the details of the law relevant to the subject but to be content with stating the essentials, to explain, if these are stated in the writer's words and not the words of the Act, that they are an approximation only, to tell members of the public where they can find fuller information and further advice, and always to make sure that people know their rights of appeal. This technique is being closely studied, in the departments concerned, by experts who have nothing to learn from me.

But there is another part of this subject: the answering of letters from correspondents about their own cases. These answers cannot be written, like pamphlets and leaflets, by people who are experts both in the subject matter and in English composition, and here I shall have some advice to give. A letter of this kind needs in some respects a special technique, but the principles of this technique are the same as those of all good writing, whatever its purpose. We have here in its most elementary form—though not on that account its least difficult—the problem of writing what one means and affecting one's reader precisely as one wishes. If therefore we begin our study of the problem of official English by examining the technique of this part of it, that will serve as a good introduction to the rest of the book, for it will bring out most of the points that we shall have to study more closely later. It is in this field of an official's duties more than any other that good English can be defined simply as English that is readily understood by the reader. To be clear is to be efficient. To be obscure is to be inefficient. Your style of letter-writing is to be judged not by literary conventions or grammatical niceties but by whether it carries out efficiently the job you have been paid to do.

This 'efficiency' must be broadly interpreted. It connotes a proper attitude of mind towards your correspondents. They may not care about being addressed in literary English, but they will care very much about being treated with sympathy and understanding. It is not easy nowadays to remember anything so contrary to all appearances as that officials are the servants of the public; but they are, and no official should foster the illusion that it is the other way round. So your style must not only be simple, but also friendly, sympathetic and natural, appropriate to one who is a servant, not a master.

Let us now translate these generalities into some practical rules.

(1) Be sure you know what your correspondent is asking before you begin to draft your reply. Study the letter in front of you carefully. If the writing is obscure, spare no trouble in trying to get at its meaning. If you conclude that the person who wrote it meant something different from what is actually on the page (as it may well prove) address yourself to the meaning and not to the words, and do not be clever at your correspondent's expense. Adapt the atmosphere of your reply to suit that of the letter you have received. If its tone is troubled, be sympathetic. If it is rude, be especially courteous. If it is muddle-headed, be especially lucid. If it is stubborn, be patient. If your correspondent is helpful, be appreciative. If you find yourself convicted of a mistake, acknowledge it freely and even with gratitude. And never let the flavour of the patronising creep in as it did into this letter received by a passenger who had lost a railway ticket:

> In the circumstances you have now explained, and the favourable enquiries made by me, I agree as a special case and without prejudice not to press for payment of the demand sent you ... and you may consider the matter closed. I would however suggest that in future you should take greater care of your railway ticket to obviate any similar occurrence.

Follow the admirable advice given in an instruction by the Board of Inland Revenue to their staff, 'that we should try to put ourselves in the position of our correspondent', for then we 'shall speedily detect how unconvincing our letters can seem, or how much we may be taking for granted'.

(2) Begin by answering the question. Do not start by examining relevant law and practice, only gradually leading up to a statement that explains how this applies to the case in hand. By doing so you keep your correspondent on tenterhooks and risk causing such befuddlement that your answer is lost. Give the answer briefly and clearly at the outset, and only then, if explanation is needed, begin your explanation. Thus your correspondent will know the worst, or the best, at once, and can choose whether or not to skip the explanation.

(3) So far as possible, confine yourself to the facts of the case you are writing about, and avoid any general statement about the law. If you do make statements about the law, you are likely to face this dilemma: that if you want to be strictly accurate you will have to use technical terms and legal diction that your correspondent will not understand, yet if you want to be simple and intelligible you will have to qualify your statement so copiously with hedging phrases like *normally, ordinarily, in most cases* and *with some exceptions*, that you will give the impression of keeping something up your sleeve and not being frank in what you say.

(4) Avoid a formal framework, if you can. This is a difficult subject, and those who supervise correspondence of this kind are still groping for a satisfactory standard practice. How are we to 'get away from the chilly formalities of the old style'?

Over the years when the 'old style' became set, official correspondence consisted mostly of interdepartmental communications. The stock formalities in these letters served as reminders that, for present purposes, both the official who wrote a letter and the official who received it were in themselves things of naught; they merely formed a conduit along which the thoughts of their political chiefs might be exchanged. It is no doubt proper that officials and the public should be reminded at all turns that min-isterial responsibility is the keystone of our democracy. But however appropriate a formal style may still be in certain circum-stances, it will not do for the sort of letter we are now concerned with. It is too flagrantly unreal, besides militating against the spirit of friendliness we have seen to be desirable.

There are two difficulties. One is how to start. The other is to whom to attribute the sentiments, opinions and decisions that the letter contains. As to the first, everyone's inclination is to follow tradition at least to the point of beginning with *In reply to your letter of*, or *With reference to your letter of*. That brings us to our first difficulty: how are we to go on?

In detail the possibilities are infinite, but the main forms are few. 'I have (or "I am") to inform you' used to be the most common. But it is unsatisfactory, not to say silly, with its mysterious suggestion of some compulsion working undisclosed in the background. 'I beg to inform you' will not do. 'In reply to your letter ... I wish to inform you' (which I have seen) is crushingly stiff. This is almost like saying *I would have you know*. The passive 'you are informed' has an aloof-ness that ought to rule it out. There is the device of plunging straight into saying what you have to say without any introductory words. But this will not do as a continuation of *In reply to your letter*. What is in reply to the letter is not the information but the giving of it. (It is nonsense to say, 'In reply to your letter of (date), the income tax law on personal allowances has been changed'.) *I regret to inform you* and *I am glad to inform you* will do nicely when there is anything to be glad or sorry about, but that will not always be the case.

Must we then conclude that we ought to abandon the stand-ard opening *In reply to your letter* unless we find we can continue naturally with *I am glad to tell you*, or *I am sorry to have to tell you*, or some such phrase? Perhaps. Nothing would be lost, and there are plenty of other ways of beginning that will not lead us into this mire. But if we turn versions of *In reply to your letter* into a full sentence we shake off our difficulties.

This must be done with discretion. Some attempts are unfortunate. For instance:

> Your letter is acknowledged, and the following would appear to be the position.

> Receipt of your letter is acknowledged. It is pointed out ...

Here is the inhuman passive. A better way of saying what these two were trying to say is 'Thank you for your letter. The position is (or the facts are) as follows ...'. Or again, in this example,

> With reference to your claim. I have to advise you that before the same is dealt with ...

there is no need to start with an ejaculatory and verbless clause. All that was needed was to begin: 'Before I can deal with your claim'. I believe that a common formula during the war was:

> Your letter of (date) about so-and-so. We really cannot see our way ...

I am told that this is fortunately dying out, perhaps because it is becoming less difficult to see our way. Another not very happy effort is:

> I refer to recent correspondence and to the form which you have completed ...

There is a faint air of bombast to this: it vaguely recalls Pistol's way of talking ('I speak of Africa and golden joys'). Probably 'Thank you for the completed form' would have been an adequate opening.

There are, however, many possible ways to do the job of *In reply to your letter* or *With reference to your letter* that make a complete sentence without getting the writer into trouble.

Thank you for your letter of (date).

I have received your letter of (date).

I am writing to you in reply to your letter of (date).

You wrote to me on such-and-such a subject.

I have looked into the question of such-and-such, about which you wrote to me.

All enable you to continue by saying what you have to say as a direct statement, with no unfriendly preliminaries like *I would inform you.*

There remains the second question. To whom are you to attribute the opinions and decisions which, having got over the initial hurdle, you then proceed to deliver? There are four possibilities. To illustrate them, let us take what must today be a common type of letter, one turning down an application. The first of them is that the letter should be written in the first person, and that the official who signs it should boldly accept responsibility:

> I have considered your application and do not think you have made out a case.

The second is that responsibility should be spread by the use of the first person plural:

> We have considered your application and do not think you have made out a case.

The third is that it should be further diluted by attributing decisions and opinions to 'the Department':

> The Department has (or have) considered your application and does (or do) not think you have made out a case.*

---

* See pp. 189–90 for choosing between the department *has* or *have*, *is* or *are*, etc.

The fourth is that responsibility should be assigned to a quarter mystically remote by the use throughout of the impersonal passive:

> Your application has been considered and it is not thought that
> you have made out a case.

This is neither sympathetic nor natural.

I cannot pretend to be an authoritative guide on the comparative merits of all of these approaches (no doubt every department makes its own rules), but there are three further points that seem to me important.

First, in letters written in the first person be careful to avoid giving the impression that you are an all-powerful individual signifying your pleasure. If the letter grants what is asked for, do not say that you are making a 'concession'. If it refuses a request never say, as in the example given, *I* do not think you have made out a case. You should imply no more than that it is your duty to decide how the case before you fits into the instructions under which you work.

Second, it is a mistake to mix these methods in one letter unless there is good reason for it. If you choose an impersonal method, such as 'the Department', you may of course need to introduce the first person in order to say something like 'I am glad to tell you that the Department has . . .'. But do not mix the methods merely for variety, saying *I* in the first paragraph, *we* in the second, *the Department* in the third and *it is* in the fourth. Choose one and stick to it.

Third, do not use the impersonal passive at all—with its formal unsympathetic phrases, *it is felt, it is regretted, it is appreciated* and so on—otherwise you will seem to your correspondent more like a robot than a human being. How feeble this sentence is: 'It is thought you will now have received the form of agreement', compared with: 'I expect that by now you will have received the form of agreement'.

(5) Be careful to say nothing that might give the impression, however mistakenly, that you think it right that your correspondent should be put to trouble in order to save you from it. Do not ask for information a second time that you have asked for and been given already unless there is some good reason for doing so; and if there is, explain the reason. Otherwise you will make it seem as though you think it proper that your correspondent should have to do what is perhaps quite a lot of work to save you the effort of turning up a back file. Do not use the phrase *Date as postmark*. This will be read by many recipients as meaning: 'I am much too important and busy a person to remember what the date is or to put it down if I did. So if you want to know you must pick the envelope out of the wastepaper basket, if you can find it, and read the date on the postmark, if you can decipher it. It is better that you should do this than that I should be delayed in my work for even a moment'.

Note. The phrase *Date as postmark* may be less popular now than it was when Gowers wrote this, but it does survive in bureaucratic writing, especially on printed matter destined to be posted without a covering letter. ~

(6) Use no more words than are necessary to do the job. Superfluous words waste your time, waste official paper, tire your reader and obscure your meaning. There is no need, for instance, to begin each paragraph with a phrase like *I am further to point out*, *I would also add*, or *you will moreover observe*. Go straight to what you have to say without striking a precautionary note, and then say it in as few words as are needed to make your meaning plain.

(7) Keep your sentences short. This will help you to think clearly and will help your correspondent to take your meaning. If you

find you have slipped into long sentences, split them up. This sentence is a long one:

> If he was not insured on reaching the age of 65 he does not become insured by reason of any insurable employment which he takes up later, and the special contributions which are payable under the Act by his employer only, in respect of such employment, do not give him title to any health benefits or pension, and moreover a man is not at liberty to pay any contributions on his own account as a voluntary contributor for any period after his 65th birthday.

This sentence contains three statements of fact linked by the conjunction *and*. Because this is its form, no reader can be quite sure until reading beyond the *and*s whether any of these statements has been completed. Only in re-reading the sentence will many people pick up the statements one by one. If they had been separated by full stops (after *later* and *pension*) and the *and* s omitted, each statement could have been grasped at first reading. The full stops would have seemed to say: 'Have you got that? Very well, now I'll tell you something else'.

(8) Be compact. Do not put a strain on your reader's memory by widely separating parts of a sentence that are closely related to one another. Why, for instance, is this sentence difficult to grasp on first reading?

> A deduction of tax may be claimed in respect of any person whom the individual maintains at his own expense, and who is (i) a relative of his, or of his wife, and incapacitated by old age or infirmity from maintaining himself or herself, or (ii) his or his wife's widowed mother, whether incapacitated or not, or (iii) his daughter who is resident with him and upon whose services he is compelled to depend by reason of old age or infirmity.

The structure of the sentence is too diffuse. The reader has to keep in mind the opening words all the way through. The last point explained is that a deduction of tax may be claimed 'in respect of any person whom the individual maintains at his own expense and who is his daughter', but *his daughter* is separated from *who is* by no fewer than thirty-two words. In a later leaflet of income tax instructions, the same sentence was rewritten to run as follows:

> If you maintain a relative of yourself or your wife who is unable to work because of old age or infirmity, you can claim an allowance of . . . You can claim this allowance if you maintain your widowed mother, or your wife's widowed mother, whether she is unable to work or not. If you maintain a daughter who lives with you because you or your wife are old or infirm, you can claim an allowance of . . .

Why is the new version so much easier to grasp than the old? Partly it is because a sentence of eighty-one words has been split into three, each making a statement complete in itself. But it is also because a device has been employed that is a most useful one when an official has to say, as an official so often must, that such-and-such a class of people who have such-and-such attributes, and perhaps such-and-such other attributes, have such-and-such rights or obligations. The device is to say: *if* you belong to such-and-such a class of people, and *if* you have such-and-such attributes, you have such-and-such a right or obligation (that is, the device is to use conditional clauses in the second person instead of relative clauses in the third). The advantage of this is that it avoids the wide separation of the main verb from the main subject. The subject *you* comes immediately next to the verb it governs, and in this way you announce unmistakably to your reader: 'I have finished describing the class of people about whom I have to tell you something, and I shall now say what that something is'.

(9) Do not say more than is necessary. The feeling that prompts you to tell your correspondent everything when you give an explanation is commendable, but you will often be of more help if you resist it, and confine yourself to the facts that make clear what has happened.

> I regret however that the Survey Officer who is responsible for the preliminary investigation as to the technical possibility of installing a telephone at the address quoted by any applicant has reported that owing to a shortage of a spare pair of wires to the underground cable (a pair of wires leading from the point near your house right back to the local exchange and thus a pair of wires essential for the provision of service for you) is lacking and that therefore it is a technical impossibility to install a telephone for you at . . .

This explanation is obscure partly because the sentence is too long, partly because the long parenthesis has thrown the grammar out of gear, and partly because the writer, with the best of intentions, says far more than is necessary even to make what is said here seem thoroughly polite and convincing. It might have run thus:

> I am sorry to have to tell you that we have found that there is no spare pair of wires on the cable that would have to be used to connect your house with the exchange. I fear, therefore, that it is impossible to install a telephone for you.

(10) Explain technical terms in simple words. You will soon become so familiar with the technical terms of the law you are administering that you will feel that you have known them all your life, and may forget that to others they are unintelligible.

Of this fault I can find no English example to equal the American one already quoted:

> The non-compensable evaluation heretofore assigned to you for your service-connected disability is confirmed and continued.

This means, I understand, that the veteran to whom it is addressed has been judged to be still not entitled to a disability pension.

I am indebted for the following example to a friend in the Board of Inland Revenue, who also supplies the comment:

> I have pleasure in enclosing a cheque for £ . . ., a supplementary repayment for . . . This is accounted for by the fact that in calculating the untaxed interest assessable the interest on the loan from Mr X was treated as untaxed, whereas it should be regarded as received in full out of taxed sources—any liability thereon being fully satisfied. The treatment of this loan interest from the date of the first payment has been correct—i.e. tax charged at full standard rate on Mr X and treated in your hands as a liability fully satisfied before receipt.

'The occasion was the issue of an unexpected cheque,' writes my friend. 'It is a difficult matter to explain, and an honest attempt has been made. The major fault is one of over-explanation in technical language. The writer could have said:

> The interest you received from Mr X on the money you lent him was included as part of your income to be taxed. This was wrong. Mr X had already paid tax on this interest, and you are not liable to pay it again. You have been repaid all the tax due to you.

With this the recipient would have been satisfied. "Treated in your hands as a liability" is an odd way of describing an asset, and the loan was of course *to* Mr X, not from him. "Interest-on-the-loan" is treated confusingly as a composite noun.'

(11) Do not use what have been called the 'dry meaningless

formulae' of commercialese. Not all of them need warning against: officials do not write *your esteemed favour to hand* or address their correspondents as *your good self*. But some of these formulae do occasionally appear. *Same* is used as a pronoun,* *enclosed please find* is written instead of *I enclose*, and foolish *begs* are common. The use of *beg* in commercialese is presumably to be accounted for by a false analogy with the reasonable use of *I beg* as a polite way of introducing a contradiction, *I beg to differ* meaning 'I beg your leave to differ'. But there is no reason why one should apologise, however faintly, for acknowledging a letter or remaining an obedient servant.

Avoid, too, that ugly and unnecessary symbol *and/or* when writing letters. It is fit only for forms and lists and specifications and things of that sort. It can always be dispensed with. Instead of writing (say) 'soldiers and/or sailors' we can write 'soldiers or sailors or both'.

Note. And/or is not fit even for 'specifications and things of that sort' unless used with care. When it is thrown into the middle of the confounding phrase 'regardless . . . or not' it becomes positively boggling, as the Department for Communities and Local Government demonstrates in one of its attempts to explain current planning law to the public:

> With all building work, the owner of the property (or land) in question is ultimately responsible for complying with the relevant planning rules and building regulations (regardless of the need to apply for planning permission and/or building regulations approval or not). ~

Do not allow *per* to get too free with the English language. Such convenient abbreviations as *mph* and *rpm* are no doubt

---

* On which see pp. 209–10.

with us for good. But generally it is well to confine *per* to its own language, e.g. *per cent*, *per capita*, *per contra*, and to avoid writing 'as *per* my letter' for 'as I said in my letter'. Even for phrases in which *per* is linked to a Latin word, there are often English equivalents that serve at least as well, and possibly better. '£100 a year' is more natural than '£100 *per annum*', and *per se* does not ordinarily mean anything more than 'by itself' or 'in itself'. Another Latin word better left alone is *re*. This is the ablative case of the Latin word *res*. It means 'in the matter of'. It is used by lawyers for the title of lawsuits, such as '*In re* John Doe deceased', and has passed into commercialese as an equivalent of the English preposition *about*. It has no business there, or in official writing. It is not needed either in a heading ('re your application for a permit'), which can stand without its support, or in the body of a letter, where an honest *about* will serve your purpose better.

A correspondent has sent me the following example of the baleful influence of commercialese:

> Payment of the above account, which is now overdue at the date hereof, appears to have been overlooked, and I shall be glad to have your remittance by return of post, and oblige.
>
> Yours faithfully,

The superfluous *at the date hereof* must have been prompted by a feeling that *now* by itself was not formal enough and needed dressing up. And the word *oblige* is grammatically mid-air. It has no subject, and is firmly cut off by a full stop from what might have been supposed to be its object, the writer's signature.

The fault of commercialese is that its mechanical use has a bad effect on both writer and reader—the writer's appreciation of the meaning of words is deadened, and the reader feels that the writer's approach lacks sincerity.

(12) Use words with precise meanings rather than vague ones. As we have seen, you will not be doing your job properly unless you make your meaning readily understood: this is an elementary duty. Yet habitual disregard of it is the commonest cause of the abuse and raillery directed against what is called officialese. All entrants into the Civil Service come equipped with a vocabulary of common words of precise meaning adequate for every ordinary purpose. But when the moment arrives for them to write as officials, most have a queer trick of forgetting these words and relying mainly on a smaller vocabulary of less common words with a less precise meaning. It is a curious fact that in the official's armoury of words the weapons readiest to hand are weapons not of precision but of rough and ready aim. Often, indeed, they are of a sort that were constructed as weapons of precision but have been bored out by the official into blunderbusses.* The blunderbusses have been put in the front rack of the armoury. The official reaches out for a word and uses one of these without troubling to search in the racks behind for one that is more likely to hit the target in the middle.

The blunderbuss *integrate*, for instance, is now kept in front of *join*, *combine*, *amalgamate*, *coordinate* and others, and the hand stretching out for one of these gets no further. *Develop* blocks the way to *happen*, *occur*, *take place* and *come*. *Alternative* (a weapon of precision whose bore has been carelessly enlarged) stands before many simple words such as *different*, *other*, *new*, *fresh*, *revised*. *Rehabilitate* and *recondition* are in front of others, such as *heal*, *mend*, *cure*, *repair*, *renovate* and *restore*. *Involve* throws a whole

* The *OED* defines a *blunderbuss* as 'A short gun with a large bore, firing many balls or slugs, and capable of doing execution within a limited range without exact aim'. Its name derives from words meaning 'thunder box'.

section of the armoury into disuse, though not so big a one as that threatened by *overall*. And rack upon rack of simple prepositions are left untouched because before them are kept the blunderbusses of vague phrases such as *in relation to*, *in regard to*, *in connection with* and *in the case of*.

It may be said that it is generally easy enough to guess what is meant. But you have no business leaving your reader to guess, even though the guess may be easy. That is not doing your job properly. If you make a habit of not troubling to choose the right weapon of precision you may be sure that sooner or later you will set your reader a problem that is past guessing.

(13) If two words convey your meaning equally well, choose the common one rather than the less common. Here again official tendency is in the opposite direction, and you must be on your guard. Do not say *regarding*, *respecting* or *concerning* when you can say *about*. Do not use *advert* instead of *refer*, or *state*, *inform* or *acquaint* when you might use *say* or *tell*. *Inform* is a useful word, but it seems to attract adverbs as prim as itself, sometimes almost menacing. In *kindly inform me* the politeness rings hollow; all it does is to put a frigid and magisterial tone into your request. *Perhaps you will inform me* means that you have *got* to inform me, and no 'perhaps' about it, and I suspect the consequences may be serious for you. *Furthermore* is a prosy word used too often. It may be difficult to avoid it in a cumulative argument (*moreover . . . in addition . . . too . . . also . . . again . . . furthermore*) but choose one of the simpler words if they have not all been used up. Do not say *hereto*, *herein*, *hereof*, *herewith*, *hereunder*, or similar compounds with *there*, unless, like *therefore*, they have become part of the everyday language. Most of them put a flavour of legalism into any document in which they are used. Use a pronoun and perhaps a preposition instead. For instance:

With reference to the second paragraph thereof. (With reference to its second paragraph.)

I have received your letter and thank you for the information contained therein. (For the information it contains.)

I am to ask you to explain the circumstances in which the gift was made and to forward any correspondence relative thereto. (Any correspondence about it.)

To take a few more examples of unnecessary choice of stilted expressions, do not say *predecease* for *die before*, *ablution facilities* for *wash basins*, *it is apprehended that* for *I suppose*, *capable of locomotion* for *able to walk*, *will you be good enough to advise me* for *please tell me*, *I have endeavoured to obtain the required information* for *I have tried to find out what you wanted to know*, *it will be observed from a perusal of* for *you will see by reading*.

These starchy words may not be bad English in their proper places, but you should avoid them for two reasons. First, some of the more unusual of them may actually be outside your reader's vocabulary, and will convey no meaning at all. Second, their use runs counter to your duty to show that officials are human. These words give the reader the impression that officials are not made of common clay but are, in their own estimation at least, beings superior and aloof. They create the wrong atmosphere. The frost once formed by a phrase or two of this sort is not easily melted. If you turn back to the example given under rule (8) you will see how careful the writer of the revised version has been about this. The word *individual* (a technical term of income tax law to distinguish between a personal taxpayer and a corporate one) was unnecessary and has disappeared. *Deduction of tax* is translated into *allowance*, *incapacitated* into *unable to work*, *is resident with* into *lives with*, and *by reason of old age or infirmity* into *because you are old or infirm*.

Here is an example of words chosen for their simplicity:

> If a worker's clothing is destroyed beyond all hope of repair by an accident on his job his employer can apply to us for the coupons needed to replace it. This does not mean of course that anyone can get coupons if his boots fall to pieces through ordinary wear or if he just gets a tear in his trousers.

'If he just gets a tear in his trousers' not only conveys a clearer meaning than (say) 'If his garments suffer comparatively minor damage and are capable of effective reconditioning', it also creates a different atmosphere. The reader feels that these words were written by a human being and not a mere cog in the bureaucratic machine—almost that the writer might be rather a decent sort.

I have called this chapter 'The Elements' because in it I have suggested certain elementary rules—'be short, be simple, be human'—for officials to follow in the duties that I have described as 'explaining the law to the millions'. These rules apply no less to official writing of other kinds, and they will be elaborated in Chapters V to VIII, in which much of what has been said in this chapter will be expanded. I can claim no novelty for my advice. Similar precepts were laid down for the Egyptian Civil Service some thousands of years ago:

> Be courteous and tactful as well as honest and diligent.
> All your doings are publicly known, and must therefore
> Be beyond complaint or criticism. Be absolutely impartial.
> Always give a reason for refusing a plea; complainants
> Like a kindly hearing even more than a successful plea.
> Preserve dignity but avoid inspiring fear.
> Be an artist in words, that you may be strong, for
> The tongue is a sword ...

If we may judge from the following letter, those brought up in this tradition succeeded in avoiding verbiage. It is from a Minister of Finance to a senior civil servant:

> Apollonius to Zeno, greeting. You did right to send the chickpeas to Memphis. Farewell.

IV

CORRECTNESS

> My Lord, I do here, in the Name of all the Learned and Polite
> Persons of the Nation, complain to Your Lordship, as *First
> Minister*, that our Language is extremely imperfect; that its
> daily Improvements are by no means in proportion to its daily
> Corruptions; that the Pretenders to polish and refine it, have
> chiefly multiplied Abuses and Absurdities; and, that in many
> Instances, it offends against every Part of Grammar.
>
> SWIFT, Proposal for Correcting, Improving and
Ascertaining the English Tongue, 1712

We will now turn to the implications of a remark I made in
Chapter I: 'Lapses from what for the time being is regarded as
correct irritate readers educated to notice errors, distract their
attention, and so make them less likely to be affected precisely as you wish'. This suggests a fourth rule to add to the three
with which we finished the last chapter—'be correct'. It applies
to both vocabulary and grammar. This chapter is concerned
with vocabulary only, and grammar will be the subject of
Chapter IX.

Correctness of vocabulary seems once to have been enforced
more sternly on officials than it is now. More than two centuries
ago the Secretary to the Commissioners of Excise wrote this
letter to the Supervisor of Pontefract:

The Commissioners on their perusal of your 2nd Round Diary observe that you make use of many affected phrases and incongruous words as 'phantation', 'preconception', 'harmony', 'scotomy', 'illegal procedure',... all which you use in a sense which the words do not naturally bear. I am ordered to acquaint you that if you hereafter continue that affected and schoolboy way of writing and to murder the language in such a manner you will be discharged for a fool. (Quoted in Edward Hughes, *Studies in Administration and Finance, 1558–1825*, 1934)

To us the punishment seems disproportionate to the offence, though the same penalty today might prove gratifying to those who think we have too many officials. That said, we can have nothing but admiration for the sentiment of the letter and for the vigorous directness of its phrasing. It serves moreover to illustrate a difficulty presented by this chapter's precept. What is correctness, and who is to be the judge of it? It cannot be the same now as it was then. A collector of customs and excise today might certainly use the expression *illegal procedure* without being called into question, and might even refer safely to 'harmony of relations with trade'. On the other hand it would not do now to say, as the Supervisor of Pontefract might have said, that the local bench was 'an *indifferent* body', meaning that they performed their duties with impartiality, or that a certain businessman *prevented* the arrival of his staff at his office, meaning that he always got there first.

English is not static—neither in vocabulary, nor in grammar, nor yet in that elusive quality called style. The fashion in prose alternates between the ornate and the plain, the elevated and the colloquial. Grammar and punctuation defy all the efforts of grammarians to force them into the mould of a permanent code of rules. Old words drop out or change their meanings; new words are admitted. What was stigmatised by the purists of one generation as a corruption of the language may a few generations later be accepted as an enrichment, and what was then common currency may have become a pompous archaism or acquired new significance.

Eminent figures with a care for the language, such as Swift, have from time to time proposed that an Authority should be set up to preserve what is good and resist what is bad. 'They will find', he said, in his *Proposal for Correcting, Improving and Ascertaining the English Tongue*, 'many Words that deserve to be utterly thrown out of our language, many more to be corrected; and perhaps not a few, long since antiquated, which ought to be restored, on account of their Energy and Sound.' Swift's plea, made in the form of a letter to the Lord Treasurer, came to nothing, causing Lord Chesterfield, Swift's contemporary, to observe dryly in an essay of 1754 that this was less than surprising, 'precision and perspicuity not being in general the favourite objects of Ministers'. A year later, in the Preface to his *Dictionary*, Dr Johnson described the task as hopeless:

> Academies have been instituted, to guard the avenues of their languages, to retain fugitives, and repulse invaders; but their vigilance and activity have hitherto been in vain; sounds are too volatile and subtile for legal restraints; to enchain syllables, and to lash the wind, are equally the undertakings of pride, unwilling to measure its desires by its strength.

More recently we have seen a Society for Pure English, with eminent leaders, inviting the support of those who 'would aim at preserving all the richness of differentiation in our vocabulary, its nice grammatical usages, its traditional idioms, and the music of its inherited pronunciation', but would oppose 'whatever is slipshod and careless, and all blurring of hard-won distinctions', while opposing no less 'the tyranny of schoolmasters and grammarians, both in their pedantic conservatism, and in their ignorant enforcing of new-fangled rules'. But it is now defunct.

Dr Johnson was right, as usual. One has only to look at the

words proposed by Swift for inclusion in his *Index Expurgatorius* to realise how difficult, delicate and disappointing it is to resist new words and new meanings. He condemns, for instance, *sham*, *banter*, *mob*, *bully* and *bamboozle*. A generation later Dr Johnson called *clever* a 'low word' and *fun* and *stingy* 'low cant'. Should we not have been poorer if Swift and Johnson had had their way in this? There is no saying how things will go. The fight for admission to the language is quickly won by some assailants, but long resistance is maintained against others. The word that excited Swift to greatest fury was *mob*, a contraction of *mobile vulgus*. Its victory was rapid and complete. So was that of *banter* and *bamboozle*, which he found hardly less offensive. And if *rep* for *reputation* has never quite risen above being slang, and *phiz* for *physiognomy* is now dead, that is not because Swift denounced them, but because public opinion did not fully embrace them.

Some words gatecrash irresistibly because their sound is so appropriate to the meaning they are trying to acquire. *Gatecrash* is itself an example. It comes from America and has only been in the language since the 1930s. We still have defenders of our tongue who scrutinise such words, condemning them as undesirables. But we ought not to forget how greatly our language has been enriched by the ebullient word-making habit of the Americans. Acquisitions of the past few decades include *debunk*, *commuter*, *cold war*, *nifty*, *babysitter*, *stockpile*, *bulldoze*, *teenager*, *traffic jam*, *underdog* and many others. I do not see why people should turn up their noses at words that usefully fill a gap. These things are a matter of taste, but one's own taste is of no importance unless it happens to reflect the general.

Reliable was long opposed on the curious ground that it was an impossible construction; an adjective formed from *rely* could only be *reli-on-able*. I remember noticing as a junior in the India Office many years ago that the Secretary of State struck it out of a draft despatch and wrote in *trustworthy*, but that must have been almost the last shot fired at it. The objection to it was a survival of a curious theory, widely held in pre-Fowler days, that no sentence could be 'good grammar', and no word a respectable word, if its construction violated logic or reason. But it is not the habit of the English to refrain from doing anything merely because it is illogical, and in any case it was less illogical to accept *reliable* than to strain at it after swallowing *available* and *objectionable*. (I shall have more to say about pedantry when we consider grammar in Chapter IX.)

Nice in the sense in which it is ordinarily used in conversation today has still not yet fully established itself in literary English, though we know from the rather priggish lecture that Henry Tilney gives about it to Catherine Morland in *Northanger Abbey* that it was trying to get over the barrier as far back as the start of the nineteenth century:

> 'Oh! it is a very nice word indeed! it does for every thing. Originally perhaps it was applied only to express neatness, propriety, delicacy, or refinement;—people were nice in their dress, in their sentiments, or their choice. But now every commendation on every subject is comprised in that one word.'
>
> 'While, in fact,' cried his sister, 'it ought only to be applied to you, without any commendation at all. You are more nice than wise.'

Equally, *haver* does not mean 'vacillate' (it means 'blather'), but almost everyone south of the Border thinks it does: there is no withstanding its suggestion of simultaneous hovering and wavering. The dictionaries do not yet recognise this, but doubtless they will soon bow to the inevitable.*

---

* Gowers was right—they did and have. In an early reprint of *The Complete Plain Words* he added his own footnote here to say that a Scottish friend had

There has been further stout resistance to certain words that attacked the barrier in the nineteenth century with powerful encouragement from Dickens—*mutual, individual* and *aggravate*. *Mutual*, not in the sense of 'reciprocated' but of 'common' or 'pertaining to both parties', as in *Our Mutual Friend*, goes back to the sixteenth century, according to the *OED*, yet some people still regard this as incorrect. Perhaps the reason it is so difficult to restrain the word to its 'correct' meaning is the ambiguity of *common*. ('Our common friend' might be taken as a reflection on the friend's manners or birth.)* The use of *individual* that is unquestionably correct is to distinguish a single person from a collective body, as it is used in the Income Tax Acts to distinguish between a personal taxpayer and a corporate one. But its use as a facetious term of disparagement was once common and still lingers. That was how Mr Jorrocks, Surtees's hero, understood it when Mr Martin Moonface described him as an 'unfortunate individual', provoking the retort 'You are another indiwidual'. Over *aggravate* the long-drawn-out struggle still continues between those who, like Dickens, use it in the sense of 'annoy' and those who would confine it to its original sense of 'make worse'.† About all these words, in the minds of purists, the issue is still in the balance.

It is around new verbs that battles rage most hotly. New verbs are ordinarily formed in one of three ways, all of which have been

---

written to him, full of reproaches, describing the English definition of *haver* as 'utterly damnable', and concluding (after further furious comment) 'I deplore your weak-kneed acquiescence'. ~

* On the redundant use of *mutual* in the phrase 'mutually contradictory', see p. 105

† The two meanings of *aggravate* continue to cause trouble, not least because it is sometimes unclear which of them is intended. What is meant, for example, when the *Daily Mail* reports that a certain footballer is 'in danger of missing out after aggravating injury'? ~

employed in the past to create useful additions to our vocabulary. The first is the simple method of treating a noun as a verb. It is one of the beauties of our language that nouns can be converted so readily into verbs and adjectives. *Elbow*, for instance, was a 600-year-old noun when Shakespeare made it into a verb in *King Lear*. The second is what is called 'back-formation', that is to say, forming from a noun the sort of verb from which the noun might have been formed had the verb come first. In this way the verb *diagnose* was formed from *diagnosis*. The third is to add *ise** to an adjective, as *sterilise* has been formed from *sterile*. All these methods are being used today with no little zest. New verbs for something that is itself new (like *pressurise*) cannot be gainsaid. *Service* is a natural and useful newcomer in an age when almost everyone keeps a machine of some sort that needs periodical attention. But it provides an interesting example of the way in which new verbs, once you give them an inch, may take a yard. *Service* is already ousting *serve*, as in

> A large number of depots of one sort or another will be required to service the town.

> To enable the Local Authority to take advantage of this provision it is essential that sites should be available, ready serviced with roads and sewers.

As I write, the credentials of to *contact* are still in dispute between those like Sir Alan Herbert, who in his book of 1935, *What a Word!*, calls it 'loathsome', and those like Ivor Brown, who, in *A Word in your Ear* of 1942, holds that it can claim indulgence on the ground that besides this 'there is no word which covers approach by telephone, letter and speech', and *contact* is

---

* On the question whether this should be *ise* or *ize* see pp. 70–71.

'self-explanatory and concise'. If I were to hazard a prophecy, it would be that *contact* will win, but for the present it still excites in some people feelings akin to those aroused by split infinitives and *those kind of things*. So do *feature, glimpse, position, sense* and *signature* when used as verbs, though all have long since found their way into dictionaries. So do the verbs *loan, gift* and *author*, though these were verbs centuries ago, and are only trying to come back again after a long holiday, spent by *loan* in America, by *gift* in Scotland and by *author* in oblivion. Whatever their fate may prove to be, we shall not be disposed to welcome such a word as *reaccessioned*, used by a librarian of a book once more available to subscribers. To *underground* (of electric cables) seems at first sight an unnecessary addition to our vocabulary of verbs when *bury* is available, but an editor to whom protest was made retorted that *bury* would not have done because the cables were 'live'.

But these words are mere skirmishers. The main body of the invasions consists of verbs ending in *ise*. Among those now nosing their way into the language are *civilianise* (replace military staff by civil), *editorialise* (make editorial comments on), *finalise* (finally settle), *hospitalise* (send to hospital), and *publicise* (give publicity to). The reason for inventing them seems to be to enable us to say in one word what would otherwise need several. Whether that will prove a valid passport time alone can show. If the words I have listed were all, they might be swallowed, though with wry faces. But they are by no means all. A glut of this diet is being offered to us (*trialise, itinerise, casualise* and *reliableise* are among the specimens sent to me), and they continue to come no matter our nausea. It is perhaps significant that at the Coronation of Queen Elizabeth II the word *Inthroning* was substituted for the first time for *Inthronisation*, used in all previous coronations. This may be symptomatic of a revolt against the ugliness of *ise* and still more of *isation*, which Sir Alan Herbert has compared to lavatory fittings, useful in their proper place but not to be multiplied beyond what is necessary for practical purposes.

Another popular way of making new words is to put *de*, *dis* or *non* at the beginning of a word in order to create one with an opposite meaning. *De* and *dis* are termed by the *OED* 'living prefixes with privative force'. 'Living' is the right word. They have been living riotously of late. Anyone, it seems, can make a new verb by prefixing *de* to an existing one. Sir Alan, still on the warpath, drew up a list of a few remarkable creations of this sort, calling them 'septic'. Among his examples were *derestrict, dewater, debureaucratise, decontaminate, dedirt, dehumidify, deratizate* (to eliminate rats), *deinsectize,** dezincify*. (The Ministry of Food, I am told, once fixed maximum prices for *defeathered* geese.)

Some of these, it is to be hoped, may prove to be freaks of an occasion and will be seen no more. But there is a class that appears permanent. This comprises verbs that denote the undoing of something the doing of which called for—or at any rate was given—a special term. If to affect with gas is to *contaminate*, to enforce a speed limit is to *restrict*, and to commandeer a house is to *requisition*, then the cancellation of those things will inevitably, whether we like it or not, be *decontaminate, derestrict* and *derequisition*, and it is no use saying that they ought to be *cleanse, exempt* or *release*, or any other words that are not directly linked with their opposites. Most of the new *dis*-words since the war have been invented by

---

* In 1950, Gowers received a modestly triumphant letter from a friend at the Ministry of Health: 'I have got "deratting" into our own Port Regulations . . . The present drafts use "deratting" and say the ship "should be cleared of rats" instead of "subjected to measures of deratisation"'. Less cheering news was that the World Health Organisation had switched from 'disinsectisation' to the barely improved 'disinsection', which Gowers's correspondent felt should mean (if anything at all) 'healing a cut'. ~

economists (several by *The Economist* itself). *Disincentive* and *disinflation*, received at first with surprised disapproval, seem to have quite settled down. It is recognised that the old-fashioned opposites of *incentive* and *inflation*—*deterrent* and *deflation*—will not do: we need a special word for the particular form of deterrent that discourages us from working hard, and for a process of checking inflation that is something less than deflation. Yet on the heels of these new arrivals come *diseconomy* and *dissaving*:

> It would yield economies that would far outweigh the diseconomies that are the inevitable price of public ownership and giant size.

> Some 13.4 million of the 22 million income earners ... kept their spending in such exact step with their incomes that they saved or dissaved less than £25 in that year.

Will these be accepted also on the ground that in the first, no positive word—neither *extravagance* nor *waste* nor *wastefulness*—would express the writer's meaning so well as 'diseconomies', and that in the second, 'dissaved' is the only way of expressing the opposite of *saved* without a clumsy periphrasis that would destroy the nice balance of the sentence? Perhaps; it is at least certain that these words spring from deliberate and provocative choice and not from mental indolence. What is deplorable is that so many of those who go in for the invention of opposites by means of 'living prefixes with privative force' do not know when to stop. It becomes a disease. 'Disincentive' replaces *deterrent*, then 'undisincentive' ousts *incentive*, and then *disincentive* itself has to yield to 'non-undisincentive'. In George Orwell's 'newspeak', which he pictured as the language of 1984, 'very bad' has become 'doubleplusungood'.

The same warning is needed about the prefix *non*. To put *non* in front of a word is a well-established way of creating a word with the opposite meaning. *Non-appearance*, *non-combatant*, *non-conformist* and *non-existent* are common examples. But the lazy habit of using *non* to turn any word upside down, so as not to have the trouble of thinking of its opposite, is becoming sadly common. 'Institutions for the care of the *non-sick*' presumably means something different from 'institutions for the care of the healthy', but the difference is not apparent. I should have said that this trick was of recent origin if Mr G. M. Young had not sent me an early example of it that would hold against any modern rival. Sir John Simon, an eminent surgeon who later became a government official, giving evidence in 1869 before a Royal Commission on Sanitary Laws, referred to 'a disease hereditarily transmissible and spreading among the non-fornicative part of the population'. Mr Young says he was surprised to come across this, because Simon was a man of culture and a friend of Ruskin. 'It just shows', he adds unkindly, 'what Whitehall can do.'

Yet another favourite device for making new words is the suffix *ee*. This is an erratic suffix, not conforming wholly to any rule. But in its main type it serves to denote the object of a verb, generally the indirect object, as in *assignee*, *referee* and *trustee*, but sometimes the direct object, as in *examinee*, *trainee* and *evacuee*. It therefore makes for confusion of language if the suffix is used to form a word meaning the subject of a verb. *Escapee* is worse than useless; we already have *escaper*. When unskilled labour is used to 'dilute' skilled labour, the unskilled ought to be called not *dilutees*, as they are officially termed, but *dilutors*. The skilled are the *dilutees*. Apart from misuse such as this, we are getting too many *ee* words. They are springing up like weeds. Their purpose seems to be the same as that of many of our new verbs: to enable us to use one word instead of several. But we have got on very well for quite a long time without such words as *expellee* and *persecutee*.

While the age-long practice of creating new words has quickened its tempo, so has the no less ancient habit of extending the meaning of established words. Here again we ought to examine the novelties on their merits, without bias. The main test for both is whether the new word, or the new meaning, fills a need in the vocabulary. If it is trying to take a seat already occupied—as the new verbs *decision* and *suspicion* are squatting in the places of *decide* and *suspect*, and the enlarged meanings of *anticipate* and *claim* in those of *expect* and *assert*—they are clearly harming the language by 'blurring hard-won distinctions'. Still more are words like *overall* and *involve* open to that charge: they are claiming the seats of half a dozen or more honest words. But those that claim seats hitherto empty may deserve to be admitted. *Stagger*, for example, has recently enlarged its meaning logically and usefully in such a phrase as 'staggered holidays'.

Nor do I see why purists should condemn the use of *nostalgic* not only for a feeling of homesickness but also for the emotion aroused by thinking of the days that are no more. An appeal to etymology is not conclusive. When a word starts to stray from its derivative meaning it may often be proper, and sometimes even useful, to try to restrain it. There are many now who would like to restrain the wanderlust of *alibi* and *shambles*. The ignorant misuse of technical terms excites violent reactions in those who know their true meanings. The popular use of *to the nth degree* in the sense of 'to the utmost' exasperates the mathematician, who knows that strictly the notion of largeness is not inherent in *to the nth degree* at all. The use of *by and large* in the sense of 'broadly speaking' exasperates the sailor, who knows that the true meaning of the phrase—alternately close to the wind and with the wind abeam or aft—has not the faintest relation to the meaning given to its present usage. But there is a point when it becomes idle pedantry to try to put back into their etymological cages words and phrases that escaped from them many years ago, and that are now settled down firmly elsewhere. To do so is to start on a path on which there is no logical stopping point short of such absurdities as insisting that *muscle* means nothing but 'little mouse', or that the word *anecdote* can only be applied to a story never told before, whereas we all know that now it generally means one told too often.

Sometimes words appear to have changed their meanings when the real change is in the popular estimate of the value of the ideas they stand for. So *imperialism*, which in 1881 Lord Rosebery, the future Liberal Prime Minister, could define as 'the greater pride in Empire ... a larger patriotism', has fallen from its pedestal. And *academic* is suffering a similar debasement owing to the waning of love of learning for its own sake and the growth of mistrust of intellectual activities that have no immediate utilitarian results. In music, according to the music critic of *The Times*, the word 'has descended from the imputation of high esteem to being a wither-ing term of polite abuse', in spite of an attempt by Stanford, the composer, to stop the rot by describing it as 'a term of opprobrium applied by those who do not know their business to those who do'.

Public opinion decides all these questions in the long run. There is little individuals can do about them. Our national vocabu-lary is a democratic institution, and what is generally accepted will ultimately be correct. I have no doubt that anyone happening to read this book in fifty years' time would find current objections to the use of certain words in certain senses as curious as we now find Swift's denunciation of the word *mob*. Lexicographers soon find this out. I have quoted Dr Johnson. Some seventy years later, Noah Webster was reported by the traveller Basil Hall to have said much the same thing in different words:

> It is quite impossible to stop the progress of language—it is like the course of the Mississippi, the motion of which, at times, is scarcely perceptible; yet even then it possesses a momentum quite irresistible ... Words and expressions will be forced into use, in spite of all the exertions of all the writers in the world.

The duty of the official is, however, clear. Just as it has long been recognised that, in salaries and wages, the Civil Service must neither walk ahead of public opinion nor lag behind it, but, in the old phrase, be 'in the first flight of good employers', so it is the duty of officials in their use of English neither to perpetuate what is obsolescent nor to give currency to what is novel, but, like good servants, to follow what is generally regarded by their masters as the best practice for the time being. Among an official's readers will be vigilant guardians of the purity of English prose, and they must not be offended. So the official's vocabulary must contain only words that by general consent have passed the barrier; and no helping hand should be given to any that are still trying to get through, even if they appear deserving.

> For last year's words belong to last year's language
> And next year's words await another voice.

Mr Eliot adds to these lines from 'Little Gidding', that in the sentence that is 'right',

> every word is at home,
> Taking its place to support the others,
> The word neither diffident nor ostentatious
> An easy commerce of the old and new,
> The common word exact without vulgarity,
> The formal word precise but not pedantic,
> The complete consort dancing together . . .

Note. Gowers remarks in the middle of this chapter, 'There is no saying how things will go'. But after more than half a century, it is at least possible to say what happened next to some of the new or 'loathsome' words that he discussed in 1954.

The verb to *signature*, for example, has failed to stick, but to *underground* survives in the jargon of the National Grid, and to *contact* has become entirely unremarkable. To *service*, which he thought a useful newcomer, almost immediately expanded its meaning into the unhappy realm of the utilitarian sex act. *Dissave* (to spend savings), *diseconomy* and *derestrict* persist as jargon, as does *derequisition*, though liberated from its narrow, post-war meaning. *Dehumidify*, another verb Gowers hoped would disappear completely, has now entered ordinary speech. To *reaccession* is still in use, but he was right that in general we should not be disposed to welcome it; and sadly, since the 1970s to *deaccession* has also found a place, 'deaccessioning', selling off exhibits, being the last resort of the impoverished gallery or museum. Purists still fume when they find *mutual* and *aggravate* given the senses of 'common' and 'annoy' (making *mutual* mean 'common' seems to have started with Shakespeare); however, a further word Gowers listed with those two, *phenomenal*, surely now means 'prodigious' in anyone's vocabulary. As a poor reflection of modern politics, *expellee* and *persecutee,* after something of a lull, are coming back into ever greater use; and *amputee*, another word Gowers thought superfluous, is now unexceptionable. (Some people argue that *amputee* should refer not to the person who has endured surgery but to the bits that got taken off: to Nelson's arm, so to speak, and not the rest of him. At least one might agree that the word itself has been lopped, and should really be 'amputatee'.)

The habit of making adjectives out of other words by adding the suffix *able* continues apace. Those who once protested that *reliable* should be *reli-on-able* would presumably also argue that today's *relatable* should be *relate-to-able*. (According to the *Daily Mail*, the Duchess of Cambridge is 'relatable' because she makes a habit of wearing the same garment twice.) Another adjective of this kind is *scalable* as it is now used in commercial English, where a 'scalable' business is always 'scale-up-able', or one that has the potential to be made larger.

Not all verbs created by means of *ise* are inexpedient, as Gowers conceded. Not all are necessary either. 'Reliableise' and 'deinsectize' may have died a quick death, but *initialise* has jumped the bounds of computer jargon and is now being used in the most general sense of to 'begin'. Again, though to *decision* and to *suspicion* may not have lasted as examples of a form Gowers deplored, modern instances proliferate: to *solution* is creeping into the language in place of to *solve* ('Prior to starting, you need to be able to solution these kinds of questions'); to *action* is used for to *put in action* or simply *do*, to *transition* is made to take the place of *move*, *shift*, *switch*, *adapt*, *change*—even, now, of to *transit*.

There are still writers who have what Gowers called 'the lazy habit of using *non* to turn any word upside down'. A recent statistical report for the Department for Work and Pensions (Research Report No 416) found that men are 'more disadvantaged by disability' than women, giving as one reason that 'a much higher proportion of non-disabled women than non-disabled men are non-employed in any case'. This could perfectly well have been written, 'Among those adults capable of work, women are much less likely than men to have jobs'.

Gowers ended this chapter on correctness with a list, given below, of words and phrases that he described as 'often used in senses generally regarded as incorrect'. Also given below are his clarifications of some knotty points of idiom and of spelling. He drew a distinction between the uses 'generally thought to be incorrect' marshalled in this chapter, and uses he considered merely 'unsuitable', examples of which are given at the end of Chapter VII ('Seductive Words') and Chapter VIII ('Clichés and Overworked Metaphors'). He acknowledged that it was hard to draw a line between the two classes, the 'incorrect' and the merely 'unsuitable', adding that it was still harder to get others to agree about where this line should fall—if they even agreed that it warranted being drawn in the first place. He concluded, 'Even if my choice is right now, it will almost certainly be out of date before long'.

It turns out, however, that by the lights of those who continue to care about these things, many of the words and phrases that he placed in the 'incorrect' category in 1954 remain there. It is true that a few of his bugbears have become so obscure that there is no longer a pressing need to warn against them. Who these days mistakes a *prescriptive* right for an *indefeasible* one, or wrongly uses *desiderate* to mean 'desire'? It is not the fashion now to use 'desiderate' at all, though this verb enshrines what must be a widespread experience, that of longing with painful regret for something we miss or lack. But these obsolete examples are the minority. The rest of his list is given below, followed by a few examples of comparable incorrect uses too recently popular for him to have warned against them. These may themselves in future come to be universally accepted as correct, and in some cases were correct in the past. But for the time being they can be expected to irritate those whom Gowers called 'vigilant guardians of the purity of English prose'. ~

WORDS AND PHRASES OFTEN USED INCORRECTLY

Alibi
Alibi is often now used in the sense of 'excuse', or of an admission of guilt with a plea of extenuating circumstances, or of throwing the blame on someone else. So we find that 'Members of the timber trade, like members of any other trade, are glad of any alibi to explain any particular increases in price'. But *alibi* is the Latin for 'elsewhere'. To plead an alibi is to rebut a charge by adducing evidence that the person charged was elsewhere at the time the criminal act was committed. The mischief is that if the novel, diluted use establishes itself, the language will lose precision, and we shall be left without a word to signify the true meaning of *alibi*.

Alternately and Alternatively
These are sometimes confused. *Alternately* means 'by turns'. *Alternatively* means 'in a way that offers choice'. 'The journey may

be made by rail or alternately by road' means, if it means anything, that every other journey is made by road. It does not mean, as the writer intended, that for every journey, the traveller has a choice between the two means of transport. Conversely, 'alternatively they sat and walked by moonlight, talking of this and that' cannot have been intended to mean that they sat and walked in the moonlight as an alternative to doing something else. What must have been intended is that they sat and walked alternately.

Anticipate

The use of this word as a synonym for *expect* is now so common that it may be a waste of time to fight it any longer. But I should like even now to put in a plea that the official will set a good example by never using *anticipate* except in its correct sense, that is to say, to convey the idea of forestalling or acting in advance of an expected event, as in the time-honoured reply of Chancellors of the Exchequer, 'I cannot anticipate my budget statement'.*

Approximate

This means 'very close'. An *approximate* estimate is one that need not be exact, but should be as near as you can conveniently make it. There is no need to use *approximately* when *about* or *roughly* would do as well or even better. Moreover, the habit of using *approximately* leads to the absurdity of saying 'very approximately' when what is meant is *very roughly*, or in other words, *not* very approximately.

Note. Gowers caved in on this point when he revised Fowler in 1965, allowing that *very approximately* was universally understood

---

* Gowers's 'time-honoured' example now marks a different sort of decline in standards, as today's Chancellors of the Exchequer appear to have few qualms about leaking details of their budget statements. ~

to mean 'very roughly'. It is worth remembering, even so, that because *proximate* means 'close' the phrase *close proximity* is tautological. ~

A Priori

Do not say *a priori* when you mean *prima facie*. In fact you can probably get by without either. It is wrong to say that if many medically advanced countries have done without a certain drug for twenty years, this 'is sufficient to show that there is an *a priori* case for its total abolition'. To argue *a priori* is to argue from assumed axioms and not from experience. (The fact that the argument here rests on the twenty-year experience of several countries makes it an argument *a posteriori*.)

Prima facie, which is probably what the writer had in mind, means 'on a first impression', before hearing fully the evidence for and against.

Beg the Question

To *beg the question* is to form a conclusion by making an assumption that is as much in need of proof as the conclusion itself. Logicians call this *petitio principii*. Brewer gives the following example: 'to say that parallel lines will never meet because they are parallel is simply to assume as a fact the very thing you profess to prove'.

Note. Gowers felt it necessary to add to this explanation that to *beg the question* did not mean (as was then commonly supposed) to 'evade a straight answer to a question'. It does not mean that today either, in common or any other use: the error he was resisting has been overwhelmed by another. The phrase to '*beg* the question' is now so far removed from its original meaning that it is freely used where to 'raise' a question would do, though the choice of *beg* can sometimes imply special urgency. If there is any lingering sense of difficulty attached to 'begging' a question, it is perhaps reflected in the peculiar new usage, to 'beggar the question'. Presumably this mutation has sprung into being as an echo of 'beggaring' belief or description (a figurative use introduced into the language by Shakespeare). But though to *beggar* means to 'exhaust' or 'outdo', a question supposedly 'beggared' is not introduced in this way because it is thought unanswerable. Rather, it has yet to be answered.

There is no hope that 'begging the question' will ever again be reserved for the censure of *petitio principii* (reserved, that is, for condemning the logic of a remark such as 'mercy killing cannot be condoned because it involves the taking of a life'). Yet even a liberal ear, happy to accept *beg* as meaning 'raise', might baulk at how *beg the question* is itself now regularly mangled. In the *Daily Mail* we find, 'the question begs: when should you give in . . . ?'; a correspondent for *The Times* writes, 'But as your question begs: where and how?'; and in a sociology journal, an academic throws out rhetorically, 'The question begs of why?' It is tempting to respond, in the words of a writer for the *Guardian*, 'The whole thing beggars several questions'. ~

Comprise

A body *comprises*, or consists of, the elements of which it is *composed*, or constituted. It is wrong to speak of the 'smaller Regional Hospitals which comprise a large proportion of those available to Regional Boards'. Here, the Regional Hospitals *form* or *constitute* a large proportion of those available.

The *OED* recognises *comprise* in the sense of 'compose', but calls it 'rare'. Once again, in the interests of precision, it should remain so. The difference between *comprise* and *include* is that *comprise* is better when all the components are enumerated and *include* when only some of them are.

Note. Perhaps it was a general anxiety about the distinction Gowers outlines above that gave rise to the garbled form 'comprises of'. This phrase is a particular favourite of estate agents in their descriptions of houses for sale, though it is made to vie for place with 'boasts of': 'the accommodation comprises of three bedrooms, generous lounge, separate dining room ...'. Though *comprises* alone (or even *boasts* alone) would be correct here, *has* is all that is really needed. ~

Definitive

This word differs from *definite* by imparting the idea of finality. A *definite* offer is an offer exact in its terms. A *definitive* offer is the last word of the person who makes it.

Dilemma

Dilemma originally had a precise meaning that it would be a pity not to preserve. It should not therefore be treated as the equivalent of a 'difficulty', or, colloquially, a 'fix' or a 'jam'. To be in a *dilemma* (or, if you want to show your learning, to be 'on the horns of a dilemma') is to be faced with two (and only two) courses of action, each of which is likely to have awkward results.

Disinterested

Disinterested, according to the *OED*, means 'unbiased by personal interest'. It is sometimes wrongly used for *uninterested*, i.e. 'not interested'. A minister recently said that he hoped an earlier speech he had given in Parliament would excuse him 'from the charge of being disinterested in this matter'. But people in such positions, dealing with public business, can never be 'charged' with being disinterested, as if it were a crime. It is their elementary duty always to be so.

i.e. and e.g.

These are sometimes confused, especially by the wrong use of i.e. to introduce an example; i.e. (*id est*) means 'that is' and introduces a definition, as one might say 'we are meeting on the second Tuesday of this month, i.e. the tenth'; e.g. (*exempli gratia*) means 'for the sake of example' and introduces an illustration, as one might say 'let us meet on a fixed day every month, e.g. the second Tuesday'.

Infer

It is a common error to use *infer* for *imply*: 'I felt most bitter about this attitude . . . it inferred great ignorance and stupidity on the part of the enemy'. A writer or speaker *implies* what a reader or hearer *infers*. 'If you see a man staggering along the road you may infer that he is drunk, without saying a word;' explains Sir Alan Herbert, 'but if you say "Had one too many?" you do not infer but imply that he is drunk.' There is authority for *infer* in the sense of *imply*, as there is for *comprise* in the sense of *compose*. But here again the distinction is worth preserving in the interests of the language.

Leading Question

This does not mean, as is widely supposed, a question designed to embarrass the person questioned. On the contrary, because it is asked in such a way as to suggest its own answer, it may be one that helps the person. 'You never meant to damage the Department's reputation, did you?' is a leading question. 'What did you do?' is not. In court, lawyers are barred from putting leading questions to witnesses whom they themselves have called.

Majority

The major part and *the majority* ought not to be used when a plain *most* would meet the case. They should be reserved for occasions when the difference between a majority and a minority is significant. Thus 'most of the members have been slack in their attendance', but 'the majority of members are likely to be against the proposal'.

Maximum

It is curiously easy to say the opposite of what one means when making comparisons of quantity, time or distance, especially if they are negative. A common type of this confusion is to be found in such statements as 'Meetings will be held at not *less* than monthly intervals', when what is meant is that the meetings will be not less frequent than once a month, that is to say, at not *more* than monthly intervals. *Maximum* and *minimum* sometimes cause a similar confusion, leading to one being used for the other, as has happened in the following sentence taken from a passage condemning the wounding of wild animals by shooting at them from too far away: 'It would be impossible to attempt to regulate shooting by laying down minimum ranges and other details of that sort'.

Mitigate

Mitigate for *militate* is a curiously common malapropism. An example is: 'I do not think this ought to mitigate against my chances of promotion'.

Note. Though Gowers saw no need to explain further, he could have added that the expression 'mitigate against' is not only curiously common but also simply curious. To *militate against* is to 'counter' or to exert a negative force on something, but to *mitigate* means to make more bearable or to 'appease'. 'Mitigate against' ought therefore to have a sense akin to 'alleviate against', which, if it means anything at all, should cancel itself out. All the same, when a former Chief of the General Staff, in an article on combat in Afghanistan, explains that 'an unlucky shot by a rocket-propelled grenade or a machinegun at close range remains a hazard that is very hard to mitigate against', this does somehow carry the ring of truth. ~

Practical and Practicable

Practical, with its implied antithesis of *theoretical*, means 'useful in practice'. *Practicable* means simply 'capable of being carried out in action', should anyone wish to do so. Something that is practicable may nevertheless be impractical (such as hoisting a loose giraffe on to the deck of a ship).

Protagonist

This word is not the opposite of *antagonist* (one who contends with another). The pair must not be used as synonyms of *supporter* and *opponent*, the *pros* and the *antis*. *Protagonist* has nothing to do with the Latin word *pro*: its first syllable is derived from a Greek word meaning 'first'. Its literal meaning is the principal actor in a play; hence it is used for the most prominent personage in any affair. It is not necessarily associated with the advocacy of anything, although it often happens to be so in fact. When we say that Mr Willett was protagonist in the movement for summer time, we are not saying that he was *pro* summer time. We are saying that he played a leading part in the movement. *Protagonist* should not be used in the sense merely of 'advocate' or 'champion'.

Resource

There is much pardonable confusion between *resource*, *recourse* and *resort*. The most common mistake is to write 'have resource to' instead of *have recourse to* or *have resort to*. The correct usage can be illustrated thus: 'They had recourse (or had resort, or resorted) to their reserves; it was their last recourse (or resort); they had no other resources'.

Transpire

It is a common error to use *transpire* as if it meant 'happen' or 'occur'. It does not. It means to 'become known'. An example of its wrong use is: 'I was in Glasgow, attending what transpired to be a very successful series of meetings'.

Note. The misuse described here dates from the eighteenth century. If nowadays you were to write that something had 'transpired' when you meant no more than that it had *happened*, you would still annoy a purist (if you could find one), whereas if you wished to suggest in a public document that something previously secret had leaked out and become known, and so correctly wrote that it had *transpired*, your precise meaning would escape all but a very few. ~

Wastage

Wastage should not be used as a more dignified alternative to *waste*. The ordinary meaning of *waste* is 'useless expenditure or consumption' of money, time, etc. The ordinary meaning of *wastage* is 'loss by use, decay, evaporation, leakage, or the like'. You may, for instance, properly say that the daily wastage of a reservoir is so many gallons. But you must not say that a contributory fact is the 'wastage' of water by householders if what you mean is that householders waste it.

Note. Though Gowers's distinction here is no longer fully supported by the *OED*, some may still find it interesting. In modern professional jargon, *waste* is frequently referred to as 'arisings', but that is another matter. ~

NOTE. SOME CURRENT EXAMPLES

Behalf

A person who acts on your *behalf* is your agent or representative. (It used to be that someone who defended your cause or sought to further your interests acted *in* your behalf, but this distinction is now largely forgotten.) Just as it would make no sense to say that you acted 'instead of' yourself, so it is wrong in correct English to use the formula, 'It was a bit of a mistake on my behalf to eat that pie'. The error here is easily corrected by saying 'It was a bit of a mistake on my part to eat that pie', but the misuse of 'on so-and-so's *behalf*' to mean 'on so-and-so's *part*' (or even '*by* so-and-so') is increasingly common.

Impunity
The *OED* defines *impunity* as meaning 'exemption from punishment or penalty', but it is starting to be used as though it means roughly the opposite. Thus a *Guardian* journalist can write that 'The committee was charged with examining how a Times reporter . . . had managed to fabricate and plagiarise dozens of stories without impunity for so long'; and a reporter for the *Independent* can explain that 'A series of legal actions will mean that the millions of users . . . can no longer post their comments without impunity'. Both examples require *impunity* to mean 'fear of punishment'—unless perhaps *without* is to be thought of as meaning 'with'.

Incredulous
Incredulous means 'disbelieving', or more loosely, 'amazed', 'thunderstruck', and so on. In an academic paper on information display systems, discussing the real case of an aeroplane whose fuel line ruptured in flight, it is stated that the pilot found himself faced by the 'sudden and unexpected presentation of apparently anomalous and incredulous information'. Information somehow capable of feeling disbelief would indeed be an anomaly: though the information may have seemed incredible, only the pilot could have been 'incredulous'.

Infinitesimal
An early press release for the Visitor Centre at CERN's Large Hadron Collider advertised an exhibition that would plunge people into the fascinating world of particles, including

'infinitesimally large' ones. It is no longer unusual to find *infinitesimally* used as though it somehow has more to it of the infinite than *infinitely* does, but in correct English *infinitesimally* is only ever used to qualify what is very small.

May

The difference between *may* and *can* is that if you *may* do something, you are permitted to do it, but to say that you *can* do it is to say no more than that, if permitted, you would be capable. Those who can build a bomb have the knowledge and wherewithal to build a bomb, but not necessarily the permission that says they may.

May may be used to express a future possibility: 'tomorrow it may be stormy'. But it is incorrectly substituted for the post-conditional *might*: 'they might have got married last year, had she not been stuck in prison'. A cricket correspondent for *The Times* makes this error: 'Had it not been for India's success in South Africa, the IPL may never have happened'. The Indian Premier League already had happened by the time these lines were written. (It is with us still.) The reporter meant that the IPL *might* never have happened.

Reticent

It is now common for people to use *reticent*, which means 'reserved' and 'likely to keep quiet', as though it has the sense of *reluctant*, or disinclined and unwilling. In a *Daily Telegraph* article about the heir to a banking family, the young man in question is described as 'famously reticent about publicity', which is then explained as meaning 'somewhat backward in coming forward'. If the young man is truly reticent about publicity, he is not reluctant to step into the limelight, but keeps his own counsel in the matter of publicity itself.

Up to Date

To keep something *up to date* is to keep it current. The substitutes 'up to day' and 'up today' are starting to creep into the language. (The next step may be 'uptoday'.) Neither version is yet over the barrier, but *Private Eye* is keen to help, saying of the MoD's hospitality register that its details are 'skimpy and not terribly up to day'. The notionally related phrase 'out of day' does not yet exist, but 'sell by day' does, bringing to mind darkened supermarket aisles haunted by revenant items from the meat counter.

Other incorrect uses that seem ever more fashionable—ones that mangle what remain the prevailing meanings of the words they confuse—include the phrase to 'make abeyance' for *make obeisance* (to be *in abeyance* is to be temporarily dormant or in suspension; to *make obeisance* is to pay homage); 'heart-rendering' for *heart-rending* (the first suggests melting the fat out of a piece of meat; the second means ripping the heart asunder); 'antidotal evidence' for *anecdotal evidence* (an *antidote* is a medicine that counters the effect of a poison; *anecdotal evidence* is evidence flimsily drawn from anecdotes); 'emerged in' for *immersed in* ('emerged in' seems to blend *immersed in* with *submerged*, but strictly means something like 'came out of in'); 'lost in the midst of time', which we all are, so that it hardly seems worth saying, for *lost in the mists of time* (i.e. 'lost in the impenetrable past'); a 'fool's economy' for a *false economy* (the second may be the first, but a *false economy* is specifically one where the pursuit of a perceived benefit will have unfortunate consequences that outweigh the desired advantage); and 'from the offing' for *from the off* (the *offing* is a nautical term for an area of sea that is visible from land but some way out from shore; the following job advertisement can therefore really only be aimed at a businesslike mermaid: 'A calm and assertive individual with plenty of commercial acumen, you will be content to work without supervision from the offing and possess outstanding organisational abilities'). ~

SOME POINTS OF IDIOM

Idiom is defined by the *OED* as 'a group of words established by usage as having a meaning not deducible from the meanings of the individual words'. When anything in this book is called 'good English idiom' or *idiomatic*, what is meant is that usage has established it as correct. Idiom does not conflict with grammar or logic as a matter of course; it may be grammatically and logically neutral. Idiom requires us to say *try to get* not 'try at getting'. Logic and grammar do not object to this, but they would be equally content with 'try at getting'. At the same time idiom is, in Otto Jespersen's phrase, a 'tyrannical, capricious, utterly incalculable thing' (*Progress in Language*, 1894), and if logic and grammar get in its way, so much the worse for logic and grammar. It is idiomatic—at least in speech—to say 'I won't be longer than I can help' and 'it's me'. That the first is logically nonsense and the second a grammatical howler is neither here nor there; idiom makes light of such things. Yet during the reign of pedantry, attempts were constantly made to force idiom into the mould of logic. We were not to speak of a criminal being 'executed', for 'the *person* is *prosecuted*, the *sentence executed*'; we were not to say 'vexed question', for 'in our English sense, many a question vexes: none is vexed'; nor 'most thoughtless', an expression 'inelegant and unhappy', for if a person is without thought there cannot be degrees in the lack of that quality; nor 'light the fire', for 'nothing has less need of lighting'; nor 'round the fireside', for that would mean that 'some of us are behind the chimney'. So, in his *Imaginary Conversations*, argued Walter Savage Landor, sometimes as himself, sometimes in the person of Horne Tooke, but in both guises a stout and undiscriminating defender of his language against the intrusion of the illogical.

In spite of Fowler and Jespersen, some trace still lingers of the idea that what is illogical 'must' be wrong, such as condemnation of *under the circumstances* and of the uses of a plural verb with *none*. The truth, in the words of Logan Pearsall Smith, is that

> a language which was all idiom and unreason would be impossible as an instrument of thought; but all languages permit the existence of a certain number of illogical expressions: and the fact that, in spite of their vulgar origin and illiterate appearance, they have succeeded in elbowing their way from popular speech into our prose and poetry, our learned lexicons and grammars, is a proof that they perform a necessary function in the domestic economy of speech.   (*Words and Idioms*, 1925)

Circumstances

It used to be widely held by purists that to say 'under the circumstances' must be wrong because what is around us cannot be over us. *In the circumstances* was the correct expression. This argument is characterised by Fowler as puerile. Its major premiss is not true ('a threatening sky is a circumstance no less than a threatening bulldog') and even if it were true it would be irrelevant, because, as cannot be too often repeated, English idiom has a contempt for logic. There is good authority for *under the circumstances*, and if some prefer *in the circumstances* (as I do), that is a matter of taste, not of rule.

Compare

There is a difference between *compare to* and *compare with*. The first is taken to liken one thing to another: 'Shall I compare thee to a summer's day?' The second is to establish that the resemblances and differences between two things are about to be weighed. Thus: 'If we compare the speaker's note with the report of his speech in *The Times* . . .'.

Consist
There is a difference between *consist of* and *consist in*. *Consist of* denotes the substance of which the subject is made: 'The writing desks consist of planks on trestles'. *Consist in* defines the subject: 'The work of the branch consists in interviewing the public'.

Depend
It is wrong in formal writing, though common in speech, to omit the *on* or *upon* after *depends*, as in: 'It depends whether we have received another consignment by then'.

Different
There is good authority for *different to*, but *different from* is today the established usage. 'Different than' is not unknown even in *The Times*:

> The air of the suburb has quite a different smell and feel at eleven o'clock in the morning or three o'clock in the afternoon than it has at the hours when the daily toiler is accustomed to take a few hurried sniffs of it.

But this is condemned by the grammarians, who would say that *than* in this example should have been *from what*.

Doubt
Idiom requires *whether* after a statement of positive doubt, and *that* after one that is negative or rhetorical. 'I doubt whether he will come today' implies an active state of doubt as to whether or not he will come. 'I doubt that he will come to day' implies that there is no expectation that he will come.

Either

Some grammarians argue that *either* means one or other of two. But it has been used to mean each of two throughout its history, as in Tennyson's lines:

> On either side the river lie
> Long fields of barley and of rye

or in, 'The concert will be broadcast on either side of the nine o'clock news'. As this usage (each of two) remains common, there does not seem to be any good ground for Fowler's dictum that it is 'archaic and should be avoided'.

First

There used to be a grammarians' rule that you must not write *firstly*; your enumeration must be *first, secondly, thirdly.* It was one of those arbitrary rules whose observance was supposed by a certain class of purist to be a hallmark of correct writing. This rule, unlike many of the sort, does not even have logic on its side. Of late years there has been a rebellion against these rules, and I do not think that any contemporary grammarian will mind much whether you say *first* or *firstly*, or indeed *first, second, third.*

Follows (as Follows)

Do not write 'as follow' for *as follows*, however numerous the things that follow. The *OED* states that 'The construction in *as follows* is impersonal, and the verb should always be used in the singular'.

Got

'Have got' for *possess* or *have*, says Fowler, is good colloquial but not good literary English. Others have been more lenient. Dr Johnson, in his *Dictionary*, said:

he has got *a good estate* does not always mean that he has acquired, but barely that he possesses it. So we say *the lady* has got *black eyes*, merely meaning that she has them.

When such high authorities differ, what is the ordinary person to think? If it is true, as I hold it to be, that superfluous words are an evil, we ought to condemn 'the lady has got black eyes' (for 'the lady has black eyes'), but not 'the lady has got a black eye' (someone hit her). Still, in writing for those whose prose inclines more often to primness than to colloquialisms, and who are not likely to overdo this use of *got*, I advise them not to be afraid of it.

Hard and Hardly
Hard, not *hardly*, is the adverb of the adjective *hard*. *Hardly* must not be used except in the sense of 'scarcely'. *Hardly earned* and *hard-earned* have quite different meanings. 'Their reward was hardly earned': they were rewarded but did little to deserve it; 'their hard-earned reward': the reward they went to great lengths to earn. (*Hardly*, like *scarcely*, is followed by *when* in a sentence such as: 'I had hardly begun when I was interrupted'. Sometimes *than* intrudes – 'hardly begun *than* I was interrupted'—from a false analogy with 'I had no sooner begun than I was interrupted'.)

Help
The expression 'more than one can help' is a literal absurdity. It means exactly the opposite of what it says. 'I won't be longer than I can help' means 'I won't be longer than is unavoidable', which is to say, longer than I *can't* help. But it is good English idiom. Sir Winston Churchill writes in *The Gathering Storm*: 'They will not respect more than they can help treaties extracted from them under duress'. Writers who find the ridiculousness of the phrase more than they can stomach can always write 'more than they must' instead.

Inculcate

One *inculcates* ideas into people (as one might urge ideas upon them), not people with ideas. *Imbue* would be the right word for that. A vague association with *inoculate* may have something to do with the mistaken use of 'inculcate with'.

Inform

Inform cannot be used with a verb in the infinitive, and the writer of this sentence has gone wrong: 'I am informing the branch to grant this application'. This should have been *telling* or *asking*.

Less and Fewer

The following is taken from *Good and Bad English* (1950) by Whitten and Whitaker:

> *Less* appertains to degree, quantity or extent; *fewer* to number. Thus, *less* outlay, *fewer* expenses; *less* help, *fewer* helpers; *less* milk, *fewer* eggs.
>
> But although 'few' applies to number do not join it to the word itself: 'a fewer number' is incorrect; say 'a smaller number.'
>
> 'Less' takes a singular noun, 'fewer' a plural noun; thus, 'less opportunity,' 'fewer opportunities.'

Prefer

You may say 'He prefers writing to dictating' or 'he prefers to write rather than to dictate', but not 'he prefers to write than to dictate'.

Prevent

You may choose any one of three constructions with *prevent*: prevent *them from coming*, prevent *them coming* and prevent *their coming*.

Purport (verb)

The ordinary meaning of this verb is 'to profess or claim by its tenor' (*OED*), e.g. 'this letter purports to be written by you'. The use of the verb in the passive is an objectionable and unnecessary innovation. 'Statements which were purported to have been official confirmed the rumours' should be 'statements which purported to be official confirmed the rumours'.

Unequal

The idiom is unequal *to*, not *for*, a task.

A FEW POINTS OF SPELLING

Note. As well as discussing the use of *ise* and *ize*, Gowers gave a few examples of words that sometimes cause confusion because, though spelled differently, they sound the same (known as *homophones*). He did not cite pairs where the words are likely to be mistaken through sheer carelessness, such as *here* and *there* and *hear* and *their*, but ones where the distinct meanings of the paired words are not always understood. The list has been very slightly expanded. ~

Ise or Ize

On the question whether verbs like *organise* and nouns like *organisation* should be spelled with an *s* or a *z* the authorities differ. The *OED* favours universal *ize*, arguing that the suffix is always in its origin either Greek or Latin, and in both languages is spelt with a *z*. Other authorities, including some English printers, recommend universal *ise*. Fowler stands between these two opinions. He points out that the *OED*'s advice over-simplifies the problem, as there are some verbs (e.g. *advertise, comprise, despise, exercise* and *surmise*) that are never spelt *ize* in this country. On the other hand, he says, 'the difficulty of remembering which these *ise* verbs are is the only reason for making *ise* universal, and the sacrifice of significance to ease does not seem justified'. This austere conclusion will not recommend itself to everyone, and the round advice to end them all in *ise* is a verdict with which I respectfully agree.

Complement /Compliment

One thing *complements* another if it fulfils or completes it. A report on efficient new ways to kill rats might *complement* a report on the estimated number of rats infesting London's Underground system. A *compliment* is an expression by which one offers praise ('Both reports were excellent').

Note. These days to *complement* is often used as though it means no more than to 'match' or 'go well with': 'She wore ruby earrings to complement her red shoes'. This dispenses with the word's more precise meaning, which the following sentence preserves: 'She wore rubies to complement her red outfit'. ~

Dependant /Dependent

In the ordinary usage of today *dependant* is a noun meaning 'a person who depends on another for support, position, etc.' (*OED*). *Dependent* is an adjective meaning relying on or subject to something else. Dependants are dependent on the person whose dependants they are.

Discreet /Discrete

Someone who is *discreet* is quiet, tactful, unobtrusive, circumspect. A *discrete* entity is one that is separate or self-contained. In the greater difficulty of selling an undesirable house, one might face the discrete problem of its having a leak in the roof.

Enquiry /Inquiry

Enquiry and *inquiry* have long existed together as alternative spellings of the same word. In America *inquiry* is dislodging *enquiry* for all purposes. In England a useful distinction is developing: *enquiry* is used for asking a question and *inquiry* for making an investigation. Thus you might 'enquire what time the Inquiry begins'.

Forego/Forgo

To *forego* is to go before ('the foregoing provisions of this Act'). To *forgo* is to go without, to waive ('I will forgo my right').

Principal/Principle

Principal means primary, leading or most important. Matters of *principle* are matters of fundamental moral belief. ('The principal point at issue is not what he did, so much as that in doing it he broke his word. It is against my principles to accept this.')

Proscribe/Prescribe

To *proscribe* is to ban or exclude. To *prescribe* is to authorise a course of action or lay down a rule. Doctors prescribe medicines, but a responsible person might proscribe the use of pills prescribed by a quack.

V

THE CHOICE OF WORDS (1)

Introductory

> The craftsman is proud and careful of his tools: the surgeon
> does not operate with an old razor-blade; the sportsman fusses
> happily and long over the choice of rod, gun, club or racquet.
> But the man who is working in words, unless he is a professional
> author (and not always then), is singularly neglectful of his
> implements.
>
> IVOR BROWN, *Just Another Word*, 1943

Here we come to the most important part of our subject. Correctness is not enough. The words used may all be words approved by the dictionary and used in their right senses; the grammar may be faultless and the idiom above reproach. Yet what is written may still fail to convey a ready and precise meaning to the reader. That it does fail on these grounds is the charge brought against much of what is written nowadays, including much of what is written by officials. In the first chapter I quoted a saying of Matthew Arnold, that the secret of style is to have something to say and to say it as clearly as you can. The basic fault of much present-day writing is that it seems to say what it has to say in as complicated a way as possible. Instead of being terse and direct, it is stilted, long-winded and circumlocutory. Instead of choosing the simple word it prefers the unusual. Instead of the plain phrase, it resorts to cliché.

This sort of writing has been called 'barnacular',* and the American word for it is 'gobbledygook'. Its nature can be studied not only in the original but also in translation. George Orwell, in his essay 'Politics and the English Language', took the passage in Ecclesiastes about the race not being to the swift nor the battle to the strong,† and put it into 'modern English': 'success or failure in competitive activities exhibits no tendency to be commensurate with innate capacity'. It may be significant that many critics have found their greatest contrasts with barnacular writing in the Bible or Prayer Book. English style over the years must have been immeasurably influenced by everyone's intimate knowledge of these two books, whose cadences were heard every day at family prayers and every Sunday at matins and evensong. Now family prayers are said no longer, and few go to church.

The forms that gobbledygook commonly takes in official writing will be examined in the following three chapters. In this one we are concerned (if I may borrow a bit of jargon from the doctors) with the aetiology of the disease, and with prescribing some general regimen to help avoid catching it.

Why do so many writers spurn simplicity? Officials are far from being the only offenders. It seems to be a morbid condition contracted in early adulthood. Children show no sign of it. Here, for example, is the response of a child of ten to an invitation to write an essay on a bird and a beast:

---

* The obscure term 'barnacular', which Ivor Brown attempted to popularise in the 1940s, was designed to invoke the Tite Barnacles of the Circumlocution Office in *Little Dorrit*. ~
† Ecclesiastes 9:11, 'I returned, and saw under the sun, that the race is not to the swift, nor the battle to the strong, neither yet bread to the wise, nor yet riches to men of understanding, nor yet favour to men of skill; but time and chance happeneth to them all'.

The bird that I am going to write about is the owl. The owl cannot see at all by day and at night is as blind as a bat.

I do not know much about the owl, so I will go on to the beast which I am going to choose. It is the cow. The cow is a mammal. It has six sides—right, left, an upper and below. At the back it has a tail on which hangs a brush. With this it sends the flies away so that they do not fall into the milk. The head is for the purpose of growing horns and so that the mouth can be somewhere. The horns are to butt with, and the mouth is to moo with. Under the cow hangs the milk. It is arranged for milking. When people milk, the milk comes and there is never an end to the supply. How the cow does it I have not yet realised, but it makes more and more. The cow has a fine sense of smell; one can smell it far away. This is the reason for the fresh air in the country.

The man cow is called an ox. It is not a mammal. The cow does not eat much, but what it eats it eats twice, so that it gets enough. When it is hungry it moos, and when it says nothing it is because its inside is all full up with grass.

The child who wrote this had something to say and said it as clearly as possible, and so unconsciously achieved style.* But why do we write, when we are ten, 'so that the mouth can be somewhere', and perhaps when we are thirty, 'in order to ensure that the mouth may be appropriately positioned environmentally'? What songs do the sirens sing to lure a writer into barnacular realms? This question, though puzzling, is not beyond all conjecture. I will hazard one or two.

---

* A slightly different version of this little essay, 'The Bird and the Beast', appears in a Classics journal of the 1940s, where it is translated into Greek. There its author is described as being an evacuee, and, in a later reprint, as a schoolgirl. ~

The first affects only the official. It is tempting to cling too long to outworn words and phrases. The British Constitution, as everyone knows, has been shaped by retaining old forms and putting them to new uses. Among the old forms that we are reluctant to abandon are those found in State documents. Every Bill begins with the words: 'Be it enacted by the Queen's Most Excellent Majesty, by and with the advice and consent of the Lords Spiritual and Temporal, and Commons, in this present Parliament assembled, and by the authority of the same, as follows. . .'. It ends its career as a Bill and becomes an Act when the Clerk of the Parliaments is authorised by the Queen to declare 'La Reine le veult'. That is all very well, because no one ever reads these traditional phrases; they are no longer intended to convey thought from one brain to another. And none of us would much like the official to say, 'That's OK by Her Majesty'. But officials, living in this atmosphere, and properly proud of the ancient traditions of their service, sometimes allow their own style of writing to be affected by it—*adverting* and *acquainting* and *causing to be informed of same*. There may even be produced in the minds of some officials the feeling that a common word lacks the dignity that they are bound to maintain.

That, I think, is one song the sirens sing to the official. Another they certainly sing to us all. Wells's Mr Polly, from a love of striking phrases, speaks of 'sesquippledan verboojuice', and there is something of Mr Polly in most of us, especially when young. But any person of sensibility may be tempted by rippling or reverberating polysyllables. *Evacuated to alternative accommodation* seems to give a satisfaction that cannot be got from *taken to another house*; *ablution facilities* strikes a chord that does not vibrate to *wash basins*. Far-fetched words are by definition 'recherché'. They are thought to give distinction, and so examples like *implement*, *optimum* and *global* acquire their vogue. A newly discovered metaphor shines like a jewel in a drab vocabulary: *blueprint, bottle-*

neck, *ceiling* and *target* are eagerly seized, and the dust settles on their discarded predecessors—*plan*, *hold up*, *limit* and *objective*.* But it will not do. Official writing is essentially of the sort of which Manilius said: 'Ornari res ipsa negat contenta doceri'—the very subject matter rules out ornament; it asks only to be put across.

Another song I am sure the sirens have in their repertoire is a call to the instinct for self-preservation. It is sometimes dangerous to be precise. Newman, in a severe passage from his *Apologia Pro Vita Sua*, characterises 'Church-of-Englandism' as a state of being in thrall to the idea that 'mistiness is the mother of wisdom'. A figure whom he calls 'your safe man and the hope of the Church' is required to guide the Church through 'the channel of no-meaning, between the Scylla and Charybdis of Aye and No'. If so, ecclesiastics are not in this respect unique. Politicians have long known the danger of precise statements, especially at election time. An astute American senator, asked to explain a declaration that 'Americanism' was to be the year's campaign issue, is said to have replied that he did not know what it meant, but that it was going to be 'a damn good word with which to carry an election'. Disraeli made the same point in his novel of 1844, *Coningsby*:

> 'And now for our cry!' said Mr Taper.
>
> 'It is not a Cabinet for a good cry,' said Tadpole; 'but then, on the other hand, it is a Cabinet that will sow dissension in the opposite ranks, and prevent them having a good cry.'
>
> '*Ancient* institutions and *modern* improvements, I suppose, Mr Tadpole?'
>
> 'Ameliorations is the better word; ameliorations. Nobody knows exactly what it means.'

---

* This list continues to grow, so that we now also have, among others, *roadmaps*, *pinch-points*, *cut-off points* and *core goals*. ~

When an official does not know a minister's mind, when perhaps the minister does not know it either, or when the minister thinks it wiser not to speak too plainly, the official's own utterances will sometimes necessarily be covered with a mist of vagueness. Civil Service methods are often contrasted unfavourably with those of business. But to make this comparison is to forget that no board of directors of a business concern have to meet a committee of their shareholders every afternoon, to submit themselves daily to an hour's questioning on their conduct of the business, to get the consent of that committee by a laborious process to every important step they take, or to conduct their affairs with the constant knowledge that there is a shadow board eager for the shareholders' authority to take their place. The systems are quite different and are bound to produce different methods. Ministers are under daily attack, and their reputations are largely in the hands of their staffs. Only civil servants who have full and explicit authority from their ministers can show in important matters that prompt boldness that is said to be businesslike.

The following extract is from a letter written by a government department to its Advisory Council:

> In transmitting this matter to the Council the Minister feels that it may be of assistance to them to learn that, as at present advised, he is inclined to the view that, in the existing circumstances, there is, *prima facie*, a case for ...

The extract was sent by a correspondent to *The Times* for ridicule, but provoked a more judicious response:

> even though mathematical accuracy may in the nature of things be unattainable, identifiable inaccuracy must at least be avoided. The hackneyed official phrase, the wide circumlocution, the vague promise, the implied qualification are comfortingly to hand. Only those who have been exposed to the temptation to use them know

how hard it is to resist. But with all the sympathy that such understanding may mean, it is still possible to hold that something
might be done to purge official style and caution, necessary and
desirable in themselves, of their worst extravagances.

It is as easy to slip into extravagant caution as it is to see the
absurdity of it when pointed out. One may surmise that the writer
of the original letter wanted the Advisory Council to advise the
Minister in a certain way, but did not want them to think that
the Minister's mind was already made up before getting their
advice. The writer might have achieved these ends without piling
qualification on qualification and reservation on reservation. All
that was needed here was to say that the Minister thought
so-and-so but wanted to know what the Advisory Council
thought before taking a decision.

This example illustrates another trap into which official writing is led when it has to leave itself a bolt-hole, as it so often
must. Cautionary clichés are used automatically, without thought
of what they mean. There are two of them here: *inclined to think*
and *as at present advised*. Being *inclined to think*, in the sense of
inclining to an opinion not yet crystallised, is a reasonable enough
expression, just as one might say colloquially 'my mind is moving
that way'. But excessive use of the phrase may provoke the captious critic to say that if being inclined to think is really something
different from thinking, then the less said about it the better until
it has ripened into something that can properly be called thought.*

* A Civil Service correspondent takes me to task for having dealt too leniently
with this phrase, which he calls a 'monstrosity': it is one, he says, that 'the
cynic regards as being typical of the civil servant, who is (in his eyes) incapable
of decisive thought'. Perhaps it is wise to avoid a form of words that can
arouse feelings of that sort in anyone. In *The Valley of Fear*, Sherlock Holmes
reacts in the same way: '"I am inclined to think —" said I. "I should do so,"
Sherlock Holmes remarked impatiently'.

We can hardly suppose that the writer of the following thought really needed time to be sure of not being mistaken:

> We are inclined to think that people are more irritated by noise that they feel to be unnecessary than by noise that they cause themselves.

As at present advised should be used only where an opinion has been formed on expert (e.g. legal) advice, never, as it is much too often, as the equivalent of saying: 'This is what the Minister thinks at present, but since the Minister is human, tomorrow all may change'. That may be taken for granted.

There is often a real need for caution, and it can tempt a writer into hedging and obscurity. But it is no excuse for either. A frank admission that an answer cannot be given is better than an answer that tries to look as if it meant something, but really means nothing. Such a reply exasperates the reader and brings the Civil Service into discredit.

Politeness plays its part too: obscurity is less likely to give offence. Politeness often shows itself in euphemism, a term defined by the dictionary as 'the substitution of a mild or vague expression for a harsh or blunt one'. It is prompted by an impulse akin to the one that led the Greeks to call the Black Sea the *Euxine* (the hospitable one) in the hope of averting its notorious inhospitableness, and the Furies the *Eumenides* (the good-humoured ladies) in the hope that they might be flattered into being less furious. For the Greeks it was the gods and the forces of nature that had to be propitiated. For those who govern us today it is the electorate. Hence the prevalence of what grammarians call *meiosis* (understatement), the use of qualifying adverbs such as *somewhat* and *rather*, and the popularity of the 'not un-' device. This last is useful in its place. There are occasions when a writer's meaning may be conveyed more exactly by (say) *not unkindly*, *not unnaturally* or *not unjustifiably*, than by *kindly*, *naturally* or *justifiably*. But the 'not un-' habit is liable to take charge, with disastrous effects, making the victim forget all straightforward adjectives and adverbs. When an Inspector of Taxes writes 'This is a by no means uncomplicated case', we may be pretty sure that it is an example of meiosis. And, 'I think the officer's attitude was not unduly unreasonable' seems a chicken-hearted defence of a subordinate. George Orwell recommended that we should all inoculate ourselves against the disease by memorising this sentence: 'A not unblack dog was chasing a not unsmall rabbit across a not ungreen field'.

Sometimes a vague word may be preferred to a precise one because the vague is less alarming. A kindred device is to change names that have acquired unpleasant associations. Thus *distressed areas* were changed to *special areas*, *the poor* have become *the lower income brackets*, *criminal lunatics* are now *Broadmoor patients*, and *rat-catchers*, *rodent operators*. This is no doubt a useful expedient in the art of democratic government, for the power of the word is great. But the expedient has its limitations. If the unpleasantness attaches to the thing itself, it will taint the new name. In course of time yet another will have to be found, and so *ad infinitum*. We do not seem to have done ourselves much good by assigning the blameless but unsuitable word *lavatory* to a place where there is nowhere to wash; we have merely blunted the language.

There remains one more siren song to mention—that of laziness. As I observed in Chapter I, clear thinking is hard work. A great many people go through life without doing it to any noticeable extent. And as George Orwell (from whom I then quoted) has pointed out, ready-made phrases 'will construct your sentences for you—even think your thoughts for you, to a certain extent'. It is as though the builder of a house did not take the trouble to select with care the materials most suitable for the purpose, but collected chunks of masonry from ruined houses built by others and stuck them together anyhow. That is not a promising way to produce anything significant in meaning, attractive in form, or of any practical use.

So much for what I have termed the 'aetiology' of barnacular writing, though the British official is not the only (nor the worst) sufferer from the disease. Before turning to treatment it may be useful to illustrate the symptoms.

Example:

> The attitude of each, that he was not required to inform himself of, and his lack of interest in, the measures taken by the other to carry out the responsibility assigned to such other under the provision of plans then in effect, demonstrated on the part of each a lack of appreciation of the responsibilities vested in them, and inherent in their positions.

Translation:

> Neither took any interest in the other's plans, or even found out what they were. This shows that they did not appreciate the responsibilities of their positions.

Example:

> To reduce the risk of war and establish conditions of lasting peace requires the closer coordination in the employment of their joint resources to underpin these countries' economics in such a manner as to permit the full maintenance of their social and material standards as well as to adequate development of the necessary measures.

This example seems to me to defy translation.

We can now turn to the question whether some general advice can be given to fortify the writer against infection. The Fowler brothers tried their hand at this in their work of 1906, *The King's English*. This is what they said:

> Anyone who wishes to become a good writer should endeavour, before he allows himself to be tempted by the more showy qualities, to be direct, simple, brief, vigorous and lucid.
>
> This general principle may be translated into practical rules in the domain of vocabulary as follows: —
>
> > Prefer the familiar word to the far-fetched.
> > Prefer the concrete word to the abstract.
> > Prefer the single word to the circumlocution.
> > Prefer the short word to the long.
> > Prefer the Saxon word to the Romance.

'These rules,' they added, 'are given roughly in order of merit; the last is also the least.' They also pointed out that

> all five rules would be often found to give the same answer about the same word or set of words. Scores of illustrations might be produced; let one suffice: *In the contemplated eventuality* (a phrase no worse than what any one can pick for himself out of his paper's leading article for the day) is at once the far-fetched, the abstract, the periphrastic, the long, and the Romance, for *if so*. It does not very greatly matter by which of the five roads the natural is reached instead of the monstrosity, so long as it *is* reached. The five are indicated because (1) they differ in directness, and (2) in any given case only one of them may be possible.

When another distinguished figure, Quiller-Couch, discussed these rules in *On the Art of Writing*, he disagreed with the advice to prefer the short word to the long and the Saxon to the Romance. 'These two precepts', he said, 'you would have to modify by so long a string of exceptions that I do not commend them to you. In fact I think them false in theory and likely to be fatal in practice.' He then gave his own rules, which, though they may be sound in content, lack the crispness he preaches, starting, 'Almost always prefer . . .' and 'Generally use . . .'

I cannot set myself up as a judge between these high authorities, but as one who is now concerned only with a particular sort of prose, and who has made a close study of its common merits and faults, I respectfully agree with Quiller-Couch in refusing primary importance to the rule that the Saxon word must be preferred to the Romance, if only because it is not given to many of us always to be sure which is which.* Any virtue that there may be in this rule, and in the rule to prefer the short word to the long, is, I think, already implicit in the rule to prefer the familiar word to the far-fetched. Even the Fowlers said that 'the Saxon oracle is not infallible; it will sometimes be dumb, and sometimes lie', and before ever they had propounded the rule or Quiller-Couch criticised it, Bradley, the second editor of the

---

* The debate here may not be wholly clear to all readers. It is possible by being selective to make a powerful argument in favour of English words of Anglo-Saxon origin. John Newton's famous hymn on the subject of 'faith's review and expectation' opens, 'Amazing grace! (how sweet the sound) That sav'd a wretch like me!' Both *sweet* and *wretch* are 'Saxon' words (*swoete* and *wrecca*) first recorded in Old English in the ninth century. Later Romance vocabulary (largely courtesy of the Norman invaders under William the Conqueror) gave English the alternatives *dulcet* and *miscreant*; and educated seventeenth-century taste spawned the further Latinate options *sacchariferous*, *mellisonant* and *reprobate*. Not a soul could believe that Newton's hymn would be improved by choosing substitutes from among these Romance barnacles: 'Amazing grace! (how sacchariferous the sound) That sav'd a miscreant like me!' Yet *grace* and *save* are also Romance words, and some of us have need of *saving graces*. As for the idea that only our 'Saxon' words are earthy: to purge English of its Latin and Old French influences would require that we deny ourselves *sex* and *violence*, and how popular would that be? ~

OED, had said what most people are likely to think is all that needs to be said on the subject:

> The cry for 'Saxon English' sometimes means nothing more than a demand for plain and unaffected diction, and a condemnation of the idle taste for 'words of learned length and thundering sound,' which has prevailed at some periods of our literature. So far it is worthy of all respect; but the pedantry that would bid us reject the word fittest for our purpose because it is not of native origin ought to be strenuously resisted.   (Henry Bradley, *The Making of English*, 1904)

What we are concerned with is not a quest for a literary style as an end in itself, but the study of how best to convey our meaning without ambiguity and without giving unnecessary trouble to our readers. This being our aim, the essence of the advice both of the Fowlers and of Quiller-Couch may be expressed in the following three rules, and the rest of what I have to say in the domain of vocabulary will be little more than an elaboration of them.

(1) Use no more words than are necessary to express your meaning, for if you use more you are likely to obscure it and to tire your reader. In particular do not use superfluous adjectives and adverbs, and do not use roundabout phrases where single words would serve.

(2) Use familiar words rather than the far-fetched, if they express your meaning equally well; for the familiar are more likely to be readily understood.

(3) Use words with a precise meaning rather than those that are vague, for the precise will obviously serve better to make your meaning clear; and in particular prefer concrete words to abstract, for they are more likely to have a precise meaning.

As the Fowlers pointed out, rules like these cannot be kept in separate compartments: they overlap. But in the next three chapters we will follow roughly the order in which the rules are set out and examine them under the headings 'Avoiding the superfluous word', 'Choosing the familiar word' and 'Choosing the precise word'.

VI

THE CHOICE OF WORDS (2)

Avoiding the superfluous word

> A Reader of *Milton* must be always upon Duty; he is surrounded
> with Sense, it rises in every Line, every Word is to the Purpose;
> There are no Lazy Intervals, All has been Consider'd, and
> Demands, and Merits Observation. Even in the Best Writers
> you Sometimes find Words and Sentences which hang on so
> Loosely you may Blow 'em off; *Milton's* are all Substance and
> Weight; Fewer would not have Serv'd the Turn, and More
> would have been Superfluous.
>
> JONATHAN RICHARDSON, *Explanatory Notes and*
> *Remarks on Milton's Paradise Lost,* 1734

The fault of verbiage (which the *OED* defines as 'abundance
of words without necessity or without much meaning') is too
multiform for analysis. But certain classifiable forms of it are
particularly common, and in this chapter we will examine some
of these, ending with an indeterminate class that we will call
'padding', to pick up what has been left outside the others.

VERBOSITY IN ADJECTIVES AND ADVERBS

In a minute written in August 1835 by Palmerston, then Foreign
Secretary, he said of one of his diplomats in South America, who
had neglected an admonition to go through his despatches
and strike out all words not necessary for fully conveying his

meaning: 'If Mr Hamilton would let his substantives and adjectives go single instead of always sending them forth by Twos and Threes at a time, his despatches would be clearer and easier to read'.

It has been wisely said that the adjective is the enemy of the noun. If we make a habit of saying 'The true facts are these', we shall come under suspicion when we profess to tell merely 'the facts'. If a *crisis* is always *acute* and an *emergency* always *grave*, what is left for those words to do by themselves? If *active* constantly accompanies *consideration*, we shall think we are being fobbed off when we are promised bare consideration. If a decision is always qualified by *definite*, a decision by itself becomes a poor filleted thing. If conditions are customarily described as *prerequisite* or *essential*, we shall doubt whether a *condition* without an adjective is really a condition at all. If a part is always an *integral part* there is nothing left for a mere part except to be a spare part.

Cultivate the habit of reserving adjectives and adverbs to make your meaning more precise, and suspect those that you find yourself using to make it more emphatic. Use adjectives to denote kind rather than degree. By all means say an *economic crisis* or a *military disaster*, but think well before saying an *acute crisis* or a *terrible disaster*. Say, if you like, 'The proposal met with noisy opposition and is in obvious danger of defeat'. But do not say, 'The proposal met with considerable opposition and is in real danger of defeat'. If that is all, it is better to leave out the adjectives: 'The proposal met with opposition and is in danger of defeat'.

Official writers seem to have a curious shrinking from certain adjectives unless they are adorned by adverbs. It is as though they were naked and must hastily have an adverbial dressing gown thrown around them. The most indecent adjectives are, it seems, those of quantity or measure such as *short* and *long*, *many* and *few*, *heavy* and *light*. The adverbial dressing gowns most favoured are *unduly*, *relatively* and *comparatively*. These adverbs can only properly be used when something has been mentioned or implied that gives a standard of comparison. But we have all seen them used on innumerable occasions when there is no standard of comparison. They then have no meaning, and are the resort of those who timidly recoil from the nakedness of an unqualified statement. If the report of an accident says, 'about a hundred people were taken to hospital but comparatively few were detained', that is a proper use of the adverb. But when a circular says that 'our diminishing stocks will be expended in a relatively short period', without mentioning any other period with which to compare it, the word signifies nothing.

Sometimes the use of a dressing-gown adverb actually makes writers say the opposite of what they intended. The writer of the circular that said, 'It is not necessary to be unduly meticulous in . . .' meant to say 'you need not be meticulous', but actually said 'you must be meticulous but need not be unduly so', with the reader left to guess when the limit of dueness in meticulousness has been reached.

Undue and *unduly* seem to be words that have the property of taking the reason prisoner. 'There is no cause for undue alarm' is a phrase I have seen used in all sorts of circumstances by all sorts of people, from a government spokesman about the plans of the enemy to a headmistress on the occurrence of a case of polio. It is, I suppose, legitimate to say 'Don't be unduly alarmed', though I should not myself find much reassurance in it. But 'there is no cause for undue alarm' differs little, if at all, from 'there is no cause for alarm for which there is no cause', and that hardly seems worth saying. *Unduly* has of course its own proper job to do, and does it in a sentence of this kind: 'The speech was not unduly long for so important an occasion'.

As some adjectives seem to attract unnecessary adverbs, so do some nouns attract unnecessary adjectives. I have mentioned *consideration*'s fondness for the company of *active*, and I shall later refer to the inseparable companionship of *alternative* and *accommodation*. *Danger* is another word that is often given support it does not need, generally *real* or *serious*.

> The special needs of children under 5 require as much consideration as those of children aged 5–7, and there is a serious danger that they will be overlooked in these large schools ... There is a real danger ... that the development of the children will be unduly forced ...

Here we have *serious*, *real* and *unduly* all used superfluously. *Serious* is prompted by a feeling that *danger* always needs adjectival support, and *real* is presumably what grammarians call 'elegant variation': an effort made to avoid repeating the same word.* *Unduly* is superfluous because the word *forced* itself contains the idea of undue. *Real* danger should be reserved for contrast with imaginary danger, as, for instance, 'Some people fear so-and-so but the real danger is so-and-so'. These things may seem trivial, but nothing is negligible that is a symptom of loose thinking.

Vague adjectives of intensification like *considerable*, *appreciable* and *substantial* are too popular. None of these three should be used without three questions being asked. Do I need an adjective at all? If so, would a more specific adjective not be better? Or, failing that, which of these three (with their different shades of meaning) is most apt? If those who write 'This is a matter of considerable urgency' were to ask themselves these questions, they would realise that 'This is urgent' serves them better. And those who write 'A programme of this magnitude will necessarily take a considerable period' will find it more effective to say 'a long time'. Strong words like *urgent*, *danger*, *crisis*, *disaster*, *fatal*,

---

* For more on 'elegant variation' see pp. 203–4.

grave, paramount and *essential* lose their force if used too often. Reserve them for strong occasions, and then let them stand on their own legs, without adjectival or adverbial support.

It would be a fairly safe bet that *respective* (or *respectively*) is wrongly or unnecessarily used in legal and official writing more often than any other word in the language. It has one simple, straightforward use, and that is to link up subjects and objects where more than one is used with a single verb. Thus, if I say 'Men and women wear trousers and skirts', you are left in doubt which wears which—which is no more than the truth nowadays. But if I add the word *respectively*, I allot (at the risk of being misleading) the trousers to the men and the skirts to the women. It can also be used in a harmlessly distributive sense, as in the sentence 'local authorities should survey the needs of their respective areas'. But it contributes nothing to the sense here. There is no risk of local authorities thinking that they are being told to survey one another's areas. Anyway, it is neater to write 'Each local authority should survey the needs of its area'. *Respective* and *respectively* are unnecessarily or wrongly used in a sentence far more often than they are used correctly, and I advise you to leave them alone. You can always get by without them. Here is a sentence that demonstrates one of the many traps set by this capricious word. The writer has tried to make it distribute two things among three, and so left the reader guessing.

> The Chief Billeting Officer of the Local Authority, the Regional Welfare Officer of the Ministry of Health, and the Local Officer of the Ministry of Labour and National Service will be able to supplement the knowledge of the Authority on the needs arising out of evacuation and the employment of women respectively.

It is as though one were to say 'Men and women wear trousers and skirts and knickers respectively'. Who has the knickers?

But any excessive fondness the official may have for *respective* and *respectively* is as nothing compared with the fascination they exercise on lawyers. These are the opening words of a coal-mining lease:

> This indenture witnesseth that in consideration of the rents reservations and covenants hereinafter respectively reserved and contained they the said A, B and C according to their several and respective shares estates rights and interests do hereby grant to the W. Company the several mines of coal called respectively X, Y and Z and also the liberty to lay down any tramroads railroads or other roads and to connect such roads trams and railroads respectively with any other roads of similar character respectively.

Five in this small compass, with none of them doing any good, and some doing positive harm! The person who drafted this lease seems to have used the word in much the same way as the psalmist uses *Selah*, flinging it down light-heartedly whenever there was the least sense of having tramped on long enough without one. A recent example, taken from a department circular, shows the magnetism of this word: 'Owing to the special difficulty of an apportionment of expenditure between (1) dinners and (2) other meals and refreshments respectively ...'. Having taken elaborate care to arrange the sentence so as to avoid the need for *respectively*, the writer found the lure of it irresistible after all.

Definite and *definitely* must be a good second to *respective* and *respectively* in any competition for the lead in adjectives and adverbs used unnecessarily. It can hardly be supposed that the adverb in the injunction — 'local authorities should be definitely discouraged from committing themselves'—would make any difference to the official who had to carry it out. The distinction between discouraging a local authority definitely and merely discouraging it is too fine for most of us. Other examples are:

This is definitely harmful to the workers' health.

The recent action of the committee in approving the definite appointment of four home visitors.

This has caused two definite spring breakages to loaded vehicles.

Sir Alan Herbert wrote in *Punch* in 1936 that he would give a prize 'to the first Foreman of the Jury to announce a verdict of "Definitely Guilty," and another to the judge who informs the prisoner that he will be "definitely hanged by the neck till he is very definitely dead"'.

It is wise to be sparing of *very*. If it is used too freely it ceases to have any meaning. It must be used with discrimination to be effective. Other adverbs of intensification, like *necessarily* and *inevitably*, are also apt to do more harm than good unless you want to lay stress on the elements of necessity or inevitability. An automatic *inevitably*, contributing nothing to sense, is common:

The Committees will inevitably have a part to play in the development of the service.

The ultimate power of control which flows inevitably from the agency relationship.

Irresistibly reminded is on the way to becoming a cliché, especially useful to after-dinner speakers who want to drag in an irrelevant story, but by no means confined to them.

Other intrusive words are *incidentally*, *specific* and *particular*. In conversation, *incidentally* (like *actually* and *definitely*) is often a noise without meaning. In writing it is an apology for irrelevance, sometimes unnecessary or even ambiguous, as here: 'Dennis Brain will play horn concertos by Haydn and Mozart, both incidentally written to order'. Is it incidental to the announcer's announcement that the concertos were written to order, or to the working practices of Haydn and Mozart?

Particular intrudes (though perhaps more in a certain type of oratory than in writing) as an unnecessary reinforcement of a demonstrative pronoun:

> No arrangements have yet been made regarding moneys due to this particular country.

> We would point out that availabilities of this particular material are extremely limited.

> On the same day on which you advised the Custodian of the existence of this particular debt.

So much fun has been made of the common use of *literally* in the sense of 'not literally but metaphorically' that it is perhaps hardly worthwhile to make more. But it would be a pity not to record some of the choicer blossoms from a recent flowering of this perennial in the correspondence columns of *The Times*:

> (In an account of a tennis match) Miss X literally wiped the floor with her opponent.

> (A comment by *Punch* on a statement in a newspaper that throughout a certain debate Mr Gladstone had sat 'literally glued to the Treasury bench') 'That's torn it,' said the Grand Old Man, as he literally wrenched himself away to dinner.

> (Of a certain horse) It literally ran away with the Two Thousand Guineas.

> (Of a rackets player) He literally blasted his opponent out of the court.

> M. Clemenceau literally exploded during the argument.

> He died literally in harness.

VERBOSITY IN PREPOSITIONS

In all utility writing today, official and commercial, the simple prepositions we have in such abundance tend to be forgotten and replaced by groups of words more imposing perhaps, but less precise. The commonest of these groups are:

> As regards
> As to
> In connection with
> In regard to
> In relation to
> In respect of
> In the case of
> Relative to
> With reference to
> With regard to

They are useful in their proper places, but are often made to serve merely as clumsy devices to save a writer the labour of selecting the right preposition. In the collection that follows, the right preposition is added in brackets:

A firm timetable *in relation to* the works to be undertaken should be drawn up (for).

It has been necessary to cause many dwellings to be disinfested of vermin, particularly *in respect of* the common bed-bug (of).

The Authority are fully conscious of their responsibilities *in regard to* the preservation of amenities (for).

It will be necessary to decide the priority which should be given to nursery provision *in relation to* other forms of education provision (over).

The rates vary *in relation to* the age of the child (with).

Coupons without restrictions *as to* how you should spend them (on).

There may be difficulties *with regard to* the provision of suitable staff (in).

Similar considerations apply *with regard to* application for a certificate (to).

The best possible estimate will be made at the conference *as to* the total number of houses which can be completed in each district during the year (of).

Note. If Gowers's examples above had been written today, it would be unsurprising to find the phrase *in terms of* used for all of them ('A firm timetable *in terms of* the works to be undertaken . . .', 'particularly *in terms of* the common bed-bug', and so on). *In terms of* is now widely used to mean not only *for, of, over, with, on, in* and *to*, but also *about, towards, against, and, by, including* and *because*, as well as *for example*. And sometimes it means nothing. It circulates in what Gowers called the 'highest places'. In 1995, the Committee on Standards in Public Life gave as its very first principle, under the heading 'Selflessness', that 'Holders of public office should take decisions solely in terms of the public interest'. It would have been enough to remind the venal public servant that official decisions should be taken 'solely *in* the public interest'.

The vagueness of *in terms of* is demonstrated by the following extract from a 'meta-evaluation', by a professor of public sector evaluation, of an external review of multiple other evaluations of a public body:

> The timing of the technical review process has limited its value in terms of improving individual evaluation reports. Because it has been undertaken after a draft evaluation report has been

produced, there has been little scope to respond to any gaps or problems in terms of terms of reference, evaluation design (methodology), data collection or analysis'.

Though substituting *in* for *in terms of* would make both these sentences clearer, perhaps more would be gained than lost by rewriting them as follows: 'This review of the general principles on which the reports were based comes too late for there to be much chance of improving the reports themselves'.

The phrase *in terms of* is sometimes rightly used to make plain that a subject is being matched to a restricted class of language. But slack use of the expression is so prevalent that if one person now says of another, 'He abused me in terms of extreme violence', it is no longer clear whether the victim has endured a shocking verbal assault, or has suffered (say) being hit over the head with a bottle. Though *in terms of* has helped itself to the meanings of numerous other single words, its three-word form is not enough for some, who prefer the inflated version *in terms of issues to do with*. In the sentence, 'How highly should issues about access to treatment rank in terms of issues to do with resource alloca- tion . . .', a mere *in* would suffice; and the authors of the sentence that starts, 'In terms of issues to do with cosmopolitanism, we will show that . . .', could have contented themselves with a simple *on*. ~

As to deserves special mention because it leads writers astray in other ways besides making them forget the right preposition. It may tempt them into a more elaborate circumlocution:

> The operation is a severe one as to the after effects. (The after effects of the operation are severe.)

> It is no concern of the Ministry as to the source of the infor- mation. (The source of the information is no concern of the Ministry.)

As to serves a useful purpose at the beginning of a sentence by way of introducing a fresh subject: 'As to your liability for previous years, I will go into this'. But it also has a way of intruding itself where it is not wanted, especially before such words as *whether, who, what, how*. All the following examples are better without *as to*:

> Doubt has been expressed as to whether these rewards are sufficient.

> I have just received an enquiry as to whether you have applied for a supplement to your pension.

> I am to ask for some explanation as to why so small a sum was realised on sale.

> I will look into the question as to whether you are liable.

Note. Gowers himself uses the form *the question whether* elsewhere in this book (e.g. 'We can now turn to the question whether some general advice can be given to fortify the writer against infection'). There may be readers who find themselves wanting to amend this to 'the question *of* whether'; but omitting *of*, though unusual these days, is not wrong, and has the merit of brevity. ~

VERBOSITY IN ADVERBIAL AND OTHER PHRASES

Certain words beget verbosity. Among them are *case* and *instance*. The sins of *case* are well known. It has been said that there is perhaps no single word so freely resorted to as a trouble-saver and consequently responsible for so much flabby writing. Here are some examples to show how what might be a simple and straightforward statement becomes enmeshed in the coils of phrases formed with *case*:

The cost of maintenance of the building would be higher than was the case with a building of traditional construction. (Than that of a building of traditional construction.)

That country is not now so short of sterling as was formerly the case. (As it used to be.)

Since the officiating president in the case of each major institute takes up his office on widely differing dates. (Since the officiating presidents of the major institutes take ...)

The National Coal Board is an unwieldy organisation, in many cases quite out of touch with the coalfields.

It is not easy to guess the meaning of this last example.

This trick of using *case* is even worse when the reader might be misled, though only momentarily, into thinking that a material case was meant:

Cases have thus arisen in which goods have been exported without the knowledge of this commission.

Water for domestic use is carried by hand in many cases from road standpipes.

There are, of course, many legitimate uses of the word, and writers should not be frightened away from it altogether. To borrow from Fowler, there are, for instance:

A case of measles.
You have no case.
In case of need, or fire, or other emergency.*
A bad case of burglary or other crime.

---

* The phrase *in case of* can, however, be ambiguous, for example as it is found on the sign that says, 'In case of fire do not use the lift'. ~

> A law case of any sort.
> Circumstances alter cases.

But do not say 'It is not the case that I wrote that letter', when you mean 'It is not true that I wrote that letter', or merely 'I did not write that letter'.

Instance beguiles writers much as *case* does into roundabout ways of saying simple things:

> In the majority of instances the houses are three-bedroom. (Most of the houses are three-bedroom.)

> Most of the factories are modern, but in a few instances the plant is obsolete. (In a few of them.)

In the first instance can generally be replaced by *first*.

Another such word is *concerned* in the phrase *so far* (or *as far*) *as . . . is concerned*. A correspondent has written asking me to

> scarify the phrase 'so far as . . . is concerned', e.g. 'the war is over so far as Germany is concerned', an actual instance; or 'so far as he was concerned interest in the game was over'. After long and vigilant watch I have still to find a case in which a single preposition would not be clearer as well as shorter.

It is perhaps putting the case too high to say that *so far* (or *as far*) *as . . . is concerned* could always be replaced by a single preposition. I do not think that the phrase can be dispensed with by those who wish to emphasise that they have blinkers on, and are concerned only with one aspect of a question. 'So far as I am concerned you may go home' implies that someone else has a say too. Or again:

> So far as the provisions of the Trading with the Enemy Act are concerned, the sum so released may . . . be utilised to reimburse you for expenses.

There is no other equally convenient way of making clear that the writer is removing only the impediment created by the Act and is not concerned with any other impediment there may be.

Possibly, though less certainly, this sentence might claim the same indulgence:

> The effect of the suggested system, so far as the pharmaceutical industry is concerned, would be to ensure rewards for research and development work until the new preparations were absorbed into the B.P.

It might be argued that we should not get quite the same meaning from 'on the pharmaceutical industry': this destroys the suggestion that there may be other effects, but the writer is not considering them.

But these are exceptions. There is no doubt that the phrase is generally a symptom of muddled thinking:

> Some were opposed to hanging as a means of execution where women were concerned. (As a means of executing women.)

> Wood pulp manufacture on a commercial scale is a very recent development so far as time is concerned. (Omit the last six words.)

> The punishments at their disposal may not be of very serious effect so far as the persons punished are concerned. (On the persons punished.)

> That is a matter which should be borne in mind because it does rule out a certain amount of consideration so far as the future is concerned.

I cannot translate this with any confidence. Perhaps it means 'That is a matter which should be borne in mind because it circumscribes our recommendations for the future'.

The fact that is an expression sometimes necessary and proper, but sometimes a clumsy way of saying what might be said more simply:

> Owing to the fact that the exchange is working to full capacity. (Because the exchange . . .)

> The delay in replying has been due to the fact that it was hoped to arrange for a representative to call upon you. (I delayed replying because I hoped to arrange for a representative to call on you.)

So too *until such time as*, which is usually merely a verbose way of saying *until*. It may be useful to convey a suggestion that the event contemplated is improbable or remote or has no direct connection with what is to last until it occurs. But it cannot do so in,

> You will be able to enjoy these facilities until such time that he terminates his agreement.

If the phrase is used, it should be *such time as*, not, as here, 'such time that'.

There cannot, I think, ever be any justification for preferring the similar phrase *during such time as* to *while*.

As has other sins of superfluity imputed to it, besides the help it gives in building up verbose prepositions and conjunctions. Dr Ballard writes that *as* has

> acquired a wide vogue in official circles. Wherever *as* can be put in, in it goes. And often it gets into places where it has no business to be. A man in the public service used to draw his salary *from* a certain date; now he draws it *as from* a certain date. Time was when officials would refer to 'the relationship between one department and another'; now they call it 'the relationship *as* between one department and another'. Agenda

papers often include as an item : 'To consider as to the question of . . .' If this sort of interpolation between the verb and its object were extended to ordinary speech, a man would no longer 'eat his dinner,' but 'eat as to his dinner'; or, to make the parallel complete, 'eat as to the diet of his dinner'. (P. B. Ballard, *Teaching the Mother Tongue*, 1921)

There is reason in saying, of a past date, 'these allowances will be payable as from the 1st January last', but there is none in saying, of a future date, 'these allowances will cease to be payable as from the 1st July next'. 'On the 1st July' is all that is needed. The phrase *as and from*, not unknown, is gibberish.

As such is sometimes used in a way that seems to have no meaning:

The statistics, as such, add little to our information.

If they do not do so as statistics, in what capacity do they? The writer probably meant 'by themselves'.

There is no objection to the sale of houses as such.

Here the context shows the writer to have meant that there was no objection of principle to the sale of houses.

Note. The word *as*, sometimes coupled with *of*, continues to be overworked. *Equally as* is used to mean *equally*, *as yet* to mean *yet*, *as of yet* to mean either *yet* or *so far*, *as of now* to mean *now* or sometimes *from now on*, and *as of soon* to mean *soon*. A needless *as* appears in all the quotations below:

The BOA is to go to court to defend the lifetime ban which has been declared as 'non-compliant' with the code . . . (*The Times*)

The bespectacled, portly joker and determined tax-reformer has gone on a diet and styled himself as 'an ordinary guy' . . .
(*Guardian*)

> While many deem the message as timely and necessary, the
> way in which authorities have gone about the visual imagery is
> seen as offensive. (*Daily Mail*) ~

Certain pairs of words have a way of keeping company without being able to do any more together than either could have done separately. *Save and except* seems to have had its day, but we still have with us *as and when*, *if and when*, and *unless and until*. *As and when* can perhaps be defended when used of something that will happen piecemeal ('Interim reports will be published as and when they are received'). Nothing can be said for the use of the pair in a sentence like this one:

> As and when the Bill becomes an Act guidance will be given on
> the financial provisions of it as they affect hospital maintenance.

Bills cannot become Acts piecemeal.

If and when might plead that both are needed in such a sentence as 'Further cases will be studied if and when the material is available', arguing that *if* alone will not do because the writer wants to emphasise that material becoming available will be studied immediately, and *when* alone will not do because it is uncertain whether the material ever will be available. But this is all rather subtle, and the wise course will almost always be to decide which conjunction suits you better, and to use it alone. I have not been able to find (or to imagine) the use of *unless and until* in any context in which one of the two alone would not have sufficed.

Note. There are new redundant pairings slowly becoming conventional in modern English. *Outside of* and *hence why* are two examples where the meaning of the second word has already been taken care of by the first:

> Wales drop outside of top 100 of FIFA's world rankings for
> the first time since 2000. (*Daily Mail*)

Met Office readings revealed that the atmosphere on Monday was as dry as desert air — hence why there were no clouds or aircraft contrails in the sky. (*The Times*)

Increasingly more is another example when misused as follows: 'Clinicians are becoming increasingly more influential' (*British Medical Journal*). But often it is the first word in a common pair that is redundant because it is an adjective that adds nothing to what it notionally describes. *Future prospects, close scrutiny, temporary respite* and *mutually contradictory* are all examples (the *Guardian* reports that 'mutually contradictory witness statements often both felt true'). It should not be necessary on the London Underground to be reminded to take one's *personal* possessions—as opposed to what kind? Above ground, the tautology 'preventive maintenance' has started to appear on the sides of Britain's white vans. This novelty may have been inspired by the phrase *preventive medicine*; but unlike medicine, which can be intended to cure, all maintenance is preventive, otherwise it is *repairs* (or so one might feel justified in supposing: *repairs* is now itself sometimes recast as 'corrective maintenance'). The formula 'becoming to be' is also on the up, as here: 'Making ends meet is becoming to be more and more of a challenge'. This should either be *becoming* on its own, or *coming to be*. ~

Point of view, viewpoint, standpoint and *angle*, useful and legitimate in their proper places, are sometimes no more than a refuge from the trouble of precise thought, and provide clumsy ways of saying something that could be said more simply and effectively. They are used, for instance, as a circumlocution for a simple adverb, such as 'from a temporary point of view' for 'temporarily'. Here are a few examples.

From a cleaning point of view there are advantages in tables being of uniform height. (For cleaning.)

I can therefore see no reason why we need to see these applications, apart from an information point of view. (Except for information.)

Bare boards are unsatisfactory from every angle. (In every respect.)

This may be a source of embarrassment to the Regional Board from the viewpoint of overall planning and administration. (The plain way of putting this is: 'This may embarrass the Regional Board in planning and administration'.)

This development is attractive from the point of view of the public convenience. (This, I am told, provoked a marginal comment: 'What is it like looking from the other direction?')

Aspect is the complement of *point of view*. As one changes one's point of view one sees a different aspect of what one is looking at. It is therefore natural that *aspect* should lead writers into the same traps as do *point of view*, *viewpoint* and *standpoint*. It induces writers, through its vagueness, to prefer it to more precise words, and lends itself to woolly circumlocution. I cannot believe that there was any clear conception in the head of the official who wrote, 'They must accept responsibility for the more fundamental aspects of the case'. *Aspect* is one of the words that should not be used without deliberation, and it should be rejected if its only function is to make a clumsy paraphrase of an adverb.

VERBOSITY IN AUXILIARY VERBS

Various methods are in vogue for softening the curtness of *will not* or *cannot*. The commonest are *is not prepared to, is not in a position to, does not see his or her way to* and *cannot consider*.

Such phrases are no doubt dictated by politeness, and therefore deserve respect. But they must be used with discretion. The recipient of a letter may feel better—though I doubt it—being told that the Minister 'is not prepared to approve' than 'the Minister does not approve'. There is not even this slender justification when what is said is that the Minister *is* prepared to approve:

> The Board have examined your application and they are prepared to allocate 60 coupons for this production. I am accordingly to enclose this number of coupons.

Are prepared to allocate should have been *have allocated*. As the coupons are enclosed, the preparatory stage is clearly over.

But there is a legitimate use of *prepared to*, as in the following:

> In order to meet the present need, the Secretary of State is prepared to approve the temporary appointment of persons without formal qualifications.

Here the Secretary of State is awaiting candidates, prepared to approve them if they turn out all right. But the phrase should never be used in actually giving approval. It is silly, and if the habit takes hold, it will lead to such absurdities as,

> I have to acknowledge your letter of the 16th June and in reply I am prepared to inform you that I am in communication with the solicitors concerned in this matter.

There are other dangers in these phrases. They may breed by analogy verbiage that is mere verbiage—and that cannot call on politeness to justify its existence. You may find yourself writing that the Minister *will take steps to* when all you mean is *will*, or that the Minister *will cause investigation to be made with a view to ascertaining*, when what you mean is that the Minister will *find out. Take steps to* is not always to be condemned. It is a reasonable way to express the beginning of a gradual process, as in:

> Steps are now being taken to acquire this land.

But it will not do, because of its literal incongruity, in a sentence such as this one:

> All necessary steps should be taken to maintain the present position.

There is a danger that some of these phrases may suggest undesirable ideas to the flippant. To be told that the Minister is 'not in a position to approve' may excite a desire to retort that the Minister might try lying on the floor, to see if that does any good. The retort will not, of course, be made, but you should not put ideas of that sort about your Minister into people's heads. Pompous old phrases must be allowed to die if they collapse under the prick of ridicule. A traditional expression such as 'I am to request you to move your Minister to do so-and-so' now runs the risk of conjuring up a risible picture—of physical pressure applied to a bulky and inert object.

VERBOSITY IN PHRASAL VERBS

The English language likes to tack an adverbial particle to a simple verb and so to create a verb with a different meaning. Verbs thus formed have come to be called 'phrasal verbs'. This habit of inventing phrasal verbs has been the source of great enrichment of the language. Pearsall Smith says that from them

> we derive thousands of the vivid colloquialisms and idiomatic phrases by means of which we describe the greatest variety of human actions and relations. We can take *to* people, take them *up*, take them *down*, take them *off*, or take them *in*; keep *in*

with them, keep them *down* or *off* or *on* or *under*; get *at* them, or *round* them, or *on with* them; do *for* them, do *with* them or *without* them, and do them *in*; make *up to* them, make *up with* them, make *off with* them; set them *up* or *down* or hit them *off*—indeed, there is hardly any action or attitude of one human being to another which cannot be expressed by means of these phrasal verbs.   (*Words and Idioms*)

But there is today a tendency to form phrasal verbs to express a meaning no different from that of the verb without the particle. To do this is to debase the language, not to enrich it. *Drown out, sound out, lose out, rest up, miss out on, meet up with, visit with* and *study up on* are all examples of phrasal verbs used in senses no different from the unadorned verb. By contrast, in the newcomer to *measure up to*, the added particles give the verb a new meaning, the sense of to 'be adequate to an occasion'.

Note. When Gowers wrote this he was under the false impression that all the 'debasing' phrasal verbs in his list had originated in America, leading him to remark that they had 'so far found little favour' in British English. Wherever they were from, British favour has been widely granted to them since, apart from *rest up* and *visit with*. The effect on Gowers of *study up on* for *study* or *drown out* for *drown* must have been comparable to the effect on a modern British ear of *imagine up* or *fall up short* (*US News & World Report* quotes an expert in benefits saying, 'half the time you have enough for retirement and half the time you fall up short'). There are, however, plenty of redundant particles littered through British writing:

It is now the fourth time that the Taliban have used 'secondary' devices in the town of Sangin in which they kill or maim with an initial bomb and then await for a stretcher party before detonating another to kill the rescuers.   (*Daily Telegraph*)

Germany's staunch refusal to step up to the plate and take the responsibility of being Europe's paymaster is causing investor sentiment to erode away day by day. (*Guardian*)

Will finds it difficult to speak of that dreadful day, but is prepared to elucidate on how he has brought up his sons. (*The Times*)

Former Labour chairman will leave parliament . . . after repaying back almost £15,000 worth of expenses claims. (*Guardian*) ~

OVERLAPPING

By this I mean a particular form of what the grammarians call *tautology*, *pleonasm* or *redundancy*. Possible varieties are infinite, but one of the commonest examples is writing 'the reason for this is because . . .' instead of either 'this is because' or 'the reason for this is that . . .'.

The Ministry of Food say that the reason for the higher price of the biscuits is because the cost of chocolate has increased. (The reason . . . is that . . .)

Other versions of this error include:

The subject of the talk tonight will be about . . . (Either 'the subject will be' or 'the talk will be about'.)

The reason for the long delay appears to be due to the fact that the medical certificates went astray. (Either 'the reason is that' or 'the delay is due to the fact that'.)

By far the greater majority . . . (Either 'by far the majority' or 'by far the greater part'.)

He did not say that all actions for libel or slander were never properly brought. (Either 'that all actions . . . were improperly brought' or 'that actions . . . were never properly brought'.)

An attempt will be made this morning to try to avert the threatened strike. (Those who were going to do this might have attempted to do it or tried to do it. But merely to attempt to try seems rather half-hearted.)

The common fault of duplicating either the future or the past is another form of this error:

The most probable thing will be that they will be sold in a Government auction. ('The most probable thing is that they will be sold . . .')

The Minister said he would have liked the Government of Eire to have offered us butter instead of cream. (He 'would have liked the Government of Eire to offer . . .')

Note. As well as using versions of *the reason why is because*, many modern writers find themselves lured into a needless repetition of terms from the cluster *both share the same equally in common.** The *Independent* reports of two public figures: 'Both share a passion for education . . .', but it is enough to say 'both have a passion for', 'they share a passion for', 'they have a common passion for', 'they are equally passionate about', or even 'they have the same passion for'. Similarly, 'Both suspects remain under armed guard in separate hospitals' should read, 'The two suspects remain under armed guard in separate hospitals'. ~

QUALIFICATION OF ABSOLUTES

Certain adjectives and adverbs cannot be properly qualified by such words as *more, less, very* and *rather*, because they do not admit of degrees. *Unique* is the outstanding example. When we

* See also pp. 178–9 for superfluous use of *both*.

say a thing is 'unique' we mean that there is nothing else of its kind in existence: 'rather unique' is meaningless. But we can of course say *almost unique*.

It is easy to slip into pedantry here, and to condemn qualification of words that are perhaps absolutes but are no longer treated as being so—*true*, for instance, and *empty* and *full*. We ought not to be exercised by 'very true', or 'the hall was even emptier today than yesterday' or 'this cupboard is fuller than that one'. But the following quotation goes too far:

> It may safely be said that the design of sanitary fittings has now reached a high degree of perfection.

Nor does the comparative seem happily chosen in 'more virgin', which a correspondent tells me he has seen in an advertisement.*

PADDING

All forms of verbosity might be described as padding, and the topic overlaps others we shall come to in the chapters on choosing the familiar word and choosing the precise word. I use *padding* here as a label for the type of verbosity Sir Winston Churchill referred to in a memorandum entitled 'Brevity' that he issued as Prime Minister on the 9th August 1940. He wrote:

> Let us have an end of such phrases as these:

---

* We seem to have grown used to the idea that 'extra virgin' is a legitimate standard of purity, but the popular phrase 'very real' is now a source of irritation to many. It is not new. In 1812 an anonymous 'Society of Gentlemen', translating the work of Emanuel Swedenborg, felt driven to explain that 'the divine truth proceeding from the divine good is the very very real'. ~

'It is also of importance to bear in mind the following considerations ...' or 'consideration should be given to the
possibility of carrying into effect ...' Most of these woolly
phrases are mere padding, which can be left out altogether, or
replaced by a single word. Let us not shrink from using the
short expressive phrase, even if it is conversational.

'Padding', in the sense in which Sir Winston used the word,
consists of clumsy and obtrusive stitches on what ought to be a
smooth fabric of consecutive thought. No doubt it comes partly
from a feeling that wordiness is an ingredient of politeness, and
that blunt statement is crude, even rude. There is an element of
truth to this: an over-staccato style is as irritating as an
over-sostenuto one. But it is a matter of degree, and official prose
is of the sort that calls for plainness rather than elegance. Moreover the habit of 'padding' springs partly from less meritorious
notions—that the dignity of an official's calling demands a certain
verbosity, and that naked truth is indecent and should be clothed
in wrappings of woolly words.

Sir Winston gave two common examples based on the word
consideration. He might equally well have chosen phrases
based on *appreciate*. 'It is appreciated that' (anticipating an objection that is to be met) and 'it will be appreciated that'
(introducing a reason for a decision that is to be given) are very
prevalent. They can almost always be omitted without harm to
the sense.*

I have already referred, in Chapter III, to one way in which
padding shows itself in official letters. Each paragraph is thought
to need introductory words—*I am to add*; *I am further to observe*;
I am moreover to remark; *Finally, I am to point out*; and so forth.

---

* For more about *appreciate* see pp. 153–4.

Here is the same phenomenon in a circular sending a form for a statistical return:

(i) *It should be noted that* the particulars of expenditure ... relate to gross costs.

(ii) *It is appreciated that* owing to staffing difficulties Local Authorities may not find it possible on this occasion to complete tables ...

(iii) *It will be noted that* in Tables ... the only overhead expenditure ... which the authorities are asked to isolate is ...

(iv) Table 4 ... is intended to provide a broad picture.

The words italicised in the first three paragraphs are padding. They are no more needed there than in paragraph (iv), where the writer has wisely done without them, perhaps fearing to run out of stock.

Other examples:

I am prepared to accept the discharge of this account by payment in instalments, but *it should be pointed out that* no further service can be allowed until the account is again in credit.

The opportunity is taken to mention that it is understood ...

I regret that the wrong form was forwarded. *In the circumstances* I am forwarding a superseding one.

It should be noted that there is the possibility of a further sale.

This form of padding deserves a special mention because the temptation affects officials more than most people, and because it is comparatively easy to resist: it shows itself more plainly than other more subtle temptations to pad. For the rest, padding can be defined as the use of words, phrases and even sentences that contribute nothing to the reader's perception of the writer's meaning.

Some seem to be especially tempting to writers. I have mentioned *consideration* and *appreciate*; among other seductive phrases are *in this connection* and *for your information*. These have their proper uses, but are more often found as padding clichés. In none of the following examples do they serve any other purpose:

> I am directed to refer to the travelling and subsistence allowances applicable to your Department, and in this connexion I am to say . . .

> The Minister's views in general in this connexion and the nature and scope of the information which he felt would assist him in this connexion was indicated at a meeting . . .

> For your information I should perhaps explain that there is still a shortage of materials.

> For your information I would inform you that it will be necessary for you to approach the local Agricultural Executive Committee.

This last example, taken from a letter I received myself, shows up the futility of this curious cliché. It was not even true that I was being told this 'for information': 'for action' would have been more appropriate.

Of course is another adverbial phrase that needs watching lest it should creep in as padding. In some contexts *of course* is used to impress readers by showing the writer's familiarity with an out-of-the-way piece of information. But the official who over-works the phrase is more likely to do so from genuine humility, putting it in so as not to seem didactic: 'Don't think that I suppose you to be so stupid that you don't already know or infer what I am telling you, but I think I ought to mention it'. Sometimes *of course* is wisely used for this purpose—if, for instance, the writer has good reason to say something so obvious that any touchy readers may feel that they are being treated like fools. It is much better in these circumstances to say 'of course' than its pompous variant 'as you are doubtless aware'. *Of course* might with advantage have been used in:

> It may be stated with some confidence that though it is possible
> for a blister-gas bomb to fall in a crater previously made by
> an H.E. bomb, the probability of such an occurrence is small.

In this example, 'It may be stated with some confidence that' is not only padding but also an absurdity. One might say with some confidence that this will not happen, or with complete confidence that it is improbable, but to feel only some confidence about its improbability is carrying intellectual timidity to almost imbecile lengths.

The following extracts, taken from two documents issued by the same Ministry at about the same time, are instructive. The first is:

> I am to add that, doubtless, local authorities appreciate that
> it is a matter of prime importance that information about
> possible breaches of Defence Regulation ... should reach the
> investigating officers of the Ministry ... with the minimum
> of delay.

The second is:

> After six years of war almost every building in this country
> needs work doing to it. The whole of the building labour force
> could be employed on nothing else but repairs and mainten-
> ance. Yet there are hundreds of thousands of families who
> urgently need homes of their own and will keep on suffering
> great hardship until houses can be provided for them.

The first of these is bad. It is the sort of thing that those who say civil servants write badly point to in support of their case. The first eighteen of its thirty-eight words are padding, and the last five are a starchy paraphrase of 'as soon as possible'. The second is excellent. It has no padding, and says what it has to say in brisk, businesslike English. Why this difference of style in the same department? We can only guess, but I do not think the guess is difficult. The first was written for the guidance of local government officials only. It was a routine matter and no trouble was taken over it. Its language is the sort that local authorities expect and understand. But the second was intended to impress the public, and the writer was at pains to use language in a way that would be grasped at once and that would carry conviction. This, I have no doubt, is the explanation, but it is not sufficient. Whatever the purpose, the first is bad and the second is good.

The following introductory sentence to a circular is, I think, wholly padding, but I cannot be sure, for I can find no meaning in it:

> The proposals made in response to this request show differences of approach to the problem which relate to the differing recommendations of the Committee's Report, and include some modifications of those recommendations.

But padding is too multifarious for analysis. It can only be illustrated, and the one rule for avoiding it is to be self-critical.

Note. The style of some of Gowers's bad examples above may now sound outmoded ('I am to add that, doubtless, local authorities appreciate that it is a matter of prime importance that ...'). But officials still resort to padding. A recent paper issued by the Ministry of Justice on 'cost protection for litigants in environmental judicial review claims' states 'in respect of' appeals that 'It should be noted in this context that it will not necessarily be the claimant who has appealed...'. Here, 'it should be noted in this context that' is pure 'wrapping of woolly words'.

Sometimes the padding in a sentence appears to have arrived

there through simple fear of a blank page. Certainly the advertising puff below, reproduced in numerous tableware catalogues, bespeaks torment on the part of a writer with not much to say. The puff attempts to champion Blue Denmark, an antique plate pattern by the Staffordshire potters, Johnson Brothers:

> Historically, blue and white ceramic design dates back to the 18th and 19th centuries—this is sufficient evidence itself to recognise the reason why Blue Denmark continues its long reign.

To put 'historically' at the start here adds nothing. To say '18th and 19th' is perverse. And to end on 'continues its long reign' is an overblown metaphorical flourish. But to take 'this is why' and pad it with the words 'sufficient evidence itself to recognise the reason' is almost surreally illiterate. Unscrambled, what this sentence has told us is the following: 'China patterns in blue and white date from the eighteenth century. This explains why Blue Denmark remains popular'. It is no great surprise to find that neither of these statements is true.

VII
THE CHOICE OF WORDS (3)

Choosing the familiar word

> Literary men, and the young still more than the old of this
> class, have commonly a good deal to rescind in their style in
> order to adapt it to business . . . The leading rule is to be content
> to be common-place,—a rule which might be observed with
> advantage in other writings, but is distinctively applicable to
> these.
>
> <div align="right">HENRY TAYLOR, <i>The Statesman</i>, 1836</div>

Boswell says of Johnson: 'He seemed to take pleasure in speaking
in his own style; for when he had carelessly missed it, he would
repeat the thought translated into it. Talking of the comedy of
"The Rehearsal," he said, "It has not wit enough to keep it sweet."
This was easy;—he therefore caught himself, and pronounced a
more rounded sentence: "It has not vitality enough to preserve
it from putrefaction"'. The mind of another famous lover of the
rotund phrase worked the opposite way: '"Under the impression,"
said Mr Micawber, "that your peregrinations in this metropolis
have not as yet been extensive, and that you might have some
difficulty in penetrating the arcana of the Modern Babylon in
the direction of the City Road,—in short," said Mr Micawber,
in another burst of confidence, "that you might lose yourself—"'.
Officials should not hesitate over which of these remarkable men
to take as their model. They should cultivate Mr Micawber's
praiseworthy habit of instinctively translating the out-of-the-way

into the everyday. Thus we might find that, even though the Board of Trade could still not resist announcing that certain surplus government factories are now 'available for reallocation', they would not leave it at that. 'In short,' they would add in a burst of confidence, 'they are to be relet.'

The present inclination of officials is in the opposite direction. They are Johnsonians rather than Micawberites,* and so handicap themselves in achieving what we have seen to be their primary object as writers: to affect the reader precisely as they wish. The simple reader is puzzled. The sophisticated one is annoyed. Here is pent-up annoyance blowing off a genial jet of steam in the leading columns of *The Times*:

> some foreign importations have shown a terrifying and uncon-
> trollable vitality, so that the sins of their original sponsors are
> visited with dreadful rigour upon succeeding generations. The
> kindly nature-lover who first liberated a pair of grey squirrels
> has a great deal to answer for, including a large share of the
> salaries of numerous civil servants engaged on the task known
> to them, rather hopefully, as pest-elimination. In the etymo-
> logical field a similar bad eminence is reserved in the minds of
> all right-thinking men, for the individual who first introduced
> into the English language the word 'personnel'. It is possible,

* The *OED* cites this sentence as its sole example of a use of the word *Micawberite*, wrongly implying by its definition that Gowers meant to invoke Micawber, the 'feckless optimist'. Gowers may have been unusual in wishing instead to pay tribute to Mr Micawber's translations into plain English (the example above is taken from chapter 11 of *David Copperfield*), but he was not the first to use 'Micawberite' itself. This term, with the *OED*'s meaning, was in circulation at least as far back as the 1880s. The *Michigan Argonaut* mentions 'obsequious Micawberites' in 1884; the *Westminster Review* in 1895 compares Micawberites to ostriches; and in a 1906 issue of the *Outlook*, a weekly review, the vulnerable Micawberite is conjured up in an attack on the hire-purchase system. ~

just possible, that a more degrading, a more ill-favoured synonym for two or more members of the human race has at one
time or another been coined; but, if it has, it has never gained
the ubiquitous and tyrannical currency of this alien collective.*

It would be churlish to accuse an onslaught so disarming of not
being quite fair. But may it not be argued that when we admitted
women auxiliaries to our armed forces the expression 'men and
material' became unsuitable; and that we found a gap in our
vocabulary and sensibly filled it, as we have so often done before,
by borrowing from the French? Still, it cannot be denied that
this word, like so many other high-sounding words of vague
import, has exercised an unfortunate fascination over the official
mind. The mischief of words of this sort is that they become such
favourites that they seduce their users from clarity of thought.
They mesmerise them and numb their discrimination.

The precept to choose the familiar word (which is probably
also the short word) must of course be followed with discretion.
Many wise figures throughout the centuries, from Aristotle to
Sir Winston Churchill, have emphasised the importance of using
short and simple words. But no one knew better than these two
authorities that sacrifice either of precision or of dignity is too
high a price to pay for the familiar word. If the choice is between
two words that convey the writer's meaning equally well, one

---

* The *Times* columnist who rejected the word *personnel* out of hand might
even so have been provoked into letting off a new jet of steam at the idea that
it would one day be being used of single members of the human race, as is
demonstrated by these instructions for 'vehicle extrication': 'To properly and
safely conduct rescue-lift air bag operation, a minimum of five personnel are
required: one personnel tending to the patient, two personnel on each side . . .,
one personnel managing the rescue-lift air bag controls, and one personnel as
the officer in control . . .'. (This list does not even add up to five, unless 'two
personnel on each side' is taken to mean *one* on each side.) ~

short and familiar and the other long and unusual, of course the short and familiar should be preferred. But one that is long and unusual should not be rejected merely on that account if it is more apt in meaning. Sir Winston does not hesitate to choose the uncommon word if there is something to be gained by it. If we were to ask whether there was any difference in meaning between *woolly* and *flocculent* we should probably say no: one was commonplace and the other unusual, and that was all there was to it. But Sir Winston, in the first volume of his *Second World War*, uses *flocculent* instead of *woolly* to describe the mental processes of certain people, and so conveys to his readers just that extra ounce of contempt that we feel *flocculent* to contain (perhaps because the combination of *f* and *l* so often expresses an invertebrate state, as in *flop*, *flap*, *flaccid*, *flimsy*, *flabby* and *filleted*). Moreover there is an ugliness of shortness as well as an ugliness of length. On the same day in different daily papers I have seen the same official referred to as 'Administrator of the Organisation for European Economic Co-operation', and as 'Aid Boss'. Neither title is euphonious, but few would unhesitatingly prefer the short one.

Still, there are no great signs at present of an urgent need to warn against the overuse of simple diction by officials. In official documents, lack of precision is much more likely to arise from the use of jargon and legal language, and from an addiction to showy words.

JARGON AND LEGAL LANGUAGE

The *OED* defines *jargon* as being a word 'applied contemptuously to any mode of speech abounding in unfamiliar terms, or peculiar to a particular set of persons, as the language of scholars or philosophers, the terminology of a science or art, or the cant of a class, sect, trade, or profession'. When it is confined to that sense, it is a useful word. But it has been handled so promiscuously of recent years that the edge has been taken off it, and now, as has been well said, it signifies little more than any speech that people feel to be inferior to their own. In the original sense its growth of late has been alarming. Modern discoveries in the older sciences, and the need of the newer ones to explain their ideas, have led to an enormous increase in that part of our vocabulary that can be classed as jargon. No doubt this is to some extent inevitable. New concepts may demand new words. The discipline of psychology, for example, can at least plead that if a new word is necessary for what my most recent dictionary defines as 'the sum total of the instinctive forces of an individual', a less pretentious one could hardly have been found than *id*—and never can so much meaning have been packed into so small a space since the sentence, 'Thy kingdom is divided and given to the Medes and Persians' was compressed into the word *Upharsin*.* But I find it refreshing when the evolutionary biologist Dr Julian Huxley says:

> We need a term for the sum of these continuities through the whole of evolutionary time, and I prefer to take over a familiar word like *progress* instead of coining a special piece of esoteric jargon. (*Evolution in Action*, 1953)

In the field of neurology Sir Francis Walshe has been provoked to a similar protest. Referring to the fondness of clinicians for

---

* It was whimsical of Gowers to mention 'Upharsin' in a paragraph on jargon. This word, from the Aramaic, appears in the Bible, in the Book of Daniel, as an element in 'the writing on the wall'. 'Mene Mene Tekel Upharsin' is inscribed by floating fingers on a piece of plaster in the palace of King Belshazzar. The King, seeing unattached fingers at work, is so terrified that the 'joints of his loins' are loosed. The words are a message from God. Only Daniel can interpret them. Daniel tells Belshazzar that he has been 'found wanting' and that his kingdom will be divided. In the night King Belshazzar is slain. ~

inventing new words for newly observed symptoms that may throw light on the mysteries of cerebral physiology, he says:

> Thus one phenomenon may have close on a dozen neologisms attached to it, and these are not always used with precision. All this has made for confusion, for it needs heroic virtues to plunge into the muddy waters of the relevant literature to pluck out truth from their depths.

Even precise words are of no use where they cannot be understood. A report in the *Evening Standard* tells how a Dr M. described the condition of a man embroiled in a Southwark court case as 'bilateral periorbital haematoma and left subconjunctival haemorrhage'. When asked what this meant, he said, 'Two lovely black eyes'.

When officials are accused of writing jargon, what is generally meant is that they affect a pompous and flabby verbosity. This is not what I mean. What I have in mind is that technical terms are used—especially conventional phrases invented by a government department—that are understood inside the department but are unintelligible to outsiders. This is true jargon. A circular from the headquarters of a department to its regional officers begins:

> The physical progressing of building cases should be confined to . . .

Without the key, nobody could say what meaning this was intended to convey. It is English only in the sense that the words are English words, but they have become a group of symbols used in conventional senses known only to parties to the convention. It may be said that no harm is done, because the instruction is not meant to be read by anyone unfamiliar with the departmental jargon. But using jargon is a dangerous habit. It is easy to forget that members of the public do not understand it, and to slip into the use of it in explaining things to them. If that is done, those seeking enlightenment will find themselves plunged in even deeper obscurity. A member of the department has kindly given me this interpretation of the words quoted above, qualified by the words, 'as far as I can discover':

'The physical progressing of building cases' means going at intervals to the sites of factories, etc., whose building is sponsored by the department and otherwise approved to see how many bricks have been laid since the last visit. 'Physical' here apparently exemplifies a portmanteau usage ... and refers both to the flesh-and-blood presence of the inspector and to the material development of the edifice, neither of which is, however, mentioned. 'Progressing', I gather, should have the accent on the first syllable and should be distinguished from pro*gress*ing. It means recording or helping forward the progress rather than going forward. 'Cases' is the common term for units of work which consist of applying a given set of rules to a number of individual problems ... 'should be confined to' means that only in the types of cases specified may an officer leave his desk to visit the site.

Let us take another example. 'Distribution of industry policy' is an expression well understood in the Board of Trade and other departments concerned with the subject. But it is jargon. Intrinsically the phrase has no certain meaning. Not even its grammatical construction is clear. So far as the words go, it is at least as likely that it refers to distributing something called 'industry-policy' as to a policy of distributing industry. Even when we know that 'distribution-of-industry' is a compound noun-adjective qualifying *policy*, we still do not give the words the full meaning that those who invented the phrase intended it to have. The esoteric meaning attached to it is 'the policy of exercising governmental control over the establishment of new factories in such a way as to minimise the risk of local mass unemployment'. No doubt it is convenient to have a label for anything that can only be explained so cumbrously. But it must not be forgotten that what is written on the label consists of code symbols unintelligible to the outsider. Forgetfulness of this kind causes perplexity and irritation. A judge recently said that he could form no idea of what was meant by the sentence: 'These prices are basis prices per ton for the representative-basis-pricing specification and size and quantity'; and the *Manchester Guardian* was once moved to describe the sense of despair produced by a document from the Ministry of Supply, quoted below, purporting to explain a (genuine) simplification in planning:

> The sub-authorisations required by its sub-contractors to re-authorise their orders as in (I) and (II) above. It should be borne in mind that sub-contractors may need re-authorisation not only of sub-authorisations already given for period II and beyond, but also for sub-authorisations of earlier periods, so as to revalidate orders or parts of orders as in (I).

Single words are sometimes given a special meaning for official purposes. This was especially true of words much used during the war. At a time when our lives were regulated at every turn by the distinction between what was and what was not 'essential', that word sprouted curiously. Its development can be traced through these three quotations:

> I can only deal with applications of a highly essential nature.

> It is impossible to approve importations from the USA unless there is a compelling case of essentiality.

> It is confirmed that as a farmer you are granted high essentiality.

In the last at any rate, the word has become jargon, given a meaning not known to the dictionaries. What the writer meant in the last one was, 'you are high on our waiting list'.

In its ordinary sense also, *essential* is frequently used unsuitably. Government departments have to issue so many instructions to all and sundry nowadays that those who draft them get tired of saying that people should or must do things, and misguidedly seek to introduce the relief of variety by saying, for instance, that it is necessary or that it is important that things should be done. And from that it is only a step to work oneself up into saying that it is 'essential' or 'vital' or even 'of paramount importance'. Here is an extract from a wartime departmental circular:

> In view of the national situation on the supply of textiles and buttons it is of paramount importance that these withdrawn garments shall be put to useful purposes . . .

To say that a thing is of paramount importance can only mean that it transcends in importance all other subjects. I cannot believe that anything to do with buttons can ever have been in that class.

Legal diction, as I have said, is necessarily a class apart, and an explanation of the provisions of a legal document must therefore be translated into familiar words simply arranged:

> With reference to your letter of the 12th August, I have to state in answer to question 1 thereof that where particulars of a partnership are disclosed to the Executive Council the remuneration of the individual partner for superannuation purposes will be deemed to be such proportion of the total remuneration of such practitioners as the proportion of his share in the partnership profits bears to the total proportion of the shares of such practitioner in those profits.

This is a good example of how not to explain. I think it means merely, 'Your income will be taken to be the same proportion of the firm's remuneration as you used to get of its profits'. I may be wrong, but even so I cannot believe that language is unequal to any clearer explanation than the one that the unfortunate correspondent received.

Here is another example of the failure to shake off the shackles of legal language:

> Separate departments in the same premises are treated as separate premises for this purpose where separate branches of work which are commonly carried on as separate businesses in separate premises are carried on in separate departments in the same premises.

This sentence is constructed with just that mathematical arrangement of words that lawyers adopt to make their meaning unambiguous. Worked out as one would work out an equation, the sentence serves its purpose. As literature, it is balderdash. The explanation could easily have been given in some such way as this:

> If branches of work commonly carried on as separate businesses are carried on in separate departments of the same premises, those departments will be treated as separate premises.

This shows how easily an unruly sentence like this can be reduced to order by turning part of it into an *if* clause.

Even without the corrupting influence of jargon or legal diction, a careless explanation may leave the thing explained even more obscure than it was before. The *New Yorker*, in August 1948, quoted from a publication called *Systems Magazine*:

> Let us paraphrase it and define Work Simplification as 'that method of accomplishing a necessary purpose omitting nothing necessary to that purpose in the simplest fashion is best.' This definition is important for it takes the mystery out of Work Simplification and leaves the essentials clearly outlined and succinctly stated.

The *New Yorker*'s comment was: 'It does indeed'.

Note. There are several warnings in this book against the use of chilly formalities. Happily, the most extreme examples that Gowers cited in 1954 have since become risible (*This document is forwarded herewith for the favour of your utilisation . . . The Minister cannot conceal from himself that X . . . AB per pro CD . . . The per stipes beneficiaries Y*, etc.). No civil servant today could pepper a document with writing of this kind unaware of the remarkable effect it must have on its reader.

But the decline of such phrases is balanced by other changes for the worse. Gowers felt in the 1950s that official writing (by contrast with the commercial and the academic) played 'a comparatively small part' in promulgating jargon. If that was really true then, it is not true now. A report recently put forward for public notice on the 'Peri-operative Care of the Higher Risk Surgical Patient' contains an obscure sentence that is representative of innumerable other obscure sentences in today's official documents:

> The adoption of an escalation strategy which incorporates defined time points and the early involvement of senior staff when necessary are strongly advised.

What is the ordinary person to make of this? It means something along the lines of, 'We strongly advise this: that hospital staff should follow a set timetable of checks, and when any results are worrying, should swiftly seek help from a doctor qualified to deal with the problem'. In a later version, the word 'are' in the original has helpfully been changed to 'is'; but the jargon remains, so that to a member of the public, the sentence must remain largely meaningless.

Another example of modern jargon is provided by the Department for Work and Pensions and the Department for Business Innovation and Skills in a document investigating the merits of 'skills conditionality'. Because this phrase has no conventional meaning, the authors go to the trouble of providing a gloss: it means, they explain, 'mandating claimants with skills needs to training' (also referred to as 'work activity'), with 'potential benefit sanctions for non-participation', though not where this would interfere with 'automatic passporting' to housing benefits. In more understandable English this means 'insisting that those who are jobless and who are deemed to need training should submit to being trained, under threat of having their welfare payments docked if they refuse, though without threat to their housing benefits'. Many ordinary speakers would be gravely unimpressed by what 'skills conditionality' turned out to mean in practice, with public protests by those who interpreted training or 'work activity' as *work*, who found the phrase 'benefit sanction' incongruous, and who accused the Government of supplying forced labour to private business.

Jargon may lead to obscurity, but the patterns of ordinary speech can be equally defeating. A leaflet issued by Oxfordshire County Council to explain its parking scheme to residents states idly that 'Permits may be renewed fourteen days before expiry on production of all documents the same as a new application'. The concerned resident is forced to struggle after the meaning here, which in the end appears to be this: 'You may renew your permit fourteen days before it runs out (and thereafter, presumably). To do so you will need the same supporting documents that we ask for with a new application'.

Despite the evidence of this parking notice, and of a wider trend towards informality in many public documents, jargon and elevated language remain greater threats to clarity than the overdoing of what Gowers called 'simple diction'. Stock phrases such as *herewith for the favour of your notice* may have gone, but an excess of dignity can often come down to a single word. The *Guardian*'s online garden centre, for example, advertises 'bulbs, bedding, perennials, annuals, shrubs and trees', then adds:

> With every order you'll receive comprehensive cultural instruc-
> tions and we promise that if you aren't delighted with your
> order we'll replace your order or give you your money back.

What, the humble gardener wonders bleakly, are these 'comprehensive cultural instructions', and why would a passing interest
in crocuses make it seem as though one needed them? *Growing*
would do perfectly well the job that 'comprehensive cultural' is
supposed to do, where the use of *cultural* for *growing* will bring
most readers to a momentary halt.

Gowers ended this chapter with a column of seductive or
'showy' words that he thought were overworked in official documents. Though he accepted that they all had their proper uses,
he warned against the temptation to use them in preference to
other words that 'would convey better the meaning you want to
express'. His advice to avoid using *moiety* for *half* is probably now
obsolete, but the rest of his list still stands. Of the hundred or so
words given below, roughly fifty are modern examples that have
come into vogue since. (It should be added that one or two of
these more recent examples barely qualify as having 'proper' uses.)
The right-hand column, meanwhile, gives other words, not necessarily synonyms, that might perhaps be used instead, 'if only, in
some cases,' as Gowers put it, 'as useful change-bowlers'. ~

Seductive words:	*Words you might use instead:*
Access (verb)	Reach; get hold of; find
Achieve	Do
Acquaint	Tell; inform
Adumbrate	Sketch; outline; foreshadow
Advert	Refer
Advise	Tell
Ameliorate	Improve; better
Apprise	Inform; tell

Seductive words:	*Words you might use instead:*
Assist	Help
Baseline	Starting point
Cease	Stop; end; finish
Commence	Begin; start
Commission	Buy
Consensual	Agreed
Consider	Think
Consortium	Group
Constellation	Group; array, arrangement
Deem	Think
Deliver	Give; provide; do
Desire	Wish; hope
Desist	Stop
Discontinue	Stop
Donate	Give
Dynamic	Strong; forceful
Enable	Help
Engage	Work with; interest
Enhance	Improve
Envisage	Think; expect; face
Establish	Show; find out; set up; prove
Eventuate	Come about; turn out; happen; result; occur
Evince	Show; display; manifest
Extrapolate	Work out from
Facilitate	Help
Factor	Fact; cause; consideration; feature; circumstance; element
Finalise	Finish; complete
Function (verb)	Work; operate; act

Seductive words:	*Words you might use instead:*
Iconic	Respected; good; loved
Impact (verb)	Affect
Implement	Carry out; do; fulfil
In isolation	By itself
Indicate	Show
Inform	Tell
Initiate	Begin; start
Initiative	Idea; plan
Inspirational	Inspiring; uplifting
Integrate	Join; mix; combine
Let go	Sack
Leverage (noun)	Influence
Leverage (verb)	Use; manipulate
Limited	Small; few
Locality	Place
Locate	Find
Major	Main; chief; principal; important
Materialise	Happen; take place; come about; occur
Meaningful	Useful; helpful; valuable
Mechanism	Method
Minimise	Underestimate; disparage; belittle; make light of
Mission	Aim; purpose
Modalities	Kinds; sorts; types; forms; modes
Modify	Change; alter
Motivational	Inspiring
Notify	Tell
Optimistic	Hopeful
Optimum	Best
Outcome	Result

Seductive words:	_Words you might use instead:_
Participate	Take part in; join in with
Perform	Do
Persons	Anyone; people
Practically	Almost; nearly; all but
Prior to	Before
Proceed	Go; carry on
Procure	Buy; get hold of
Provide	Give; do
Purchase	Buy
Purport (noun)	Upshot; gist; tenor; substance
Question (noun)	Matter; problem; subject; topic
Rationalise	Cut; sack
Render	Make
Require	Want; need
Reside	Live
Residence	Home
Restructuring	Job losses
Rightsizing	Job losses
Shake up	Job losses
Spectrum	Range
State	Say
Streamlining	Job losses
Submit	Give; send
Suboptimal	Unsatisfactory; inadequate
Sufficient	Enough
Symposium	Meeting
Terminate	End
Transmit	Send; forward
Undertake	Agree; do
Unilateral	One-sided
Utilise	Use

Seductive words:	*Words you might use instead:*
Virtually	Almost; nearly; all but
Vision	Plan; aim; hope
Visualise	Imagine; picture

VIII
THE CHOICE OF WORDS (4)

Choosing the precise word

And even things without life giving sound, whether pipe or harp, except they give a distinction in the sounds, how shall it be known what is piped or harped? For if the trumpet give an uncertain sound, who shall prepare himself to the battle? So likewise ye, except ye utter by the tongue words easy to be understood, how shall it be known what is spoken?

ST PAUL, First Epistle to the Corinthians

THE LURE OF THE ABSTRACT WORD

The reason for preferring the concrete to the abstract is clear. Your purpose must be to make your meaning plain. Even concrete words have a penumbra of uncertainty round them, but an incomparably larger one surrounds all abstract words. If you are using an abstract word when you might use a concrete one you are handicapping yourself in your task, difficult enough in any case, of making yourself understood.

Unfortunately the very vagueness of abstract words is one of the reasons for their popularity. To express one's thoughts accurately is hard work, and to be precise is sometimes dangerous. We are tempted by the safer obscurity of the abstract. It is the greatest vice of present-day writing. Numerous writers seem to find it more natural to say 'Was this the realisation of an anticipated liability?' than 'Did you expect to have to do this?'; to say

'Communities where anonymity in personal relationships prevails' than 'Communities where people do not know one another'. To resist this temptation, and to resolve to make your meaning plain to your reader even at the cost of some trouble to yourself, is more important than any other single thing if you would convert a flabby style into a crisp one.

An excessive reliance on the noun at the expense of the verb will, in the end, detach the mind of the writer from the realities of here and now, and from when and how and in what mood the thing was done. It will insensibly induce a habit of abstraction and vagueness. To what lengths this can go may be illustrated by these two examples:

> The desirability of attaining unanimity so far as the general construction of the body is concerned is of considerable importance from the production aspect.

> The actualisation of the motivation of the forces must to a great extent be a matter of personal angularity.

The first, which says that it 'relates to the building of vehicles', means, I suppose, that in order to produce vehicles quickly it is important to agree on a standard body. The meaning of the second is past conjecture. (Its perpetrator was an economist, not an official.)

Here are two less extreme examples of the habit of using abstract words to say in a complicated way something that might be said simply and directly:

> A high degree of carelessness, pre-operative and post-operative, on the part of some of the hospital staff, took place. (Some of the hospital staff were very careless both before and after the operation.)

> The cessation of house-building operated over a period of five years. (No houses were built for five years.)

Note the infelicity of 'a cessation operated'. 'Operate' is just what cessations cannot do.

Sometimes abstract words are actually invented, so powerful is the lure of saying things this way:

> The reckonability of former temporary service for higher leave entitlement.

The following is not official writing, but as it appeared in a newspaper that never shrinks from showing up the faults of official writing, it deserves a place:

> Initiation of a temporary organisation to determine European economic requirements in relation to proposals by Mr Marshall, American Secretary of State, was announced in the House of Commons this evening.

This way of expressing oneself seems to be tainting official speech as well as writing. 'We want you to deny indirect reception,' said the goods clerk of my local railway station, telephoning me about a missing suitcase. 'What does that mean?' I asked. 'Why,' he said, 'we want to make sure that the case has not reached you through some other station.'

Exponents of the newer sciences are fond of expressing themselves in abstractions. Perhaps this is unavoidable, but I cannot help thinking that they sometimes make things unnecessarily difficult for their readers. I have given an example on the last page of an economist's wrapping up his meaning in an impenetrable mist of abstractions. Here is one from psychology:

> Reserves that are occupied in continuous uni-directional adjustment of a disorder, as is the case in compensative existence, are fixed or mortgaged reserves. They are no longer available for use

in the ever-varying interplay of organism and environment in the spontaneity of mutual synthesis.

(I. H. Pearse and L. H. Crocker, *The Peckham Experiment*, 1943)

In official writing the words *availability*, *lack* and *dearth* contribute much to the same practice, though they do not produce the same obscurity. Perhaps the reason those words are so popular is that we have suffered so much from what it is fashionable to call a 'lack of availability' of so many useful things:

The actual date of the completion of the purchase should coincide with the availability of the new facilities. (The purchase should not be completed until the new facilities are available.)

'There is a complete lack of spare underground wire' is not the natural way of saying 'We have no spare underground wire', or 'A dearth of information exists' for 'We have very little information'.

POSITION AND SITUATION

The words *position* and *situation* greatly fascinate those who are given to blurring the sharp outlines of what they have to say. A debate takes place in the House of Commons about an acute scarcity of coal during a hard winter. A speaker wants to say that it is hard to imagine how the Government could have made sure of there being enough coal. Does the speaker say this? No; the thought is enveloped in a miasma of abstract words, and is given like this instead: 'In view of all the circumstances I do not see how this situation could have been in any way warded off'. Later, someone speaking for the Government wants to strike a reassuring note, and to express confidence that we shall get through the winter without disaster. 'We shall', says the second speaker, also taking refuge in abstractions, 'ease through this position without any deleterious effect on the situation.'

It fell to a master of words to make an announcement at a time of grave crisis. Sir Winston Churchill did not begin his broadcast of the 17th June 1940, 'The position in regard to France is extremely serious'. He began: 'The news from France is very bad'. He did not end it, 'We have absolute confidence that eventually the situation will be restored'. He ended: 'We are sure that in the end all will be well'.

Position and *situation*, besides replacing more precise words, have a way of intruding into sentences that can do better without them. These words should be regarded as danger signals, and if you find yourself using one, try to think whether you cannot say what you have to say more directly:

> It may be useful for Inspectors to be informed about the present situation on this matter. (To know how this matter now stands.)

> Unless these wagons can be moved the position will soon be reached where there will be no more wagons to be filled. (There will soon be no more . . .)

> Should the position arise where a hostel contains a preponderance of public assistance cases . . . (If a hostel gets too many public assistance cases . . .)

All three sentences run more easily if we get rid of the *situation* and the *position*s.

Position in regard to is an ugly expression, not always easy to avoid, but used more often than it need be. 'The position in regard to the supply of labour and materials has deteriorated' seems to come more naturally to the pen than 'It is now harder to get labour and materials'. 'No one has any doubt', writes the *Manchester Guardian*, 'that deceased senior officials of the Civil Service have *in regard to* engraved on their hearts; and their successors to-day show no recovery from this kind of hereditary lockjaw.'

But it is not fair to put all the blame on officials. Even *The Times* is capable of saying, 'The question of the British position in regard to the amount of authorisation', rather than 'the question how much Britain is to get of the amount authorised'.

Note. When Gowers came to revise Fowler, he added an entry under the heading 'abstractitis': the disease, he said, was endemic, and he warned that the habit of using misty, abstract words would slowly cloud a person's thoughts, making the difficult business of clear writing even harder.

As no cure for this disease has yet been discovered, today's body of English is abundantly spotted with new abstract words. Academics must discover their own 'positionality' or be damned, translators are forced to ruminate on the 'situationality' of what they are translating, businesses find themselves worrying about how to 'organisationalise' useful data, old buses are 'allocated for air-conditionisation', and companies that deliver parcels require 'sortation facilities' for their toiling 'sortation facility operatives'.

Official writing too is nowadays speckled with words like *proportionality, conditionality, operationality, interoperationality* and *operationalisation*. Herefordshire Council is standing up for 'greater transactionalisation' of its services; one has the dim sense that this means getting more people to use them. The Government's Committee on Radioactive Waste Management must face down the 'necessary provisionality' of the advice it receives: the fact that specialists cannot be sure how long their advice will stand. The Government in Scotland is worried about the 'occupationalisation' of unpaid carers, defined as 'a task based approach to caring which looks not at the carer but only at the caring tasks'—thereby, the explanation continues, putting at risk the opportunity for unpaid carers 'to be all that they are and want to be', which would seem to set the bar for improving their lot rather high. A Department for Transport document on 'highways assignments modelling techniques' gives as its first objective, 'To review current and foreseeable wider modelling requirements and policy analysis requirement to identify the functionality that highway assignment modelling needs to provide to meet them'. Plainly put, this means, 'To decide how detailed our estimates of road use need to be now, and will need to be in future, so that we can work out how to produce the required estimates'. On its own, the phrase to 'provide functionality' means nothing much more than to be *able to do* something.

If there were ever an ugliness contest for words of this sort, 'operationalisation' would be a fair bet to win. It is most often used as though it means roughly 'making X work'. For instance, in a report for the Department of Social Security on ways of encouraging pensioners to claim certain benefits, it is stated that a given method 'should be ... capable of operationalisation across all Benefits Agency offices'. Here 'should be ... capable of operationalisation' means simply *should work*, or indeed *must work*. In a more insidious example, a report for the Department of Work and Pensions on 'persistent employment disadvantage' concerns itself deeply with the fact that how you define *disabled* governs who is classed as disabled. The author observes that those devising a census form must make up their minds on this matter, and speaks of a sinister 'census operationalisation of disability'. This appears to mean that classing people as disabled *makes* them disabled, with the politically seductive corollary that those whom you refuse to class as disabled somehow become, and thus may (more cheaply) be treated as being, fully fit.

THE ABSTRACT APPENDAGE

This brings us to what has been called the 'abstract appendage'; for *position*, *situation* and *conditions* find themselves in that role more commonly than any other words. In a letter to *The Times* objecting to the phrase 'weather conditions', the writer quotes two lines from Thomas Hardy's poem, 'Weathers':

> This is the weather the shepherd shuns,
> And so do I . . .

The BBC, the correspondent suggests, would be more likely to say, 'These are the weather conditions the shepherd shuns . . .'.

'Weather conditions' can perhaps be defended as importing a larger idea than *weather* alone does (it embraces the conditions created by yesterday's weather and the likelihood of tomorrow's weather changing them). But the attack, though badly aimed, was directed against a real fault in official English. If the attack had been made the next day on the announcement that *blizzard conditions* had returned to the Midlands, it could not have been met with any such plea. It was not 'blizzard conditions' that had returned, it was a blizzard. Similarly it is both unnecessary and quaint to say that temperatures will return to 'normal values' instead of merely that they will return to normal. *Level* has also been greatly in demand of late as an abstract appendage. A correspondent has kindly presented me with a collection of hundreds of specimens, ranging from 'pub-and-street-corner-level' to 'world-level' through every conceivable intermediate level. This passion for picturing all our relationships with one another as stratifications is an odd phenomenon at a time when we are supposed to be developing into a classless State.

THE HEADLINE PHRASE

Serious harm is also being done to the language by excessive use of nouns as adjectives. In the past, as I have said, the language has been greatly enriched by this free-and-easy habit. We are surrounded by innumerable examples—War Department, Highway Code, Nursery School, Coronation Service, Trades Union

Congress and so on. But something has gone wrong recently with this useful practice, and its abuse is corrupting English prose. It has become natural to say 'World population is increasing faster than world food production' instead of 'The population of the world is increasing faster than the food it produces'; 'The eggs position exceeds all expectation' instead of 'Eggs are more plentiful than expected'. It is old fashioned to write of the 'state of the world'; it must be the 'world situation'. As was observed by Lord Dunsany, writer, marksman and friend of Yeats, in his *Donnellan Lectures* of 1943, the fact is that 'too many *of*s have dropped out of the language, and the dark of the floor is littered with this useful word'. And so we meet daily with headlines like 'England side captain selection difficulty rumour'.

This sort of language is no doubt pardonable in a newspaper, where as many stimulating words as possible must be crowded into spaces so small that *treaties* have had to become *pacts*; *ambassadors*, *envoys*; *investigations*, *probes*; and all forms of human enterprise, *bids*. Headlines have become a language of their own, knowing no law and often quite incomprehensible until one has read the article that they profess to summarise. 'Insanity Rules Critic' and 'W. H. Smith Offer Success' have quite different meanings from their apparent ones. Who could know what is meant by 'Hanging Probe Names Soon' without having read on and discovered that 'The names of the members of the Royal Commission on Capital Punishment will shortly be announced'? Who could guess that the headline 'Unofficial Strikes Claim' introduces a report of a speech by a member of Parliament who said that there was abundant evidence that unofficial strikes were organised and inspired by Communists as part of a general plan originating from abroad? I do not see how those three words by themselves can have any meaning at all. To me they convey a vague suggestion of the discovery of oil or gold by someone who ought not to have been looking for it. And if the announcement 'Bull Grants

Increase' is construed grammatically, it does not seem to deserve a headline at all: one would say that that was no more than was to be expected from any conscientious bull.

But what may be pardonable in headlines will not do in the text, nor is it suitable in English prose generally. For instance:

> Food consumption has been dominated by the world supply situation. (People have had to eat what they could get.)

> An extra million tons of steel would buy our whole sugar import requirements. (All the sugar we need to import.)

The only thing that can be said for the following sentence is that it does not end 'sites preparation':

> Everything is being done to expedite plant installation within the limiting factors of steel availability and the preparation of sites.

This should have run: 'So far as steel is available and sites can be prepared, everything is being done to expedite the installation of plant'.

An exceptionally choice example is:

> The programme must be on the basis of the present head of labour ceiling allocation overall.

Here *head of labour* means *number of workers*. *Ceiling* means *maximum*. *Overall*, as usual, means nothing.* The whole sentence means 'The programme must be on the assumption that we get the maximum number of workers at present allotted to us'.

The use of a noun as an adjective should be avoided where the same word is already an adjective with a different meaning. Do

---

* For more on *overall*, see pp. 159–161.

not, for instance, say 'material allocation' when you mean 'allocation of material', but reserve that expression against a time when you may want to make clear that the allocation you are considering is not a spiritual one. For the same reason this phrase is not felicitous:

> In view of the restrictions recently imposed on our capital economic situation . . .

By way of emphasising that the official is by no means the only offender, I will add an example from an American sociological book discussed in an article in *The Economist*:

> Examination of specific instances indicated that in most cases where retirement dissatisfaction existed advance activity programming by individuals had been insignificant or even lacking.

I translate with diffidence, but the meaning seems to be:

> Examination of specific instances indicated that most of those who did not wish to retire had given little or no thought to planning their future.

Note. The humour of Gowers's example above, 'our capital economic situation', has dated (few people now use *capital* to mean *splendid*), but the Vatican milks a lasting joke on the same grammatical lines for the title of its weekly radio show, 'The Latin Lover'. Of course where a double meaning of this sort has been arrived at by mistake, context will usually forestall confusion over what sense was intended. Yet faced solely with the headline, 'Tussaud Giant Delivery Mixup Nightmare', a reader would have no way of knowing whether a great number of standard waxwork figures had gone astray, or a single seven-footer.

Gowers's capital joke may now be a little dusty, but his warning against the excessive use by officials of nouns as adjectives is not. The Chief Executive of the Higher Education Funding Council for England wrote recently that 'concerns are beginning to be expressed that the level of widening participation activity delivered in future may decline'. What this seems to mean, 'declines of level-delivery' and all, is: 'People are starting to worry that in future fewer students from wide-ranging backgrounds will be successfully encouraged to go to university'. (Perhaps, though, 'activity' refers to the actual effort put into encouraging them.) In the same vein, the Office for Fair Access wishes to know about the 'access' efforts of 'School Centred Initial Teacher Training providers'. These appear to be schools that train teachers on the job. The Department for Education has seen fit to sponsor an 'Emotional abuse recognition training evaluation study'; and so it goes on. ~

ABSTRACT ADJECTIVAL PHRASES

By this I mean using a phrase consisting of an adjective and an abstract noun (e.g. *character, nature, basis, description, disposition*) where a simple adjective would do as well. This too offends against the rule that you should say what you have to say as simply and directly as possible in order that you may be readily understood:

> These claims are of a far-reaching type. (These claims are far reaching.)

> The weather will be of a showery character. (It will be showery.)

> The wages will be low owing to the unremunerative nature of the work.

The translation of the last example will present no difficulty to a student of Mr Micawber, who once said of the occupation of selling corn on commission: 'It is not an avocation of a remunerative description—in other words, it does *not* pay'.

Proposition is another abstract word used in the same way:

> Decentralisation on a regional basis is now a generally practical proposition. (Is now generally feasible.)

> Accommodation in a separate building is not usually a viable proposition. (Is not usually feasible.)

> The high cost of land in clearance areas makes it a completely uneconomic proposition to build cottages in those areas. (Makes it completely uneconomic to build cottages there.)

Basis is especially likely to lead writers to express themselves in roundabout ways. When you find you have written 'on a … basis' always examine it critically before letting it stand:

> Such officer shall remain on his existing salary on a mark-time basis. (Shall mark time on his existing salary.)

> The organisation of such services might be warranted in particular localities and on a strictly limited basis. (Scale.)

> The machines would need to be available both day and night on a 24-hour basis. (At any time of day or night.)

> Please state whether this is to be a permanent installation or on a temporary line basis. (Or a temporary line.)

A legitimate use of *basis* is:

> The manufacturers are distributing their products as fairly as possible on the basis of past trading.

Note. The formula 'on an X basis' has not gone away. Thus *permanently* becomes 'on a permanent basis'; *individually*, 'on a case-by-case basis'; *as we go along,* 'on a rolling basis'; *all the time,* 'on a 24/7 basis'. In a recent internal review by the Ministry of Defence (of a 'control framework' that failed to prevent the waste of hundreds of millions of pounds) the authors declare, 'we report on an exception basis only', apparently meaning 'we report only on what has gone wrong' (which probably did take up a lot of space). The Department for Transport has revealed that a new Order will 'enable local authorities and the Secretary of State to operate the statutory highway functions listed in the Order on a contracted out basis'. The ending here presumably means 'using private contractors', though whether *functions* can be *operated* is another matter. The document carries on, unhelpfully, 'These functions include ... street works functions'. But at last comes the explanation: 'Street works are works carried out by, or on behalf of, undertakers operating under a statutory right...', which brings to mind the unwelcome image of gravediggers plugging large potholes with unclaimed corpses. ~

CLICHÉS AND OVERWORKED METAPHORS

In the course of this book I have called numerous expressions clichés. A cliché may be defined as a phrase whose aptness in a particular context when it was first invented has won it such popularity that it has become hackneyed, and is now used without thought in contexts where it is no longer apt. Clichés are notorious enemies of the precise word. To quote from Eric Partridge:

> Clichés range from fly-blown phrases ('much of a muchness'; 'to all intents and purposes'), metaphors that are now pointless ('lock, stock and barrel'), formulas that have become mere counters ('far be it from me to ...')—through sobriquets that have lost all of their freshness and most of their significance ('the Iron Duke')—to quotations that are nauseating ('cups that cheer but not inebriate') and foreign phrases that are tags ('longo intervallo'; 'bête noire'). (*A Dictionary of Clichés*, 1947)

A cliché, then, is by definition a bad thing, not to be employed by self-respecting writers. Judged by this test, some expressions are unquestionably and in all circumstances clichés. This is true in particular of verbose and facetious ways of saying simple things (*conspicuous by its absence*, *tender mercies*) and of phrases so threadbare that they cannot escape the suspicion of being used automatically (*leave no stone unturned*, *acid test*). But a vast number of other expressions may or may not be clichés. It depends on whether they are used unthinkingly as reach-me-downs, or have been deliberately chosen as the best means of saying what a writer wants to say. Eric Partridge's *Dictionary* contains some thousands of entries. But, as he says in his preface, what is a cliché is partly a matter of opinion. It is also a matter of occasion. Many of those in his dictionary may cease to be clichés if used carefully. Writers would be needlessly handicapped if they were never permitted such phrases as *cross the Rubicon*, *sui generis*, *swing of the pendulum*, *thin end of the wedge* and *white elephant*. These may be the fittest way of expressing what is meant. If you choose one of them for that reason you need not be afraid of being called a cliché-monger.

The trouble is that writers often use a cliché because they think it fine, or because it is the first thing that comes into their heads. It is always a danger signal when one word suggests another and Siamese twins are born—*part and parcel*, *intents and purposes**and the like. There is no good reason why *inconvenience* should always be said to be *experienced* by a person who suffers it and *occasioned* by the person who causes it. Single words too may become clichés, used so often that their edges become blunt while

---

* In the decades since Partridge and Gowers wrote disparagingly of the cliché *to all intents and purposes*, it has given rise to a corrupted version of itself, 'to all intensive purposes'. This is no improvement on the original. ~

more exact words are neglected. Some indeed seem to attract by their very drabness.

Those who resort carelessly to cliché are also given to overworking metaphors. I have already said that newly discovered metaphors shine like jewels. They enable a writer to convey briefly and vividly ideas that might otherwise need tedious exposition. What should we have done, in our present economic difficulties, without our *targets*, *ceilings* and *bottlenecks*? But the very seductiveness of metaphors makes them dangerous. New ones, in particular, tend to be used indiscriminately and soon get stale, but not before they have elbowed out words perhaps more commonplace but with meanings more precise. Sometimes metaphors are so absurdly overtaxed that they become a laughing stock and die of ridicule.*

Another danger in the use of metaphors is that of falling into incongruity: for as long as they remain 'live', they must not be given in a context that would be absurd if the words used metaphorically were being used literally. By a 'live metaphor' I mean one that evokes in the reader a mental picture of the imagery of its origin. A dead one does not. If we write 'the situation is in hand' and 'he has taken the bit between his teeth', we are going to horsemanship for our metaphors; but to most readers 'in hand' will be a dead metaphor, unconnected to managing a horse, so that using it would have an impact no different from 'the situation is under control'. It is possible the second metaphor still has a little life in it, calling up for a few people, however faintly and momentarily, a horse that has taken the 'bit' under its own control. But 'taking the bit between the teeth' is probably close to dead also.

Almost all writers fall occasionally into the trap of using a live metaphor infelicitously. It is worth taking great pains to avoid

* Gowers confidently gave as examples *explore every avenue* and *leave no stone unturned*, but decades later both soldier on, yet to hit the buffers. ~

doing so, because the reader who notices it will deride you. The statesman who said that sections of the population were being 'squeezed flat by inflation' was not then in his happiest vein, nor was the writer who claimed for American sociology the distinction of having always 'immersed itself in concrete situations', nor the enthusiastic scientist who announced the discovery of a 'virgin field pregnant with possibilities'.*

OVERWORKED WORDS OFTEN USED IMPRECISELY

Among clichés and overworked metaphors represented by single words, the following deserve comment. We cannot but admit that there is no hope of checking the astonishing antics of *target*, and of bringing that flighty word within reasonable bounds. But we do not want any more metaphors getting out of hand like that.

Affect

Affect has won undeserved popularity because it is colourless—a word of broad meaning that saves the writer the trouble of thought. It is useful in its place, but not when used from laziness. It may be easier to say 'The progress of the building has been *affected* by the weather', but it is better to use a more precise word—*hindered*, perhaps, or *delayed* or *stopped*. I used to think during the war when I heard that gas mains had been affected by a raid that it would have been more sensible to say that they had been broken.

Alternative

The use of *alternative* for such words as *other*, *new*, *revised* or *fresh* is rife. It is generally regarded as pedantry to say that, because of

---

* The Deputy Prime Minister not so long ago roundly declared, 'We will not balance the books on the backs of the poor'. ~

its derivation, *alternative* must not be used where there are more than two choices. But it is certainly wrong to use it where there is no choice at all. For instance, the Ministry of Health announced one spring that owing to the severe winter the house-building programme for the year had been abandoned, and added that no 'alternative programme' would be issued. They might have said *other*, *new*, *fresh* or *revised*, but *alternative* must be wrong. There is nothing for it to be an alternative to: the old programme is torn up. Even in that popular phrase *alternative accommodation*, the adjective is generally incorrect, for the person to whom the accommodation is offered usually has no alternative to taking it. Innumerable examples could be given of this misuse. Here are two:

> The Ministry of Transport are arranging alternative transport for the passengers of the *Empire Windrush* [which is at the bottom of the Mediterranean].

> Billeting Authorities are requested to report any such cases as they are unable to rebillet, in order that alternative arrangements may be made.

Alternative must imply a choice between two or more things.

Appreciate

The ordinary meaning of *appreciate*, as a transitive verb, is to form an estimate of the worth of anything, or to set a value on it. It is therefore not surprising that it is useful to polite officials corresponding with members of the public who want more than they can get, as most of us do today. Refusals are softened by a phrase such as 'I appreciate how hard it is on you not to have it'. But there can be no doubt that *appreciate* is being used by writers of official letters and circulars with a freedom that passes reason. It is often used merely by way of courteous padding, or where it would be more suitable to say *understand, realise, recognise, be grateful, be obliged*. 'It would be appreciated if' can usually be translated into 'I shall be glad (or grateful, or obliged, or even pleased) if . . .'. 'You will appreciate' can often be better expressed by 'you will realise' or even 'of course'. An effective way of curbing *appreciate* might be to resolve never to use it with a *that* clause ('I appreciate that there has been a delay'), but always to give it a noun to govern ('I appreciate your difficulty').

Appropriate

This is an irreproachable word. But so too are *right, suitable, fitting* and *proper*, and I do not see why *appropriate* should have it all its own way. In particular, the Whitehall cliché *in appropriate cases* might be confined more closely than it is now to cases in which it is appropriate.

Note. A new cliché is *appropriate*'s opposite, *inappropriate*. So imprecise has *inappropriate* become as a term of condemnation that it is often applied in circumstances where no 'appropriate' contrast exists (the 'inappropriate' disclosure of a jury's deliberations, or an 'inappropriate' sexual liaison between a teacher and a schoolchild). ~

Blueprint

This word has caught on as a picturesque substitute for *scheme* or *plan* and the shine is wearing off.

Note. *Blueprint* started out as a Victorian photographic term for a white image printed on a blue background. Blueprints were usually used to reproduce plans. Other examples of vocabulary springing from the Industrial Revolution and quickly taken into metaphorical use are *deadbeat, backlash, safety valve, gas bag, dynamo* and *powerhouse*. The word *cliché* is itself an example: it was adopted from French into English in the 1830s, and was originally a printing term for a stereotype block. If the shine was wearing off *blueprint* in the 1950s, it is surely now a 'dead' metaphor, with no confusing blueness implied. But it is perhaps still worth remembering that, as Gowers noted, 'in the engineering industries, where it comes from, the blueprint marks the final stage of a paper design'. ~

Bottleneck

Bottleneck is useful as a metaphor to denote the point of constriction of something that ought to be flowing freely. Its use as a metaphor is not new, but it has had a sharp rise in popularity, perhaps because our economy has been so full of bottlenecks. It needs to be handled with care in order to avoid absurdity. Examples recently held up to ridicule in *The Times* include the 'overriding bottleneck', the 'drastic bottleneck', the 'worldwide bottleneck' and the 'vicious circle of interdependent bottlenecks'. A correspondent from America has written to me of an official praised for his ability to 'lick bottlenecks'.

Note. Though we are now also detained by metaphorical *pinchpoints*, *chokes* and phases of *gridlock* (even where there are no grids), 'bottlenecks' have not gone away. 'We should not', wrote Gowers, 'refer to the biggest bottleneck when what we mean is the most troublesome one, for that will obviously be the narrowest.' This thought cannot have struck the correspondent for *The Economist* who wrote recently that 'Most Nigerians are unlikely to receive more than a few hours of mains electricity per day for many years—the single biggest bottleneck in the economy'. ~

Ceiling

This is one of the bright young metaphors that are now so fashionable, and are displacing the old fogeys. *Ceiling*'s victims are *maximum* and *limit*. There is no great harm in that, so long as those who use the word remember to treat it as a metaphor.

Note. Gowers objected to ceilings being 'increased' rather than *raised*, let alone to them being 'waived', and added that 'our normal relationship to a ceiling is to be under it, not within it'. He particularly despaired of metaphorical *ceilings* being mixed up with metaphorical *floors* ('The effect of this announcement is that the total figure for 1950–51 of £410 million can be regarded as a floor as well as a ceiling'), or indeed with actual floors ('In determining the floor-space, a ceiling of 15,000 square feet should normally be the limit').

Those who use *ceiling* comparably freely today would no doubt argue that, with *blueprint* and *bottleneck*, it has become a dead metaphor. (The more particular *glass ceiling* is, by contrast, still live, continually being smashed and shattered, or not smashed and shattered but bumped against and longingly peered through.) But a metaphorical *ceiling* can still be abused in ways that risk suggesting 'undesirable ideas to the flippant'. Another recent contributor to *The Economist*, writing about euro bonds, reported on the unconvincing suggestion that a 'flexible ceiling would act as an automatic stabiliser . . .', and on the belief that 'the respective share of wayward countries would be reduced as their ceilings were reduced . . .' (presumably 'lowered'), the counter view being that 'if the ceiling was in any way perceived as being soft . . . the disciplining effect . . . disappears'. It is a fearful thought that anybody should seek to maintain discipline by emphasising the hardness of a ceiling. ~

Decimate

To *decimate* is to reduce *by* one-tenth, not *to* one-tenth. It meant originally to punish mutinous troops by executing one man in ten, chosen by lot. Hence by extension it means to destroy a large proportion. The suggestion it now conveys is usually of a loss much greater than a tenth, but because of the flavour of exactness that still hangs about it, it should not be used with an adverb or adverbial phrase. We may say 'The attacking troops were decimated', meaning that they suffered heavy losses, but we must not say 'The attacking troops were badly decimated', and still less 'decimated to the extent of 50 per cent or more'. The following truly remarkable instance of the misuse of *decimate* (and *literally*), taken from a penny dreadful, was given in the course of correspondence in *The Times*: 'Dick, hotly pursued by the scalp-hunter, turned in his saddle, fired and literally decimated his opponent'.

Note. Gowers's account here is of the Roman origin of *decimate*. When the word was first imported into medieval English, it was used to mean taking a tax of one-tenth, and a 'decimator' was a tax collector. But its use in the imprecise sense of inflicting huge damage has been common in English for at least two centuries. Those who continue to believe that this meaning is incorrect because it defies the word's etymology commit themselves, by the same argument, to insisting that a *journey* can last only one day, and a period of *quarantine*, forty. Nevertheless, enough people do know the strict meaning of *decimate* that to manhandle the word as Gowers describes above is still to risk seeming under-informed. ~

Involve

The meaning of this popular word has been diluted to a point of extreme insipidity. Originally it meant *wrap up in something, enfold*. Then it acquired the figurative meaning *entangle a person in difficulties or embarrassment*, and especially *implicate in a crime or a charge*. Then it began to lose colour, and to be used as though it meant nothing more than *include, contain* or *imply*. It has thus developed a vagueness that makes it the delight of those who dislike the effort of searching for the right word, and is therefore much used, generally where some more specific word would be better and sometimes where it is merely superfluous. (In its super-fluous uses, it is matched by *entail*.)

Here are a few examples:

The additional rent involved will be £1. (Omit *involved*.)

We have been informed that the procedure involved would necessitate lengthy negotiation. (Omit *involved*.)

Much labour has been involved in advertising. (... expended in advertising.)

This would possibly involve the creation of a precedent that might embarrass the Government. (This would possibly create a precedent that ...)

The Company would oppose this application unless compensation involving a substantial sum were paid. (... unless a substantial sum were paid in compensation.)

Such are some of the sadly flabby uses to which this word of character is put. Reserve it for more knotty purposes and especially for use where there is a suggestion of entanglement or complication, as we would use *involved* when we say 'this is a most involved subject'.

Issue

This word has a very wide range of proper meanings as a noun, and should not be made to do any more work—the work, for instance, of *subject*, *topic*, *consideration* and *dispute*.

Note. The workload of *issue* has grown enormously since Gowers wrote this, not least because it now also doubles up on the job hitherto done by *problem*. Thus a government department these days might release a disastrous consultation paper in terms of issues to do with interoperability issues, even as a Minister has personal issues that threaten to become an issue in the press, causing the Prime Minister to have a major issue with the Minister. In short, Gowers's warning went unheeded, and *issue* is being made to labour harder than ever. ~

Overall

The favour that this word has won over the past few years is astonishing. It is an egregious example of the process I described as boring out a weapon of precision into a blunderbuss. Indeed the word seems to have a quality that impels people to use it in settings in which it has no meaning at all.

Examples of its meaningless use are:

The overall growth of London should be restrained.

Radical changes will be necessary in the general scheme of Exchequer grants in aid of local authorities, therefore, to secure that overall the policy of the Government in concentrating those grants as far as possible where the need is greatest is further developed. (Here *overall* is an adverb.)

The Controller should assume a general overall responsibility for the efficient planning of all measures.

When *overall* is not meaningless, it is commonly used as a synonym for some more precise word, especially *aggregate, average* and *total*, but also *supreme, overriding, comprehensive, absolute* and others.

For *aggregate*:
Compared with the same week a year ago, overall production of coal showed an increase of more than 100,000 tons. (i.e. 'deep-mined plus opencast'.)

For *average*:
The houses here are built to an overall density of three to the acre.

For *total*:
I have made a note of the overall demand of this company for the next year.

For *supreme*:
Vice-Admiral Duncan, of the United States Navy, was in overall command.

For *overriding*:
They came forward as witnesses because of the overall fear of being involved in a capital charge.

For *comprehensive*:
An overall plan for North Atlantic Defence measures was approved yesterday by the Defence Minister at the Hague.

For *bird's-eye*:
Our observer will be in the control tower, where he will have an overall view of the aerodrome.

For *absolute*:
The Conservatives will have an overall majority in the new Parliament.

For *on balance*:
The purpose of the plan is to enable a larger initial payment to be made and correspondingly lower payments subsequently, entailing an overall saving to the customer. (... leading on balance to a saving for the customer.)

Overall is also used to mean *altogether, whole, on the whole, generally, complete*. According to the dictionaries, it means 'including everything between the extreme points', as one speaks of the overall length of a ship. For this purpose it is useful, but it is high time that its excursions into the fields of other words were checked. So pervasive is the word now that it is a pleasant surprise to come across an old-fashioned *general* in such sentences as:

> These reports may be used for obtaining a general picture of the efficiency of a given industry.

> Although Europe's general deficit with the outside world fell by over $2 billion during 1949, its deficit with the United States fell hardly at all.

Most writers today would say 'overall picture' and 'overall deficit' almost automatically.

Percentage, Proportion, Fraction

Do not use the expression *a percentage* or *a proportion* when what you mean is *some*, as in:

> This drug has proved of much value in a percentage of cases.

> The London Branch of the National Association of Fire Officers, which includes a proportion of station officers . . .

Here *percentage* and *proportion* pretend to mean something more than *some*, but do not really do so. They fail to give the reader any idea of the number or proportion of successful cases, or of station officers. One per cent is just as much 'a percentage' as 99 per cent. So for that matter is 200 per cent.

Do not forget the simple words *many, few* and *some*: use *percentage* or *proportion* only if you want to express not an absolute number but the relation of one number to another, and can give at least an approximate degree of exactitude. Though you may not be able to put an actual figure on the percentage or proportion, you can at any rate say 'a high percentage', 'a large proportion', 'a low percentage', 'a small proportion'.

But *fraction* is different. It has become so common to use 'only a fraction' in the sense of 'only a small fraction' that it would be pedantry to object that 999/1000 is as much a fraction as 1/1000, just as it would certainly be to point out to anyone who says 'He has got a temperature' that 98 degrees is just as much 'a temperature' as 104.

Realistic

This word is becoming dangerously popular. What is realistic is what the writer thinks sensible. *Realistic* is ousting words like *practical, feasible, sensible* itself, and *workmanlike*. Everything nowadays seems to be either 'academic' or 'realistic.'

Target

Of all the metaphors that have been called on to help in restoring our balance of trade, *target* has been the most in demand. We are urged not only to reach and attain our targets, but also to fight for them, to achieve them and obtain them. We must not be lulled by a near target. It is discouraging to be a long way short of our target and (what seems to amount to the same thing) to be a long way behind it, but it is splendid to be a long way beyond it. 'Target in danger' means that it is in no danger of being hit, and 'target in sight' is intended to be exceptionally encouraging to those who are trying to hit it. In fact targets have got completely out of control. We must regard the life of this metaphor as having been as short as it certainly has been merry, and treat it as dead, driven into an early grave by overwork. Then we can all do anything we like to a target without giving offence to anyone. But readers ought not to be tried too hard. Not even the exigencies of newspaper language can excuse the headline 'Export Target Hit' to introduce the news that, owing to a dock strike, the export target is unlikely to be hit.

Note. Gowers's metaphorical shoulders would no doubt have sagged even further had he known that for 'minimum standards' the Department for Education would one day substitute 'floor targets', with much trumpeting of 'rising floor targets' (see '*Ceiling*' above).

Some institutions have now succumbed instead to 'goal-directed motivational systems', but *targets* remain hugely popular, and have even reached the point of striking back—or so the *Guardian* reports, saying of a new set of exam standards: 'targets will hit disadvantaged'. ~

THE HANDLING OF WORDS

Proper Words in proper Places, makes the true Definition
of a Style.

Swift, A Letter to a Young Gentleman,
Lately Entr'd into Holy Orders, 1721

If language is not correct, then what is said is not what is
meant; if what is said is not what is meant, then what ought to
be done remains undone.

Confucius

We must now return to what I called in Chapter IV 'correctness',
and consider what it means not in the choice of words but in
handling them when chosen. That takes us into the realm of
grammar and syntax, as well as of idiom—three words that overlap and are often used loosely, with grammar as a generic term
covering them all.

Grammar has fallen from the high esteem that it used to enjoy.
In 1818, in his work *A Grammar of the English Language*, William
Cobbett wrote that 'Grammar, perfectly understood, enables us,
not only to express our meaning fully and clearly, but so to express
it as to enable us to defy the ingenuity of man to give to our words
any other meaning than that which we ourselves intend them to
express'. The very name of grammar school serves to remind us
that grammar was long regarded as the only path to culture and

learning. But that was Latin grammar. When our mother tongue encroached on the paramountcy of the dead languages, questions began to be asked. Even at the time when Cobbett was writing his grammar, Sydney Smith, one of the founders of the *Edinburgh Review*, was fulminating about the unfortunate boy who was 'suffocated with the nonsense of grammarians, overwhelmed with every species of difficulty disproportionate to his age, and driven by despair to peg, top, or marbles'.

Very slowly over the years since, the idea seems to have gained ground that the grammar of a living language, which is changing all the time, cannot be fitted into the rigid framework of a dead one. Nor can the grammar of a language such as Latin, which changes the forms of its words to express different grammatical relations, be profitably applied to a language such as English, which has got rid of most of its inflections, and expresses grammatical relations by devices like prepositions and auxiliary verbs, and by the order of its words. The Board of Education itself declared in 1910: 'There is no such thing as English grammar in the sense which used to be attached to the term'.

In 1912, George Saintsbury, the classicist and critic, denounced the futility of trying to 'draw up rules and conventions for a language which is almost wholly exception and idiom'. Jespersen preached that the grammar of a language must be deduced from a study of how good writers of it in fact write, not how grammarians say it ought to be written. George Orwell, in 'Politics and the English Language', went so far as to say that correct grammar and syntax 'are of no importance so long as one makes one's meaning clear'. And in 1951, in his book *Grammar Without Tears*, Hugh Sykes Davies—after surveying the development of our language from the clumsy and tortuous synthetic beginnings of its Gothic origins to the grace and flexibility of its present analytical structure—showed how, in this great and beneficent reform, the hero is what he calls the 'lowly man', and the villain, the grammarian, who constantly tried to hamper the freedom of the lowly man to go his own way. Mr Sykes Davies, surrealist, Communist and university lecturer in English at Cambridge, has advocated a 'grammatical moratorium' in which we may all be free to disregard the rules of grammar and continue the good work.

The old-fashioned grammarian certainly has much to answer for, having created a false sense of values that still lingers. I have ample evidence in my own correspondence that too much importance is attached to the fetishes of grammarians even now, and too little to choosing the right words. But we cannot have grammar jettisoned altogether; that would mean chaos. There are certain grammatical conventions that are, so to speak, a code of good manners. They change, but those current at the time must be observed by writers who wish to express themselves clearly and without offence to their readers. Mr Sykes Davies himself says that his 'grammatical moratorium' must be preceded by some instruction in the principles of language 'which will not shy from the inescapable necessity of starting from nowhere else than the position we stand in at the moment, conditioned by the past'.

In this chapter I shall concern myself with some common troubles in the handling of words on which I have noticed guidance to be needed. After an opening section on the arrangement of words, these troubles will be classified under those with Conjunctions (p. 176), Negatives (p. 184), Number (p. 189), Prepositions (p. 196), Pronouns (p. 201), and Verbs (p. 222).

TROUBLES IN ARRANGEMENT

Of these three—grammar, syntax and idiom—it is syntax, in its strict sense of 'orderly arrangement', that is of the greatest practical importance. The quotation that heads this chapter says that 'proper words in proper places' makes the true definition of a style. But something more than 'style' depends on putting words in their proper places. In a language like ours, which, except in some of its pronouns, has got rid of its different forms for the subjective and objective cases, your very meaning may depend on your arrangement of words.

In Latin, the subject of the verb will have a form that shows it is 'in the nominative', and the object one that shows it is 'in the accusative'. You may arrange them as you like, and the meaning will remain the same. But English is different. In the two sentences 'Cain killed Abel' and 'Abel killed Cain' the words are the same, but when they are reversed the meaning is reversed too.

If all you want to say is a simple thing like that, there is no difficulty. But you rarely do. You probably want to write a more complicated sentence describing not only the central event but also its how, why and where. The Americans have popularised a useful word, *modifier*, as a label for 'words or groups of words that restrict, limit or make more exact the meaning of other words'. The 'modifiers' bring all the trouble.

The rule is easy enough to state. As was said in 1795 by the American grammarian Lindley Murray, in the construction of sentences 'the words or members, most nearly related, should be placed as near to each other as possible, so as to make their mutual relation clearly appear'. But this rule is not so easy to keep. We do not always remember that what is clear to us may be far from clear to our readers. Sometimes it is not clear even to us which 'words or members' are 'most nearly related'. And if there are many 'modifiers' we may be confronted with difficulties of the jigsaw kind.

The simplest type of faulty arrangement, and the easiest to fall into, is illustrated by the following examples. Their offence is that they obscure the writer's meaning, albeit only momentarily, and suggest a sense that is absurd:

> There was a discussion yesterday on the worrying of sheep by dogs in the Minister's room.

The official statement on the marriage of German prisoners with girls made in the House of Commons ...

It is doubtful whether this small gas company would wish to accept responsibility for supplying this large area with all its difficulties.

... the hotel lobby door opened and a young woman carrying a baby and her husband entered.

(Quoted by the *New Yorker* from a novel.)

Care should always be taken to avoid the 'false scent' that comes from grouping words in a way that suggests a different construction from the one intended, however fleeting that suggestion may be:

Behind each part of the story I shall tell lies an untold and often unsuspected story of hard work ...

The words 'I shall tell lies' irresistibly group themselves together until the eye has passed on.*

Faulty and misleading arrangement is not unknown even in model regulations issued by government departments to show local authorities how things ought to be done:

No child shall be employed on any weekday when school is not open for a longer period than four hours.

---

* It is a particular danger of the truncated language of a newspaper headline that its words will group themselves together to suggest an unintended meaning, as in this example, which introduces a report on an auction of Nazi artefacts: 'Cards from Himmler to mother as Nazis spread across Europe on sale'. But no such excuse can be made for the following sentence, taken from the *Guardian*: 'The statement effectively casts doubt on psychiatry's predominantly biomedical model of mental distress—the idea that people are suffering from illnesses that are treatable by doctors using drugs'. ~

'For a longer period than four hours' qualifies *employed*, not *open*, and should therefore come immediately after *employed*. And in departmental regulations themselves:

> Every woman by whom ... a claim for maternity benefit is made shall furnish evidence that she has been, or that it is to be expected she will be, confined by means of a certificate given in accordance with the rules ...

It is not surprising that a department that sets such an example should receive a letter like this:

> In accordance with your instructions I have given birth to twins in the enclosed envelope.

I shall have something more to say on this subject in pointing out the danger of supposing that disorderly sentences can be set right by vagrant commas.* But one cause of the separation of 'words or members most nearly related' is so common that, although I have already touched on it,† an examination of some more examples may be useful. That is the separation of the subject from the verb by intervening clauses, usually defining the subject:

> Officers appointed to permanent commissions who do not possess the qualifications for voluntary insurance explained in the preceding paragraphs and officers appointed to emergency commissions direct from civil life who were not already insured at the date of appointment (and who, as explained in para. 3, are therefore not required to be insured during service) may be eligible ...

* See p. 246.
† See p. 251.

The cases where a change in the circumstances affecting the fire prevention arrangements at the premises is such that, if the number of hours stated on the certificate were recalculated, there would be a reduction (or an increase) in the number of hours of fireguard duty which the members concerned would be liable to perform for the local authority in whose area they reside, stand, however, in an entirely different position.

In these examples the reader is kept waiting an unconscionable time for the verb. The simplest way of correcting this will generally be to change the order of the words, or to convert relative clauses into conditional, or both. For instance:

Officers appointed to permanent commissions may be eligible though they do not possess the qualifications for voluntary insurance explained in the preceding paragraph. So may officers appointed to emergency commissions direct from civil life who . . . etc.

The circumstances affecting the fire prevention arrangements at the premises may, however, so change that, if the number of hours stated in the certificate were recalculated, there would be a reduction, or an increase, in the number of hours of fireguard duty which the members concerned would be liable to perform for the local authority in whose area they reside. These cases stand in an entirely different position.

Sometimes the object allows itself to be driven a confusing distance from the verb. Poets can plead the exigencies of rhyme for separating the two, and say, as C. S. Calverley did in 'Evening':

> O be careful that thou changest,
> On returning home, thy boots.

But officials have no such excuse. They must invert the order and say 'It is of paramount importance'—for that may be the expression they will be tempted to use—'that young ladies after standing in wet grass should change their boots on returning home'.

In the following example the writer has lumbered ponderously along without looking ahead, and arrives at the object with a bump:

> One or two of the largest Local Authorities are at present employing on their staff as certifying officers and as advisers to the Mental Deficiency Act Committees officers having special qualifications or experience in mental deficiency.

By making the effort to turn the sentence round, the writer could have saved the reader some trouble:

> Officers having special qualification or experience in mental deficiency are at present being employed on the staff of one or two of the largest Local Authorities as certifying officers and as advisers to the Mental Deficiency Act Committees.

Two other common errors of arrangement that are likely to give unnecessary trouble, and may actually bewilder the reader, are letting the relative get a long way from its antecedent, and letting the auxiliary get a long way from the main verb. Here, a relative, *which*, is separated from its antecedent:

> Enquiries are received from time to time in connection with requests for the grant of leave of absence to school children during term time for various reasons, which can give difficulty to those who must decide.

What is the antecedent of *which*? Is it *enquiries*, *requests* or *reasons*? Probably *enquiries*, but if so, it is a long way off. In this sentence it matters little, but in other sentences similarly constructed it might be important for the antecedent to be unmistakable. The surest way of avoiding ambiguity, when you have started a sentence like this, is to put a full stop after *reasons*, and begin the next sentence *These enquiries* or *These requests* or *These reasons*, whichever is meant.

These are examples of the verb separated from the auxiliary:

> The Executive Council should, in cases of approved institutions employing one doctor, get in touch with the committee.

> The Council should accordingly, after considering whether they wish to suggest any modifications in the model scheme, consult with the committee . . .

It is a bad habit to put all sorts of things between the auxiliary and the verb in this way. It leads to unwieldy sentences and irritated readers.

Adverbs sometimes get awkwardly separated from the words they qualify. In his work of 1904, *An Advanced English Syntax*, C. T. Onions, the fourth editor of the *OED*, states that they 'should be so placed in a sentence as to make it impossible to doubt which word or words they are intended to affect'. If they affect an adjective or past participle or another adverb, their place is immediately in front of it (*helpfully* placed, *perfectly* clear). If they affect another part of the verb or a whole phrase, they may be in front or behind. It is usually a matter of emphasis: *he came soon* emphasises his promptitude; *he soon came* emphasises his coming.

The commonest causes of adverbs going wrong are the fear, real or imaginary, of splitting an infinitive, and the waywardness of the adverbs *only* and *even*. *Only* is a capricious word. It is much given to deserting its post and taking its place next to the verb, regardless of what it qualifies. It is more natural to say 'he only spoke for ten minutes' than 'he spoke for only ten minutes'.

Pillorying misplaced *only*s has a great fascination for some people: *only*-snooping seems to have become as popular a sport with some purists as split-infinitive-snooping was a generation ago.* A book in this vein, devoted to the exposing of errors of diction in contemporary writers, contained several examples, such as:

> He had only been in England for six weeks since the beginning of the war.

> This only makes a war lawful: that it is a struggle for law against force.

> We can only analyse the facts we all have before us.

These incur the author's censure. By the same reasoning, one would have to condemn Sir Winston Churchill for writing in *The Gathering Storm*:

> Statesmen are not called upon only to settle easy questions.

Fowler, in *Modern English Usage*, took a different view. Of a critic who protested against 'He only died a week ago' instead of 'He died only a week ago', Fowler wrote:

> There speaks one of those friends from whom the English language may well pray to be saved, one of the modern precisians who have more zeal than discretion . . .

But it cannot be denied that the irresponsible behaviour of *only* does sometimes create real ambiguity. Take this sentence:

> His disease can only be alleviated by a surgical operation.

---

* For more on split infinitives, see pp. 232–6.

We cannot tell what this means, and must rewrite it in one of two ways:

> Only a surgical operation can alleviate his disease (it cannot be alleviated in any other way).

> A surgical operation can only alleviate his disease (it cannot cure it).

Again:

> In your second paragraph you point out that carpet-yarn only can be obtained from India, and this is quite correct.

The writer must have meant 'can be obtained only from India', and ought to have written this, or, at the least, 'can only be obtained from India'. The original sentence, though not actually ambiguous (for it can hardly be supposed that carpet-yarn is India's only product), is unnatural, and sets the reader puzzling for a moment.

So do not take the *only*-snoopers too seriously. But be on the alert. It will generally be safe to put *only* in what a plain person would feel to be its natural place. Sometimes that will be its logical position, sometimes not. When the qualification is more important than the positive statement, it is an aid to being understood to bring the *only* in as soon as possible; it prevents the reader from being put on a wrong scent. In the sentence 'The temperature will rise above 35 degrees only in the south-west of England', *only* is carefully put in its right, logical place. But the listener would have grasped more quickly the picture of an almost universally cold England if the announcer had said, 'the temperature will only rise above 35 degrees in the south-west of England'.

A purist might condemn:

> I am to express regret that it has only been possible to issue a licence for part of the quantity for which application was made.

But the ordinary reader will think that this conveys the writer's meaning more readily and naturally than:

> I am to express regret that it has been possible to issue a licence for only part of the quantity for which application was made.

Even has a similar habit of getting in the wrong place. The importance of putting it in the right one is aptly illustrated in *An ABC of English Usage* by Treble and Vallins, 1936, where it is added to the sentence 'I am not disturbed by your threats':

> *Even* I am not disturbed by your threats (let alone anybody else).

> I am not *even* disturbed by your threats (let alone *hurt, annoyed, injured, alarmed*).

> I am not disturbed *even* by your threats (*even* modifies the phrase, the emphasis being on the *threats*).

As the authors note: 'It is also possible, though perhaps rather awkward, to put *even* immediately before *your*, and so give *your* the emphasis (*your* threats—let alone anybody else's)'.

Unnecessary repetition of a word—the right word for its sense put in the wrong place for its sound—is another form of poor arrangement that can be irritating to a reader. If you are able to avoid this in a natural way, you should. For instance, in the comment 'the Minister has considered this application, and considers that there should be a market in Canada', the repetition of *consider* gives the sentence a clumsy air. The second one might just as well have been *thinks*. Similarly, it would have been easy to avoid the ugly repetition of *essential* in the sentence 'it is essential that the Minister should be provided with outline programmes of essential works'. But where the same thing or act is repeatedly mentioned, it is better to repeat a word than to avoid it in a laboured or obvious way.

Irritating repetition of a sound is usually mere carelessness:

The controversy as to which agency should perform the actual contractual work . . .

Reverting to the subject of the letter the latter wrote . . .

In view of the very serious perturbation about the situation in the motor car industry . . .

Since a certain amount of uncertainty still appears to exist . . .

I feel sure that what really existed was an uncertain amount of certainty.

TROUBLES WITH CONJUNCTIONS

This is an elastic heading. It may for instance be said that neither *both* nor *like* is strictly a conjunction, but their caprices make it convenient to include them in the list below.

(1) *And.* There used to be an idea that it was inelegant to begin a sentence with *and*. The idea is now as good as dead. To use *and* in this position can be a useful way of indicating that what you are about to say will reinforce what you have just said.

(2) *And which.* There is a grammarians' rule that it is wrong to write *and which* (and similar expressions such as *and who, and where, but which, or which,* etc.) except by way of introducing a second relative clause with the same antecedent as the one that has just preceded it. It is an arbitrary and pointless rule (unknown in French) that will probably be destroyed in the end by usage, but for the present its observance is expected from those who would write correctly. According to this rule, Nelson was wrong grammatically, as well as in other more important ways, when he wrote to Lady Nelson in 1793 after his first introduction to Lady Hamilton:

> She is a young woman of amiable manners and who does honour to the station to which she is raised.

To justify the *and who* grammatically, a relative is needed in the first part of the sentence, for example:

> She is a young woman whose manners are amiable and who does honour to the station to which she is raised.

Conversely, the writer of the following sentence has got into trouble by being shy of *and which*:

> Things which we ourselves could not produce and yet are essential to our recovery.

Here *which* cannot double the parts of being the object of *produce* and the subject of *are*. To set the grammar right the relative has to be repeated:

> Things which we ourselves could not produce and which are essential to our recovery.

The wisest course is to avoid the inevitable clumsiness of *and which*, even when used in a way that does not offend the purists. Thus these two sentences might be written:

> She is a young woman of amiable manners who does honour to the station to which she has been raised.

> Things essential to our recovery that we ourselves cannot produce.

(3) *As.*　We say 'as good *as* ever' and 'better *than* ever'. But should we use *as* or *than*, or both, if we say 'as good or better'? The natural thing to say is 'as good or better than ever', ignoring the *as* that *as good* logically needs—and you commit no great crime if that is what you do. But if you want both to run no risk of offending the purists and to avoid the prosy 'as good as or better than', you can write 'as good as ever, or better'. Consider this sentence:

> Pamphlets have circulated as widely, and been no less influential, than those published in this volume.

This can be changed into:

> Pamphlets have circulated as widely as those published in this volume, and have been no less influential.

Note. Gowers also wrote here: '*As* must not be used as a preposition, on the analogy of *but* (see '*But*' below). So you may say, "no one knows knows the full truth but me", but you must not say "no one knows the truth as fully as me". It must be ". . . as fully as I". The first *as* is an adverb, the second, a conjunction'.

Anyone choosing to follow this advice who fears that the formula 'as fully as I' now sounds stiff, can easily soften it by adding a verb, e.g. 'as fully as I do'. ~

(4) *Both*.   When using *both . . . and*, be careful that these words are in the right position and carry equal weight. Nothing that comes between the *both* and the *and* can be regarded as carried on after the *and*: if words are to be carried on after the *and*, they must precede the *both*; if they do not precede the *both* they must be repeated after the *and*. For instance:

> He was both deaf to argument and entreaty.

Because 'deaf to' comes after *both* it cannot be 'understood' again after *and*. We must adjust the balance in one of the following ways:

> He was deaf both to argument and entreaty.
>
> He was deaf to both argument and entreaty.
>
> He was both deaf to argument and unmoved by entreaty.

An extreme example of the unbalanced *both* is:

> The proposed sale must be both sanctioned by the Minister and the price must be approved by the District Valuer.

Do not use *both* where it is not necessary (where the meaning of the sentence is no less plain if you leave it out):

Both of them are equally to blame. (They are equally to blame.)

Please ensure that both documents are fastened together. (Please ensure that the documents are fastened together.)

(5) *But.*   Where *but* is used in the sense of *except*, it is sometimes treated as a preposition, sometimes as a conjunction. Mrs Hemans would not have been guilty of 'bad grammar' in her poem 'Casabianca' if she had written 'whence all but him had fled', but in preferring *he* she conformed to formal practice. That is the worst of personal pronouns: by retaining the case-inflections that nouns have so sensibly shed, they pose these tiresome and trivial questions.* If the sentence could have been 'whence all but the boy had fled' no one could have known whether *but* was being used as a conjunction or a preposition, and no one need have cared.

When *but* is used as a conjunction, it is an easy slip to put it where there should be an *and*, forgetting that the conjunction you want is one that does not go contrary to the clause immediately preceding, but continues in the same sense. Consider the following:

> It is agreed that the primary condition of the scheme is satisfied, but it is also necessary to establish that your war service interrupted an organised course of study for a professional qualification comparable to that for which application is made, *but* as explained in previous letters, you are unable to fulfil this qualification.

The italicised *but* should be *and*. The line of thought has already been turned by the first *but*; it is now going straight on.

* For more on '*I* and *me*' and on '*who* and *whom*' see pp.207–8 and 218–20.

A similar slip is made here:

> The Forestry Commission will probably only be able to offer you a post as a forest labourer, or possibly leading a gang of forest workers, but there are at the moment no vacancies for Forest Officers.

Either *only* must be omitted, or the *but* must be changed to *as*.

(6) *If.* The use of *if* for *though* or *but* may give rise to ambiguity or absurdity. It is ambiguous in a sentence such as,

> There is evidence, if not proof, that he was responsible.

Its absurdity is demonstrated by Sir Alan Herbert's imaginary example from *What a Word!*: 'Milk is nourishing, if tuberculous'.

Care is also needed in the use of *if* in the sense of *whether*, for this too may cause ambiguity:

> Please inform me if there is any change in your circumstances.

Does this mean 'Please inform me now whether there is any change', or 'If any change should occur please inform me then'? The reader cannot tell. If *whether* and *if* become interchangeable, unintentional offence may be given by the lover who sings:

> What do I care
> If you are there?

Note. Since Gowers wrote this, *if* has encroached yet further on the territory of *whether*, so that an academic publisher is prepared to allow this comment: 'there is no saying if or not other similar troves exist'. (Those who consider this extraordinary might find themselves less worried by 'there is no saying if other similar troves exist or not'.) Nevertheless, because muddling *if* and *whether* blunts the language, it remains good practice to use *if* in a conditional sense: 'Please let me know if you marry him' (but if you remain unmarried, I do not need to hear), and *whether* for possibilities and alternatives: 'Please let me know whether you marry him' (please let me know, some time hence, whether or not you did marry him). ~

(7) *Inasmuch as.* This is sometimes used in the sense of *so far as* and sometimes as a clumsy way of saying *because* or *since*. It is therefore ambiguous, and might well be dispensed with altogether.

(8) *Like.* Colloquial English admits *like* as a conjunction, and would not be shocked by the sentence 'Nothing succeeds like success does', or by 'It looked like he was going to succeed'. But in formal English prose neither of these will do: *like* must not be treated as a conjunction. So we may say 'nothing succeeds like success'; but it must be 'nothing succeeds *as* success does' and 'it looked *as if* he were going to succeed'.

(9) *Provided that.* It is better to use this form to introduce a stipulation than *provided* without the *that*, and much better to use it than a bald *providing*. The phrase itself should be reserved for a true stipulation, as in:

He said he would go to the meeting provided that I went with him.

It should not be used loosely for *if*, as in:

I expect he will come tomorrow, provided that he comes at all.

Sometimes the misuse of *provided that* for *if* will obscure the meaning of a sentence and create difficulties for a reader:

Such emoluments can only count as qualifying for pension provided that they cannot be converted into cash.

This would have been clear with *if*.

(10) *Than.* Writers can find themselves tempted to use *than* as a preposition, like *but* (see above), in a sentence such as 'he is older than me'. Examples of this can be found in good writers, including a craftsman as scrupulous as Mr Somerset Maugham.

Yet the *OED* observes that this is 'considered incorrect': it should be 'he is older than I' (i.e. 'than I am'). We may say 'I know more about her than him' if what we mean is that my knowledge of her is greater than my knowledge of him. But if we mean that my knowledge of her is greater than his knowledge of her, we must say 'I know more about her than he (does)'.

Note. The *OED*'s warning stands to this day. But 'he is older than I am' (with the verb added at the end) now sounds a lot less starchy than 'he is older than I'. ~

A sole exception is recognised—*whom*. We must say *than whom*, and not 'than who', even though the only way of making grammatical sense of it is to regard *than* as a preposition. But that is rather a stilted way of writing, and can best be left to poetry, as when Milton remarks parenthetically of Beelzebub:

> . . . than whom, Satan except, none higher sat . . .

Be careful not to slip into using *than* with words that take a different construction. *Other* and *else* (and *otherwise* and *elsewhere*) are the only words besides comparatives that take *than*. *Than* is sometimes mistakenly used with such words as *preferable* and *different*, and is also sometimes used where a purist would prefer *as*:

> Nearly twice as many people die under 20 in France than in Great Britain, chiefly of tuberculosis.

(11) *That.* The conjunctive *that* often leads the writer into error, especially in long sentences. This is not so much a matter of rule as of being careful:

> It was agreed that, since suitable accommodation was now available in a convenient position, and that a move to larger offices was therefore feasible, Treasury sanction should be sought for acquiring them.

Here a superfluous *that* has slipped into the sentence. The first *that* was capable of doing all the work.*

(12) *When.* It is sometimes confusing to use *when* as the equivalent of *and then*.

> Let me have full particulars when I will be able to advise you. (Please let me have full particulars. I shall then be able to advise you.)

> Alternatively the Minister may make the order himself when it has the same effect as if it has been made by the Local Authority. (Alternatively the Minister may make the order himself, and it then has the same effect ...)

(13) *While.* It is safest to use this conjunction only in its temporal sense ('your letter came while I was away on leave'). That does not mean that it is wrong to use it also as a conjunction without any temporal sense, equivalent to *although* ('while I do not agree with you, I accept your ruling'), but this can lead to ambiguities:

> While he is feeling unwell, he should impress the Panel with his charm.

It should certainly not be used in these two different senses in the same sentence, as in:

> While appreciating your difficulties while your mother is ill ...

Moreover, once we leave the shelter of the temporal sense, we are on the road to treating *while* as a synonym for *and*:

> Nothing will be available for some time for the desired improvement, while the general supply of linoleum to new offices may have to cease when existing stocks run out.

---

* For more on the awkwardness of *that*, see p. 216.

There is no point in saying *while* when you mean *and*. If you are too free with *while* you are sure sooner or later to land yourself in the absurdity of seeming to say that two events have occurred simultaneously that could not possibly have done so:

> The first part of the concert was conducted by Sir August Manns ... while Sir Arthur Sullivan conducted his then recently composed *Absent Minded Beggar*.

TROUBLES WITH NEGATIVES

(1) Double negatives.　It has long been settled doctrine among English grammarians that two negatives cancel each other and produce an affirmative. As in mathematics − (−*x*) equals +*x*, so in speech 'he didn't say nothing' must be regarded as equivalent to *he said something*.

It is going too far to say, as is sometimes said, that this proposition is self-evident. The ancient Greeks did not think that two negatives made an affirmative. On the contrary, the more negatives they put into a sentence, the more emphatically negative the sentence became. Nor did Chaucer think so. In a much-quoted passage, he wrote:

> He nevere yet no vileynye ne sayde
> In al his lyf unto no maner wight.
> He was a verray, parfit gentil knyght.

Nor did Shakespeare, who made King Claudius say of Hamlet:

> Nor what he spake, though it lacked form a little,
> Was not like madness ...

Nor do the many thousands of people who find it natural today to deny knowledge by saying 'I don't know nothing'. And the comedian who sings 'I ain't going to give nobody none of mine' is not misunderstood.* Jespersen, in his *Essentials of English Grammar* of 1933, notes that a speaker of this kind, 'who wants the negative sense to be fully apprehended', will attach it

> not only to the verb, but also to other parts of the sentence: he spreads, as it were, a thin layer of negative colouring over the whole of the sentence instead of confining it to one single place. This may be called pleonastic, but is certainly not really illogical.

Still, the grammarians' rule continues to stand in formal English. Breaches of it are commonest with verbs of surprise or speculation ('I shouldn't wonder if there wasn't a storm'; 'I shouldn't be surprised if he didn't come today'). Indeed, this is so common that it is classed by Fowler as one of his 'sturdy indefensibles'. A recent speech in the House of Lords affords a typical instance of the confusion of thought bred by double negatives:

> Let it not be supposed because we are building for the future rather than the present that the Bill's proposals are not devoid of significance.

What the speaker meant, of course, was 'Let it not be supposed that the Bill's proposals *are* devoid of significance'. Another example is:

> There is no reason to doubt that what he says in his statement . . . is not true.

---

* This appears to be a reference to the early jazz song, 'I Ain't Gonna Give Nobody None of my Jelly Roll'. Gowers writes that his comic singer is 'not misunderstood' (even though the song title given here is a shade more euphemistic than the original). But what he fails to mention is that 'ain't' makes the statement a triple negative, which is much more complicated than a mere double. That said, it is presumably true even of this example that no one is likely to misunderstand the *not* giving. ~

Here the speaker meant, 'There is no reason to doubt that his statement *is* true'. And another:

> It must not be assumed that there are no circumstances in which a profit might not be made.

Avoid multiple negatives when you can. Even if you dodge the traps they set and succeed in saying what you mean, you give your reader a puzzle to solve in sorting the negatives out. Indeed it is wise never to make a statement negatively if it could be made positively. A correspondent sends me this:

> The elementary ideas of the calculus are not beyond the capacity of more than 40 per cent of our certificate students.

He comments, 'I am quite unable to say whether this assertion is that two-fifths or three-fifths of the class could make something of the ideas'. If the writer had said that the ideas were within the capacity of at least 60 per cent, all would have been clear. Here are two more examples of sentences that have to be unravelled before they yield any meaning:

> Few would now contend that too many checks cannot be at least as harmful to democracy as too few.

> The Opposition refused leave for the withdrawal of a motion to annul an Order revoking the embargo on the importation of cut glass.

(2) *Neither . . . nor.*   Some books tell you that *neither . . . nor* should not be used where there are more than two alternatives. But if you decide to ignore this advice as pedantry you will find on your side not only the translators of the Bible:

> neither death, nor life, nor angels, nor principalities, nor powers, nor things present, nor things to come, nor height, nor depth,

nor any other creature, shall be able to separate us from the love
of God ... (Romans 8:38–9)

but also, though not quite so profusely, Sir Harold Nicolson:

Neither Lord Davidson nor Sir Bernard Paget nor Mr Arthur
Bryant will suffer permanently or seriously from the spectacle
which they have provided. (*Spectator*, 1949)

(3) *Nor* and *or*. When should *nor* be used and when *or*? If a
neither or an *either* comes first there is no difficulty; *neither* is
always followed by *nor* and *either* by *or*. There can be no doubt
that it is wrong to write: 'The existing position satisfies neither
the psychologist, the judge, or the public'. It should have been
'neither the psychologist, nor the judge, nor the public'. But when
the initial negative is a simple *not* or *no*, it is often a puzzling
question whether *nor* or *or* should follow. Logically it depends
on whether the sentence is so framed that the initial negative
runs on into the second part of it or is exhausted in the first.
Practically, it may be of little importance which answer you give,
for the meaning will be clear.

He did not think that the Bill would be introduced this month,
nor indeed before the recess.

'He did not think' affects everything that follows *that*. Logically
therefore *nor* produces a double negative, as though one were to
say 'he didn't think it wouldn't be introduced before the recess'.

The blame for this disorder does not rest with Parliament, or
with the bishops, or with the parish priests. Our real weakness
is the failure of the ordinary man.

Here the negative phrase 'does not rest' is carried right through
the sentence, and applies to the bishops and the parish priests as

much as to Parliament. There is no need to repeat the negative, and *or* is logically right. But *nor* is so often used in such a construction that it would be pedantic to condemn it: if logical defence is needed one might say that 'did he think it would be introduced' in the first example and 'does it rest' in the second were understood as repeated after *nor*. By changing the framework of the sentence, it is a positive verb, *rests*, that runs through:

> The blame for this disorder rests not with Parliament nor with the bishops, nor with the parish priests, but with the ordinary man.

The original negative (*not*) is attached not to the verb but to *Parliament*, and exhausts itself in exonerating Parliament. The negative must be repeated, and *nor* is rightly used.

(4) *Not all.* It is idiomatic English, to which no exception can be taken, to write 'All officials are not good at drafting legal documents' when you mean that only some of them are (compare 'All that glitters is not gold'). But it is clearer, and therefore better, to write 'Not all officials are good at drafting legal documents'.

(5) *Not . . . but.* It is also idiomatic English to write 'I did not go to speak but to listen'. It is pedantry to insist that, because logic demands it, this ought to be 'I went not to speak but to listen'. But if the latter way of arranging a 'not . . . but' sentence runs as easily and makes your meaning clearer, as it often may, it should be preferred.

(6) *Not . . . because.* *Not* followed by *because* sometimes leads to ambiguity. 'I did not write that letter because of what you told me' may mean either 'I refrained from writing that letter because of what you told me' or 'It was not because of what you told me that I wrote that letter'. Avoid this ambiguity by rewriting the sentence.

TROUBLES WITH NUMBER

The rule that a singular subject requires a singular verb, and a plural subject a plural verb, is an easy one to remember and generally to observe. But it has its difficulties.

(1) Collective words
In using collective words or nouns of multitude (*department, parliament, government, committee* and the like), ought we to say 'the government have decided' or 'the government has decided'; 'the committee are meeting' or 'the committee is meeting'? There is no rule. Either a singular or a plural verb may be used. The plural is more suitable when the emphasis is on the individual members, and the singular when it is the body as a whole. 'A committee *was* appointed to consider this subject'; 'the committee *were* unable to agree'. Sometimes the need to use a pronoun settles the question. We cannot say 'the committee differed among itself', nor 'the committee were of one mind when I sat on them'. But the number ought not to be varied in the same document without good cause. Accidentally changing it is a common form of carelessness:

> The firm *has* given an undertaking that in the event of *their* having to restrict production ...

> The industry *is* capable of supplying all home requirements and *have* in fact been exporting.

> It will be for each committee to determine in the light of *its* responsibilities how far it is necessary to make all these appointments, and no appointment should be made unless the committee *are* fully satisfied of the need.

Conversely, a subject plural in form may be given a singular verb if it signifies a single entity such as a country ('the United

States has agreed') or an organisation ('the United Nations has resolved') or a measure ('six miles is not too far'; 'twelve months is a long time to wait').

Note. It is hard to argue against emphasising the singular when two people have just united in marriage, yet the following will probably strike most British readers as awkward: 'A South Korean couple on its honeymoon was found alive and in good condition two decks below the waterline' (*New York Post*). ~

(2) Words linked by *and*

To the elementary rule that two singular nouns linked by *and* should be given a plural verb, justifiable exceptions can be found where the linked words form a single idea. The stock example is taken from Kipling's poem 'Recessional': 'The tumult and the shouting dies'. *The tumult and the shouting*, it is explained, are equivalent to 'the tumultuous shouting'. (Even if that were not true, the singular *die* would not have allowed for the rhyme with the line 'Still stands Thine ancient sacrifice', and rhyming poets must be allowed some licence.)

Perhaps these official examples might be justified in the same way:

> Duration and charge was advised at the conclusion of the call.
> Your desire and need for a telephone service is fully appreciated.

It might be argued that *duration and charge* were equivalent to 'the appropriate charge for the duration', and that *your desire and need* were equivalent to 'the desire arising from your need'. But it is safer to observe the rule, and to leave these questionable experiments to the poets.

Other instances of singular verbs with subjects linked by *and* cannot be so easily explained away. They are frequent when the verb comes first. Shakespeare has them ('Is Bushy, Green, and the

Earl of Wiltshire dead?'), and so have the translators of the Bible ('Thine is the Kingdom, the power and the glory'). If we may never attribute mere carelessness to great writers, we must explain these by saying that the singular verb is more vivid, and should be understood as repeated with each noun – 'Is Bushy, (is) Green, and (is) the Earl of Wiltshire dead?' Those who like to have everything tidy may get some satisfaction from this, but writers of official English should forget about these refinements and stick to the simple rule.

(3) Words linked by *with*

In a sentence stating that 'X *with* Y did such-and-such', the subject is X alone. If X is singular, the verb should be too: 'The boss with his partners is responsible'; 'The Secretary of State together with the Under-Secretary is coming'.

(4) Alternative subjects

Either and *neither* must always have a singular verb if the alternative subjects are singular. It is a very common error to write sentences like these:

> I am unable to trace that either of the items have been paid.

> Neither knowledge nor skill are needed.

Have and *are* should be *has* and *is*. But where a plural subject is included, the verb should be plural:

> Neither knowledge nor sophisticated skills are needed.

(5) *Each*

When *each* is the subject of a sentence the verb is singular and so is any pronoun:

> Each man has a room to himself.

When a plural noun or pronoun is the subject, with *each* in apposition, the verb is plural:

> They have a room each.

(6) Attraction

The verb must agree with the subject, and not allow itself to be attracted into the number of the complement. Modern grammarians will not pass 'the wages of sin is death'. The safe rule for the ordinary writer in such sentences is to regard what precedes the verb as the subject and what follows it as the complement, and so to write 'the wages of sin are death' and 'death is the wages of sin'.

A verb some way from its subject is sometimes lured away from its proper number by a noun closer to it, as in:

> We regret that assurances given us twelve months ago that a sufficient supply of suitable local labour would be available to meet our requirements has not been fulfilled. (Assurances ... have not been fulfilled.)

> So far as the heating of buildings in Government occupation are concerned ... (So far as the heating ... is concerned ...)

Sometimes the weight of a plural pushes the verb into the wrong number, even though they are not next to one another:

> Thousands of pounds' worth of damage have been done to the apple crop.

Here *have* is a blunder. And so (as we have just seen) is the common attraction of the verb into the plural when the subject is *either* or *neither* in such sentences as 'neither of the questions have been answered' or 'either of the questions were embarrassing'.

However, in one or two exceptional instances the force of this attraction has conquered the grammarians. With the phrase *more than one* the pull of *one* is so strong that the singular is always used (e.g. 'more than one question was asked'); and owing to the pull of the plural in a sentence such as, 'none of the questions were answered', *none* has come to be used indifferently with a singular or a plural verb. Conversely, owing to the pull of the singular *a* in the expression *many a*, it always takes the singular verb. 'There's many a slip twixt cup and lip' is idiomatic English, as 'there are many a slip' is not.

(7) *There are* or *were*

It is a common mistake to write *there is* or *there was* where a plural subject requires *there are* or *there were*. The following is wrong:

> There was available one large room and three small ones.

This should be

> There were available ...

It is true that Ophelia said 'there is Pansies; that's for thoughts', but she was not herself at the time.

(8) Certain nouns are sometimes puzzling

(*a*) *Agenda*, though in form plural, has been admitted from Latin into English as a singular word. Nobody would say 'the agenda for Monday's meeting *have* not yet reached me'. If a word is needed for one of the components of the agenda, say 'item No. so-and-so of the agenda', not 'agendum No. so-and-so', which would be the extreme of pedantry. If a plural is wanted for *agenda* itself, it must be *agendas* or *agenda papers*.

Note. When he wrote this, Gowers contrasted the singular *agenda* with what he considered the definitely plural *data*. These days, however, many authorities use *data* as a singular word too ('the data was inconclusive'). *Media* is similarly treated as both plural and singular. In the singular, an *agenda* is being thought of as a (singular) list of things to be done, the *data* as a (singular) set of items of information, and the *media* as a (singular) range of different forms of communication. But where *criteria* and *phenomena* are used as though singular ('it was an amazing phenomena'; 'they judged it on one criteria alone'), this is simply incorrect.

There are other words, not all Latin in origin, that are treated as both singular and plural in English, e.g. *politics*, *headquarters*, *whereabouts*, *livestock* and *variety*. Sticklers tend to use them in the singular ('The whereabouts of our bull *is* unknown. Our livestock *was* already in decline. A variety of them *is* sick'). ~

(*b*) *Means* in the sense of 'means to an end' is a curious word. It may be treated either as singular or plural. Suppose, for instance, that you want to write about means having been sought to do something. You may if you choose treat the word as singular and say 'a means was sought' or 'every means was sought'. Or you may treat it as plural and say 'all means were sought'. Or again, if you use just the word *means* without any word such as *a* or *every* or *all* to show its number, you may give it a singular or a plural verb as you wish: you may say either 'means was sought' or 'means were sought'; both are idiomatic. Perhaps on the whole it is best to say 'a method (or way) was sought' if there was only one, and 'means were sought' if there was more than one.

Means in the sense of monetary resources is always plural.

(*c*) *Number*, like other collective nouns, may take either a singular or a plural verb. Unlike most of them, it admits of a simple and logical rule. When all that it is doing is forming part of a composite plural subject, it should have a plural verb, as in:

A large number of people are coming today.

But when it is standing on its own legs as the subject it should have a singular verb, as in:

The number of people coming today is large.

The following are accordingly unidiomatic:

> There is a number of applications, some of which were made before yours.
>
> There is a large number of outstanding orders.

The true subjects are not *a number* and *a large number* but *a-number-of-applications* and *a-large-number-of-outstanding-orders*.

Of the following examples, the first has a singular verb that should be plural, and the second a plural verb that should be singular:

> There was also a number of conferences calling themselves peace conferences which had no real interest in peace.
>
> The number of casualties in HMS *Amethyst* are thought to be about fifteen.

(*d*) *Those kind of things* is a phrase commonly heard in conversation, and instances of the use of the plural *these* or *those* with the singular *kind* or *sort* can be found in good authors. As I mentioned in Chapter IV, the phrase *those kind of things* (like *different to*, *very pleased*, *drive slow* and the split infinitive) used to be among the shibboleths by which it was supposed to be possible to distinguish those who were instructed in their mother tongue from those who were not. In 1910, *Punch* published a poem containing these lines:

> Did you say those sort of things
>   Never seemed to you to matter?
> Gloomily your poet sings,
> *Did* you say 'those sort of things'?
> Frightened love would soon take wings,

> All his fondest hopes you'd shatter,
> Did you say those sort of things
> Never seemed to you to matter.

We have a better sense of values today. But even now it is as well to humour the purist by writing *things of that kind*.

TROUBLES WITH PREPOSITIONS

(1) Ending sentences with prepositions
Do not hesitate to end a sentence with a preposition if your ear tells you that that is where the preposition goes best. There used to be a rather half-hearted grammarians' rule against doing this, but no good writer ever heeded it, except Dryden, who seems to have invented it. The translators of the Authorised Version did not know it ('But I have a baptism to be baptized with'). The very rule itself, if phrased 'do not use a preposition to end a sentence with', has a smoother flow and a more idiomatic ring than 'do not use a preposition with which to end a sentence'.

Dean Alford, in *The Queen's English* of 1864, protested at this so-called rule. 'I know', he said, 'that I am at variance with the rules taught at very respectable institutions for enabling young ladies to talk unlike their elders; but this I cannot help.' The story is often repeated of the nurse who performed the remarkable feat of ending a sentence with two prepositions (*to* and *for*) and a compound preposition (*out of*) by asking her charge, 'What did you choose that book to be read to out of for?' She may have broken Dryden's rule several times over, but she said what she wanted to say perfectly clearly in words of one syllable, and what more can one ask? Morris Bishop, in the *New Yorker*, outdid even the nurse in his comic response to a preposition supposedly hidden under a chair: 'What should he come up from out of in under for?'

Sometimes, when the final word is really a verbal particle, and the verb's meaning depends on it, they form a phrasal verb*—*put up with* for instance—and to separate them makes a nonsense. It is said that Sir Winston Churchill once made this comment against a sentence that clumsily avoided a prepositional ending: 'This is the sort of English up with which I will not put'. The ear is a pretty safe guide.

Note. The comic examples Gowers gives here are not completely helpful. (No one forced to reject an invitation to dance would do so in the grammar of the Authorised Version: 'But I have a partner to be partnered with; and how am I straitened till this partnership be accomplished!') Gowers does, however, provide his own, utilitarian examples of sentences that end with prepositions, for instance: 'The peculiarities of legal English are often used as a stick to beat the official with'. Though the rule he flouted by this arrangement of words may have struck him as half-hearted, there are readers who, coming upon this sentence earlier in the book, will have had an instinct to rearrange it ('a stick with which to beat the official'). But why?

The answer is that the ear is a pretty safe guide not only to grammar but also to rhetoric. A writer may sometimes seek the effect of a dying fall (it could be for comic or bathetic reasons), but a strong sentence will usually reserve its main burden of sense to the end, and this burden is not usually carried by a loose preposition. When Gowers took the sentence 'do not use a preposition to end a sentence with' and corrected it to conform to the rule it expresses, he did so in a deliberately awkward manner: 'do not use a preposition with which to end a sentence'. It is perfectly possible to recast this in a simple and direct manner that avoids violating the advice itself, yet finishes on the main point: 'Do not

---

* On phrasal verbs see also pp. 108–110.

end a sentence with a preposition'. The following quotation, about Harold Shipman, the doctor and serial murderer, will leave many an ear with the impression that its final word, the preposition *for*, has been left swinging in the wind:

> This concern with the right medication was often echoed in his advice to inmates, whom he would tell which drugs to ask the prison doctors for. (Darian Leader, *What is Madness?*, 2011)

This sentence would be stronger if it ended on another verb, e.g. 'whom he would tell which drugs to ask the prison doctors to prescribe'. Better yet, it could be rewritten to end with what the author seems to wish to emphasise most: 'This concern with prescribing the right medication continued in prison, where he would advise sick inmates to ask for drugs he himself had recommended'. ~

(2) Cannibalism by prepositions
'Cannibalism' is the name given by Fowler to a vice that prepositions are especially prone to, though it may infect any part of speech. One of a pair of words swallows the second:

> any articles for which export licences are held or for which licences have been applied.

The writer meant 'or for which export licences have been applied for', but the first *for* has swallowed the second.

(3) Some particular prepositions
(*a*) *Between* and *among*. The *OED* tells us not to heed those who tell us that *between* must only be used of two things, and that when there are more, the preposition must be *among*. *Between*, it says,

> is still the only word available to express the relation of a thing to many surrounding things severally and individually, *among*

expressing a relation to them collectively and vaguely: we should not say 'the space lying among the three points,' or 'a treaty among three powers,' or 'the choice lies among the three candidates in the select list,' or 'to insert a needle among the closed petals of a flower'.

(*b*) *Between . . . or* and *between . . . and between*.   If *between* is followed by a conjunction, this must always be a simple *and*. It is wrong to say 'the choice lies between Smith or Jones', or to say 'we had to choose between taking these offices and making the best of them and between perhaps finding ourselves with no offices at all'. If a sentence has become so involved that *and* is not felt to be enough, it should be recast. This mistake is not unknown in high places:

> It is thought that the choice lies between Mr Trygve Lie continuing for another year or the election of Mr Lester Pearson.

(*c*) For *between you and I*, see '*I and me*', p. 207.

(*d*) *Due to*.   *Owing to* long ago established itself as a prepositional phrase, and it must be admitted that the prepositional use of *due to* is also now very common and may have come to stay. But the orthodox still keep up the fight against it: they maintain that *due* is an adjective and should not be used otherwise. That means that it must always have a noun to agree with. You may say: 'Floods due to a breach in the river bank covered a thousand acres of land'. But you must not say: 'Due to a breach in the river bank a thousand acres of land were flooded'. In the first, *due to* agrees properly with *floods*, and these were in fact due to the breach. In the second, it can only agree with *a thousand acres of land*. These were not due to the breach, or to anything else except the Creation.

Due to is rightly used in:

> The closing of the telephone exchange was due to lack of equipment. (*Due to* agrees with *closing*.)

> The delay in replying was due to the fact that it was hoped to call upon you. (*Due to* agrees with *delay*.)

Due to is wrongly used in:

> We must apologise to listeners who missed the introduction to the talk due to a technical fault. (*Due to* agrees with *talk*, implying a 'talk due to a technical fault'.)

Fowler remarked about *due to* used as a preposition: 'perhaps idiom will beat the illiterates, perhaps the illiterates will beat idiom'. The illiterates will probably win.

Note. When, ten years after making this prediction, Gowers sat down to revise Fowler's *Modern English Usage*, he wrote that he now felt the battle to resist Fowler's 'illiterates' was indeed lost. This entry may therefore be thought of as a curiosity, though there are writers who still observe the rule it explains. ~

(*e*) *Prior to.* There is no good reason to use *prior to* as a preposition instead of *before*. *Before* is simpler, better known and more natural, and therefore preferable. It is, moreover, at least questionable whether *prior to* has established itself as a preposition. By all means use the phrase a *prior engagement*, where *prior* is doing its proper job as an adjective. But do not say that you made an engagement *prior to* receiving the second engagement.

> Mr X has requested that you should submit to him, immediately prior to placing orders, lists of components . . .

> Sir Adrian Boult is resting prior to the forthcoming tour of the BBC Symphony Orchestra.

In sentences such as these, *prior to* cannot have any advantage over the straightforward *before*.

Note. The same could be said of *previous to*. Gowers also wrote that *following* used as a preposition was a 'pretentious substitute' for *after* ('following heavy rain last night the wicket is very wet'). The *OED*'s earliest example of this use is dated 1947. It then cites Gowers himself, who in 1948 had written: 'Perhaps the fight against *following* as a preposition ought to be regarded as lost'. He still thought it was pretentious. ~

TROUBLES WITH PRONOUNS

Of pronouns, Cobbett wrote in his grammar that 'The use of them is to prevent the repetition of Nouns, and to make speaking and writing more rapid and less encumbered with words'. In more than one respect they are difficult parts of speech to handle.

(1) It is an easy slip to use a pronoun without a true antecedent

He offered to resign but it was refused.

Here *it* is lacking a true antecedent. It would have had one if the sentence had begun 'He offered his resignation'. This is a purely grammatical point, but unless care is taken over it a verbal absurdity may result. Cobbett gives this example from Addison:

There are, indeed, but very few who know how to be idle and innocent, or have a Relish of any Pleasures that are not Criminal; every Diversion they take is at the Expence of some one Virtue or another, and their very first Step out of Business is into Vice or Folly.

As Cobbett points out, the only possible antecedent to *they* and *their* is the 'very few who know how to be idle and innocent', and that is the opposite of what Addison means.

(2) Be sure there is no real ambiguity about the antecedent
This is more than a grammatical point; it affects the intelligibility of what you write. Special care is needed when, for example, the pronouns are *he* and *him*, and more than one male person has been mentioned. Robert Louis Stevenson, in a letter of 1892, wrote: 'When I invent a language, there shall be a direct and an indirect pronoun differently declined'. He gave an example of what he meant, to show the freedom that this would provide:

> Ex.: HE seized TUM by TUS throat; but TU at the same moment caught HIM by HIS hair. A fellow could write hurricanes with an inflection like that!

A fellow could, but English affords no such aids. Handicapped as we are by the lack of this useful artifice, we must be careful to leave no doubt about the antecedent of our pronouns, and must not make our readers guess, even though it may not be difficult to guess right. As Jespersen points out in his *Essentials of English Grammar*, a sentence like 'John told Robert's son that he must help him' is theoretically capable of six different meanings. It is true that Jespersen would not have us trouble overmuch when there can be no real doubt about the antecedent, and he points out that there is little danger of misunderstanding the theoretically ambiguous sentence:

> If the baby does not thrive on raw milk, boil it.

Nevertheless, he adds, it is well to be very careful about one's pronouns.*

---

* Babies remain vulnerable to ambiguity about antecedents, as a story from the *Guardian* shows: 'Breastfeeding babies will need their own tickets for 2012 Olympics—even if they weren't conceived when they went on sale'. The Chairman of the London Games, challenged on this point, described it as an anomaly that some people had bought 'tickets that have subsequently had babies'. ~

Here are one or two examples to show how difficult it can be to avoid ambiguity:

> Mr S. told Mr H. he was prepared to transfer part of his allocation to his purposes provided that he received £10,000.

The *his* before *purposes* refers, it would seem, to Mr H., and the other three pronouns to Mr S.

> Mr F. saw a man throw something from his pockets to the hens on his farm, and then twist the neck of one of them when they ran to him.

Here the change of antecedent from the man to Mr F. and back again to the man is puzzling at first.

There are several possible paths to removing ambiguities such as these. Let us take by way of illustration the sentence, 'Sir Henry Ponsonby informed Mr Gladstone that the Queen had been much upset by what he had told her', and let us assume that the ambiguous *he* refers to Mr Gladstone. We can make the antecedent plain by

(*a*) Not using a pronoun at all, and writing 'by what Mr Gladstone had told her'.

(*b*) Parenthetic explanation—'by what he (Mr Gladstone) had told her'.

(*c*) The *former-latter* device—'by what the latter had told her'.

(*d*) By rewriting the sentence—'The Queen was much upset by what Mr Gladstone had told her, as Mr Ponsonby then informed him'.

(*e*) The device Henry Sidgwick called 'the polite alias' and Fowler, 'elegant variation', writing (say) 'by what the Prime Minister had told her', or the 'G.O.M.' or 'the veteran statesman'.

It may safely be said that the fifth device should seldom if ever be adopted,* and the third only when the antecedent is very close.

(3) Do not be shy of pronouns

So far we have been concerned in this section with the dangers that beset the user of pronouns. But for officials no less a danger is that of not using pronouns when they ought. Legal language, which must aim above all things at removing every possible ambiguity, is more sparing of pronouns than ordinary prose, because of an ever-present fear that the antecedent may be uncertain. For instance, opening a random Act of Parliament, I read:

> The Secretary of State may by any such regulations allow the required notice of any occurrence to which the regulations relate, instead of being sent forthwith, to be sent within the time limited by the regulations.

Anyone not writing legal language would have avoided repeating *regulations* twice, and would instead have put *they* in the first place and *them* in the second.

Officials have so much to read and explain that is written in legal language that they become infected with pronoun-avoidance. The result is that what they write is often, in Cobbett's phrase, more 'encumbered with words' than it need be:

> The Ministry of Agriculture and Fisheries are anxious that the Rural Land Utilisation Officer should not in any way hinder the acquisition or earmarking of land for educational purposes,

---

* 'Elegant variation' used to be an accepted feature of fine writing, as is shown by this remarkable extract from *The Times* of 1848, in which readers are alerted to a demonstration of M. Molk's newly invented 'electric searchlight': 'At this period of the evening the moon will be in its zenith, but M. Molk does not apprehend any sensible diminution of the lustre of his light from the presence of that beautiful luminary'.

> but it is the duty of Rural Land Utilisation Officer (his duty)
> to ensure ...

> Arrangements are being made to continue the production of
> these houses for a further period, and increased numbers of
> these houses (them) will, therefore, be available.

Often the repeated word is embroidered by *such*:

> the admission of specially selected Public Assistance cases,
> provided that no suitable accommodation is available for such
> cases (them) in a home ...

This is no doubt due to infection by legal English, where this use
of *such* is an indispensable device for securing economy of words:
in legal writing, where the concern is to make the meaning certain beyond the possibility of error, it is sensible to avoid pronouns
lest there should be an ambiguity about their antecedents. The
official need not usually be so punctilious.

But using *such* in the way that lawyers use it is not always out
of place in ordinary writing. Sometimes it is proper and useful:

> One month's notice in writing must be given to terminate this
> agreement. As no such notice has been received from you ...

Here it is important for the writer to show that the second sentence refers to the same sort of notice as the first, and the *such*
device is the neatest way of doing it.

(4) It is usually better not to allow a pronoun to precede its
principal
If the pronoun comes first the reader may not know what it refers
to until arriving at the principal:

> I regret that it is not practicable, in view of its size, to provide
> a list of the agents.

Here, it is true, the reader is only momentarily left guessing what *its* refers to. But even that brief doubt could have been avoided if the sentence had been written:

> I regret that it is not practicable to provide a list of the agents as there are too many of them.

(5) *Each other*

Grammarians used to say that *each other* is the right expression when only two persons or things are referred to and *one another* when there are more than two. But Fowler, quoted with approval by Jespersen, says of this so-called rule, 'the differentiation is neither of present utility nor based on historical usage'.

Note. Gowers proved his own indifference to 'this so-called rule' in this very chapter, with the sentence: 'Sometimes the weight of a plural pushes the verb into the wrong number, even though they are not next to one another'. But today's sticklers continue to protest against the usage. To return to the story of the writing on the wall (see p. 123), we are told that when the unattached fingers inscribed 'Mene Mene Tekel Upharsin' on the plaster in King Belshazzar's palace, he was so frightened that his knees 'smote one against another'. A reader in whose mind this produces the image of a man with at least three knees might choose to side with the sticklers. ~

(6) *Former* and *latter*

Do not hesitate to repeat words rather than use *former* or *latter* to avoid doing so. The reader will probably have to look back to see which is which, and will be annoyed at the waste of time. And there is no excuse at all for using *latter* merely to serve as a pronoun, as in:

In these employments we would rest our case for the exclusion of young persons directly on the grounds of the latter's moral welfare. (Their moral welfare.)

Remember that *former* and *latter* can refer to only two things, and if you use them of more than two you may puzzle your reader. If you want to refer otherwise than specifically to the last of more than two things, say *last* or *last-mentioned*, not *latter*.

(7) *I* and *me*

The practice of using *I* for *me* in combination with some noun or other pronoun is increasingly popular, e.g. 'between you and I' or 'he must let you and I go'. But why this has become so prevalent is not easy to say. Perhaps it comes partly from an excess of zeal in correcting the opposite error. When Mrs Elton said, 'Neither Mr Suckling nor me had ever any patience with them', and Lydia Bennet, 'Mrs Forster and me are *such* friends!', they were guilty of a vulgarism that was, no doubt, common in Jane Austen's time, and is far from unknown today. One might suppose that this mistake was corrected by teachers of English in our schools with such ferocity that their pupils are left with the conviction that such combinations as *you and me* are in all circumstances ungrammatical. But that explanation will not quite do. It might account for a popular broadcaster's saying 'that's four to Margaret and I', but not for why Shakespeare had a character in *The Merchant of Venice* write: 'all debts are cleared between you and I'.

It is the combination of oneself with someone else that proves fatal. The official who wrote: 'I trust that it will be convenient to you for my colleague and I to call upon you next Tuesday' would never, if proposing to come alone, have written, 'I trust that it will be convenient to you for I to call upon you . . .' A sure and easy way of avoiding this blunder is to ask oneself what case the personal pronoun would have been in—would it have been *I* or *me*—if it had stood alone. It should remain the same in partnership as it would have been by itself.

The association of someone else with oneself sometimes prompts the use of *myself* where a simple *I* or *me* is all that is needed, e.g. 'the inspection will be made by Mr Jones and myself'. *Myself* should be used only for emphasis ('I saw it myself') or as the reflexive form of the personal pronoun ('I have hurt myself').

Note. Gowers also wrote under this heading: 'About the age-long conflict between *it is I* and *it is me*, no more need be said than that, in the present stage of the battle, most people would think "it is I" pedantic in talk and "it is me" improper in writing'. Now, however, most people would find 'it is I' disquietingly fey in any modern context, written or not. By contrast, the misuse of *myself* is flourishing. The Deputy Prime Minister, for one, clearly believes that *myself* confers a certain something that *I* and *me* both lack: 'Myself and the Prime Minister are saying exactly the same thing'; 'There is not a cigarette paper between myself and the Prime Minister on this issue', 'But all of us in this government, including the Prime Minister and myself, are not willing to compromise . . .' etc. ~

(8) *It*

This pronoun is especially troublesome because the convenient English idiom of using *it* to anticipate the subject of a sentence tends to produce a plethora of *it*s. A correspondent sends me this example:

> It is to be expected that it will be difficult to apply A unless it is accompanied by B, for which reason it is generally preferable to use C in spite of its other disadvantages.

This could be put more effectively and tersely by writing:

C is generally preferable, in spite of its disadvantages, because of the difficulty of applying A without B.

As Cobbett said, 'Never put an *it* upon paper without thinking well of what you are about. When I see many *its* in a page, I always tremble for the writer'.

(9) *One*

(*a*) *One* has a way of intruding in a sentence such as 'the problem is not an easy one'. 'The problem is not easy' may be a neater way of saying what you mean.

(*b*) What pronoun should be used with *one*? *His* or *one's*, for example? That depends on what sort of a *one* it is, whether 'numeral' or 'impersonal', to use Fowler's labels. For instance:

> One hates most of *her* teachers, but another delights in them all (numeral).

> One despairs of *one's* weaknesses, yet *one's* virtues can be equally hampering (impersonal).

But any sentence that needs to repeat the impersonal *one* is bound to be inelegant, and you will do better to rewrite it.

(*c*) '*One of those who* . . .' A common error in sentences of this sort is to use a singular verb instead of a plural, as though the antecedent of *who* were *one* and not *those*—to write, for instance, 'it is one of the exceptional cases that calls for (instead of *call* for) exceptional treatment'.

(10) *Same*

When the Thirty-nine Articles were drawn up in the sixteenth century, it was good English idiom to use *the same* as a pronoun where we should now say *he* or *she*, *him* or *her*, *they* or *them*, or *it*:

> The Riches and Goods of Christians are not common, as touching the right, title, and possession of the same; as certain Anabaptists do falsely boast.

This is no good reason for the present pronominal use of *the same* and *same*, which survives robustly in commercialese. It is to be found to some extent in official writing also, especially in letters on business subjects. This use of *same* is now by general consent reprehensible because it gives an air of artificiality and pretentiousness:

> As you have omitted to insert your full Christian names, I shall be glad if you will advise me of same. (I shall be glad if you will let me know what they are.)

> I enclose the necessary form for agreement and request that you kindly complete and return same at your earliest convenience. (That you will kindly complete and return it.)

The following sentence is curious:

> I am informed that it may be decided by X Section that this extra will not be required. I await therefore their decision before taking further action in an attempt to provide.

I like to think that the writer stopped abruptly after *provide*, leaving it objectless, in order to check the urge to write *same*. But *it* might harmlessly have been used here instead.

(11) *They* for *he* or *she*

It is common in speech, and not unknown in serious writing, to use *they* or *them* as the equivalent of a singular pronoun of common sex, as in: 'Each insisted on their own point of view, and so the marriage came to an end'. This is stigmatised by grammarians as a usage grammatically indefensible. The Judge ought, they would say, to have explained that 'He insisted on his own point of view and she on hers'. Jespersen says about this that 'In the third person it would have been very convenient to have a common-sex pronoun, but as a matter of fact English has none', and that we must therefore use one of three 'makeshift expedients'. These he exemplifies as follows:

(*a*) 'Nobody prevents you, do they?' (Thackeray, in *Pendennis*); 'God send everyone their heart's desire' (Shakespeare, *Much Ado About Nothing*).

The official writer will be wise for the present not to be tempted by the convenience of using *they* or *their* in this fashion as a singular common-sex pronoun, though necessity may eventually force it into the category of accepted idiom. And whatever justification there may be for it, there can be no excuse for this practice when only one sex is referred to, as in,

> The female manipulative jobs are of a type to which by no means everyone can adapt themselves with ease.

There is no reason why *herself* should not have been written, instead of *themselves*.

Note. Since Gowers wrote these remarks, the use of *they* and *them* as singular pronouns has become so widespread that his earlier quotation about the theft of a chicken (used to illustrate ambiguous antecedents of pronouns) might strike the modern reader as doubly opaque:

> Mr F. saw a man throw something from his pockets to the hens on his farm, and then twist the neck of one of them when they ran to him.

Did all the chickens dash over, whereupon a single unlucky bird paid the price, or did a sole, suicidal chicken run to the man with pockets? There is no doubt that by '*they* ran', the original author of this sentence meant all the hens; but a modern speaker and indeed writer might well say 'one of them when they ran to him' meaning a single chicken. It nevertheless remains safer in formal English to treat as incorrect, still, a remark such as, 'The reader may toss their book aside'. And it is inexcusably slack that Part 10 on the application form for a United Kingdom passport should carry this isolated sentence: 'If a countersignature is needed, they must fill in this section after the rest of the form has been filled in'. ~

(*b*) 'The reader's heart (if he or she have any) . . .' (Fielding, *Tom Jones*).

The Ministry of Labour and National Service have adopted a new device derived from this second expedient. It is ugly, and suitable only for forms:

> Each worker must acknowledge receipt by entering the serial
> number of the supplementary coupon sheet issued to him/her
> in column 4 and signing his/her name in column 5.

Note. Him/her, *his/hers* and *he/she*—let alone *s/he*—have not ceased to be ugly devices. *He or she, him or her*, etc., may sometimes get a writer out of a hole, but repeated use of this expedient will render the best prose inelegant. ~

(*c*) 'He that hath ears to hear, let him hear' (Authorised Version).

Note. About this third expedient, where *he* is made to stand for anyone and everyone ('the reader may toss his book aside'), Gowers said no more in 1954 than that it was 'for the present' preferable to expedients (*a*) and (*b*). He still thought so when he came to revise Fowler in 1965 (using *they* and *them*, he said, set his teeth on edge). But he now described using *he* as a 'risk', and removed a sentence from the original book, of 1926, in which Fowler disparaged as a 'sectional' interest the efforts of various 'ladies' to make English more neutral. Gowers added to his edition of Fowler the following sentence (from a Civil Service document), with a note conceding that the all-embracing *his* and *him* were used in it with a 'boldness surprising':

> There must be opportunity for the individual boy or girl to go
> as far as his keenness and ability will take him.

This sentence may appear particularly ridiculous, but it is logically no more so than 'the reader will probably throw his book in the bin'. The formula Gowers called a risk decades ago has become much riskier since, and a sentence such as the one above of a boldness surprising is worth rewriting (here, using the plural) to stop it sounding perverse:

> Boys and girls must have the opportunity to go as far as their
> individual keenness and ability will take them. ~

(12) *What*

What, in the sense of *that which*, or *those which*, is an antecedent and relative combined. Because it may be either singular or plural in number, and either subjective or objective in case, it needs careful handling.

Fowler says that its difficulties of number can be solved by asking the question, 'What does it stand for?'

> What is needed is more rooms.

Here Fowler would say that *what* means *the thing that*, and the singular verb is right. On the other hand, in the sentence 'He no doubt acted with what are in his opinion excellent reasons', *are* is right because *what* is equivalent to *reasons that*. But this is perhaps over-subtle, and there is no great harm in treating *what* as a plural in such a construction whenever the complement is plural ('what is needed are more rooms'). It may be thought to sound more natural.

Because *what* may be subjective or objective, writers may find themselves making the same word do duty in both cases, a practice condemned by grammarians. For instance:

This was what came into his head and he said without thinking.

What here is being made to do duty both as the subject of *came* and as the object of *said*. If we want to be punctiliously grammatical we will write this:

This is what (subjective) came into his head and what (objective) he said without thinking.

Preferably, we will say:

This is what came into his head, and he said it without thinking.

(13) *Which*
The *New Yorker*, in an issue of 1948, quoted a request sent to the *Philadelphia Bulletin*:

My class would appreciate a discussion of the wrong use of *which* in sentences like 'He wrecked the car which was due to his carelessness'.

The *Bulletin*'s reply, also quoted by the *New Yorker*, was:

The fault lies in using *which* to refer to the statement *'He wrecked the car'*. When *which* follows a noun it refers to that noun as its antecedent. Therefore in the foregoing sentence it is stated that the car was due to his carelessness, which is nonsense.

What, the *New Yorker* wanted to know, was nonsense here? Carelessness? Which shows how dangerous it is to dogmatise about the use of *which* with an antecedent consisting not of a single word but of a phrase. *Punch* has provided an illustration of the same danger (from a novel):

Mrs Brandon took the heavy piece of silk from the table, unfolded it and displayed ... an altar cloth of her own exquisite embroidery ... upon which, everyone began to blow their nose ...

The fact is that this is a common and convenient usage, but one that needs to be handled with discretion to avoid ambiguity or awkwardness.

Here it is unnecessary:

> The required statement is in course of preparation and will be forwarded as soon as official records are complete, which will be in about a week's time.

The sentence can be improved by omitting the words *which will be*, thereby getting rid of the relative altogether.

> The long delay may make it inevitable for the authorities to consider placing the order elsewhere which can only be in the United States which is a step we should be anxious to avoid.

Here the writer has used *which* in this way twice in a single sentence, and shown how awkward its effect can be. It would be better to put a full stop after *elsewhere*, and then say: 'That can only be in the United States, and is a step we should be anxious to avoid'.

(14) *Which* and *that*

On the whole it makes for smoothness of writing not to use the relative *which* where *that* would do as well, and not to use either if a sentence makes sense and runs pleasantly without. But that is a very broad general statement, subject to many exceptions.

Grammarians speak of a 'commenting' *which*, and a 'defining' *that*:

> The mouse, which was brown, died. (It happened to be brown. It died.)

> The mouse that was brown died. (The brown mouse died, unlike the rest of the mice—not brown, and still alive.)

That cannot be used with a commenting clause, the relative must be *which*.* With a defining clause either *which* or *that* is permissible, but *that* is to be preferred. When in a defining clause the relative is in the objective case, it can often be left out altogether. Thus we have three variants:

> This case ought to go to the Home Office, *which* deals with police establishments. (Commenting relative clause.)

> The Department *that* deals with police establishments is the Home Office. (Defining relative clause.)

> This is the case you said we ought to send to the Home Office. (Defining relative clause in which the relative pronoun, if it were expressed, would be in the objective case: 'This is the case *that* you said . . .'.)

That is an awkward word because it may be one of three parts of speech—a conjunction, a relative pronoun and a demonstrative pronoun. The three are illustrated in the order given in the following sentence:

> I think that the paper that he wants is that one.

It is a sound rule that *that* should be dispensed with whenever this can be done without loss of clarity or dignity. For instance, the sentence just given might be written with only one *that* instead of three:

> I think the paper he wants is that one.

Some verbs seem to need a conjunctive *that* after them more than others do. *Say* and *think* can generally do without. The more formal words like *state* and *assert* cannot.

---

* See also pp. 243–5 for punctuating relative clauses.

We have already noted that the conjunctive *that* can lead a writer into the error of careless duplication.* The following *that* defies both sense and grammar:

> As stated by the Minister of Fuel and Power on the 8th April, a standard ration will be available for use from 1st June, 1948, in every private car and motor cycle currently licensed and that an amount equivalent to the standard ration will be deducted ...

The writer forgot how the sentence began and concluded as though the opening had been 'On the 8th April, the Minister of Fuel and Power stated that ...'

> The Ministry of Food allow such demonstrations only if the materials used are provided by the staff and that no food is sold to the public.

In this sentence the use of *that* for *if* is even less excusable because the writer had less time to forget the beginning.

> Their intention was probably to remove from the mind of the man in question that he was in any way bound to work, and that the Government would protect him from bad employers.

This example shows the need of care in a sentence in which *that* has to be repeated. If you do not remember what words introduced the first *that*, you may easily find yourself, as here, saying the opposite of what you mean. What this writer was trying to say was that the intention was to remove the first idea and replace it with the second, not, as accidentally stated, to remove both.

Note. Gowers remarks above that 'With a defining clause either *which* or *that* is permissible, but *that* is to be preferred'. He may have used a distancing passive here because he was less than

---

* See pp. 182–3.

scrupulous about following this advice himself. Quotations throughout the book show other writers ignoring it too: Sir Harold Nicolson, when he comments that neither X nor Y nor Z 'will suffer permanently or seriously from the spectacle which they have provided'; Logan Pearsall Smith, who says 'a language which was all idiom and unreason would be impossible as an instrument of thought'; Churchill, who is quoted in Chapter X declaring rousingly: 'no future generation of English-speaking folks . . . will doubt that . . . we were guiltless of the bloodshed, terror and misery which have engulfed so many lands'. It is as well to be aware that in some readers these uses of *which* will provoke an immediate corrective spasm: 'from the spectacle *that* they have provided'; 'a language *that* was all idiom and unreason'; 'the bloodshed, terror and misery *that* have engulfed so many lands'. ~

(15) *Who* and *whom*

Who is the subjective case and *whom* the objective. The proper use of the two words should present no difficulty. But we are so unaccustomed to different case-formations in English that when we are confronted with them we are liable to lose our heads. In the matter of *who* and *whom* good writers have for centuries been perverse in refusing to do what the grammarians tell them. They will insist on writing sentences like 'Who should I see there . . .', as Steele did in the *Spectator*; 'Young Ferdinand, (whom they suppose is drowned)': Shakespeare, in *The Tempest*; and 'Whom do men say that I am?', asked by Christ in the Bible. Now, any schoolchild can see that, by the rules, *who* in the first quotation, being the object of *see*, ought to be *whom* ('Whom should I see there'), and that *whom* in the second and third quotations, being in the one the subject of *is*, and in the other the complement of *am*, ought to be *who* (Young Ferdinand, 'who, they suppose, is drowned'; 'Who do men say that I am?'). What, then, is the ordinary person to believe?

There are some who would have us do away with *whom* altogether, as nothing but a mischief-maker. That might be a useful way out. But then, as was asked in the correspondence columns of the *Spectator* by someone under the name 'A. Wood-Owl':

> Regarding the suggested disuse of 'whom', may I ask by who a lead can be given? To who, to wit to who of the 'cultured' authorities, can we appeal to boo whom, and to boom who?   (December, 1948)

Whom will take some killing. Shakespeare has his distinguished followers, such as Sir Winston Churchill ('The slaves of the Lamp ... render faithful and obedient service to whomsoever holds the talisman'), Mr E. M. Forster ('a creature whom we pretend is here already ...'),* Lord David Cecil in *Two Quiet Lives* ('and whom, he knew, would never be seduced away from him by the tawdry glitter of the world'), *The Times* ('He was not the man whom the police think may be able to help them'), and even Mr Somerset Maugham, in a story from *The Trembling of a Leaf* ('Bateman could not imagine whom it was that he passed off as his nephew'). This usage is, moreover, defended by Jespersen.

Of course the opposite mistake is also made:

> He was a chancellor who, grudging as was the acknowledgement he received for it, everyone knew to have saved his party.

Note. Gowers concluded by saying that 'it has not yet become pedantic—at any rate in writing—to use *who* and *whom* in what grammarians would call the right way', and he therefore advised ordinary writers to ignore the 'vagaries of the great'.

---

* This quotation is taken from Forster's essay of 1935 'The Menace to Freedom'. When he later republished it in *Two Cheers for Democracy*, he corrected the line to read 'a creature who, we pretend, is here already ...'. ~

Using *whom* for *who* is still a mistake, whether Shakespeare once did it or not, and those who notice this error in contemporary writing are likely to interpret it as that dreaded thing, a 'genteelism'. But it is no longer so necessary to worry about what Gowers calls the opposite mistake. He found using *who* for *whom* to be rarer than *whom* for *who*, but now it is in many circumstances entirely normal to do this. Indeed, the question 'Whom should I see theres . . .' (Steele corrected) would these days strike most people as absurdly stiff. It is not yet idiomatic to put *who* for *whom* immediately after a preposition, as a *Guardian* writer does here: 'my ex with who I was still in love'; but ordinary British English accepts and even expects, 'my ex, who I was still in love with'. The slow decline of *whom* does leave room for confusion. Nowadays 'Who am I to love?' could be taken to mean either 'What person should be the object of my affections?' or 'Worm that I am, how dare I love at all?' But it has to be admitted that outside the confines of formal prose, the worm's perspective on this question is dying away. ~

(16) *Whose*

There lingers a grammarians' rule that *whose* must not be used of inanimate objects: we may say 'authors whose books are famous' but we must not say 'books whose authors are famous'. For the second, we must fall back on an ugly roundabout way of putting it, and say 'books the authors of which are famous'. This rule is a cramping one, and produces not only ugly sentences but a temptation to misplace commas:

> There are now a large number of direct controls, the purpose of which is to allocate scarce resources of all kinds between the various applicants for their use.

Here the writer, having duly respected the prejudice against the inanimate *whose*, finds that *controls the purpose* is an awkward juxtaposition, and so opts to put a comma after *controls*. But the relative clause is a defining one (these are 'controls that have the purpose of allocating scarce resources ...'), not a commenting one ('these controls, the purpose of which is X, are numerous'). The comma is therefore misleading.

> Sir Alexander Cadogan added that legislatures were not unaccustomed to ratifying decisions the entry into force of which was contingent on circumstances beyond their control.

In this instance the writer has properly resisted the temptation to lessen the inevitable ugliness of the construction by putting a comma after *decisions*. But how much more smoothly each sentence would run if the writer had felt at liberty to say *controls whose purpose* and *decisions whose entry*.

The rule is so hampering and pointless that even the grammarians are in revolt against it. Fowler said:

> Let us in the name of common sense prohibit the prohibition of *whose inanimate*; good writing is surely difficult enough without the forbidding of things that have historical grammar and present intelligibility and obvious convenience on their side, and lack only—starch.

There are welcome signs that Fowler's advice is now being followed in official publications:

> The hospital whose characteristics and associations link it with a particular religious denomination ...

> That revolution the full force of whose effects we are beginning to feel ...

> There has been built up a single centrally organised blood transfusion service whose object is ...

TROUBLES WITH VERBS

(1) *ing* endings

Words ending with *ing* are mostly verbal participles or gerunds, and, as we shall see, it is not always easy to say which is which. By way of introduction it will be enough to observe that when they are of the nature of participles they may be true verbs ('I was *working*'), or adjectives ('a *working* agreement'), or in rare cases prepositions ('*concerning* this question') or conjunctions ('*supposing* this happened'). But if they are of the nature of gerunds they are always nouns ('I am pleased at his *coming*')—or rather a hybrid between a noun and a verb, for you may use the gerund with the construction either of a noun ('after the careful *reading* of these papers') or of a mixture between a verb and a noun ('after carefully *reading* these papers'). It is most confusing, but fortunately we are seldom called on to put a label on these words, and so I have preferred to give this section an indeterminate title.

Numerous pitfalls beset the use of *ing*-words. Here are some of them.

(*a*) Absolute construction. This is, in itself, straightforward enough. The absolute construction, in the words of the *OED*, is a name given to a clause 'not syntactically dependent on another part of the sentence'. In the sentence 'The teacher having restored order, the class resumed', the phrase 'the teacher having restored order' forms an absolute construction. But there is no absolute construction in the sentence 'The teacher, having restored order, called on her cowed pupils to continue'. Here *the teacher* is the subject of the sentence. Because of a confusion with that type of sentence, it is a curiously common error to put a comma in the absolute construction ('the teacher, having restored order, the class resumed').*

---

* For this misuse of a comma see also pp. 245–6

(*b*) Unattached or dangling participle. This blunder is rather like the last. A writer begins a sentence with a participle (which, since it is a sort of adjective, must be given a noun to support it) and then forgets to give it its noun, thus leaving it 'dangling':

> Arising out of a collision between a removal van and fully loaded bus in a fog, Mr X, removal van driver, appeared on a charge of manslaughter.

Grammatically in this sentence it was the van driver who arose out of this collision, not the charge against him. He probably did, but that was not what the writer meant.

> Whilst requesting you to furnish the return now outstanding you are advised that in future it would greatly facilitate X . . . if you were to Y.

Here *requesting* is unattached. If the structure of this rather clumsy sentence is to be retained it must run 'Whilst requesting you . . . I advise you that . . .'

As I have said, some *ing*-words have won the right to be treated as prepositions. Among them are *regarding, considering, owing to, concerning* and *failing*. When any of these is used as a preposition, there can be no question of its being misused as an unattached participle:

> Considering the attack that had been made on him, his speech was moderate in tone.

If, however, *considering* were used not as a preposition-participle but as an adjective-participle, it could be unattached. It is so in:

> Considering the attack on him beneath his notice, his speech was moderate in tone.

Here, if the first part of the sentence must stand, the second needs to be amended: 'Considering the attack on him beneath his notice, the man gave a speech that was moderate in tone'.

Past participles, as well as present, may become unattached:

> Administered at first by the National Gallery, it was not until 1917 that the appointment of a separate board and director enabled a fully independent policy to be pursued.

The writer must have started with the intention of making the Tate Gallery (the true topic here) the subject of the sentence, but by the end, *administered* has been left unattached.

> Formal application is now being made for the necessary way-leave consent, and as soon as received the work will proceed.

Grammatically *received* can only be attached to *work*, and that is nonsense. The writer should have said, 'as soon as this is received'.

(*c*) Unattached gerund.   A gerund can become unattached in much the same way as a participle:

> Indeed we know little of Stalin's personality at all: a few works of Bolshevik theory, arid and heavy, and speeches still more impersonal, without literary grace, repeating a few simple for-mulas with crushing weight—after reading these Stalin appears more a myth than a man.

Grammatically, 'after reading these' means after Stalin has read them, not after we have.

The use of unattached participles and gerunds is becoming so common that grammarians may soon have to throw in their hand and recognise it as idiomatic. But as they have not done so yet, it should be avoided.

Note. Not all grammarians are prepared to throw in their hand on this one even now. After all, if the reader is left free to decide on the intent behind such constructions, the danger arises of an ambiguity that cannot be unscrambled. Take the sentence 'Having been brought up with lax morals, I did not fully blame the bag-snatcher': in a grammatical free-for-all, how is one to know whether this implies two people with lax morals, or one with lax morals, and another with a soft, forgiving heart? ~

(*d*) Gerund versus infinitive.   In what seems to be a completely arbitrary way, some nouns, adjectives and verbs like to take an infinitive, and some a gerund with a preposition. For instance:

Capable of doing	Able to do
Ban from doing	Forbid to do
Shrink from doing	Scruple to do

Instances could be multiplied. There is no rule. It can only be a matter of observation and consulting a dictionary when in doubt.

(*e*) The 'fused participle'.   All authorities agree that it is idiomatic English to write 'the *Bill's* getting a second reading surprised everyone'—that is to say, it is correct to treat *getting* as a gerund requiring *Bill's* to be in the possessive. What they are not agreed about is whether it is also correct to treat *getting* as a participle, and write 'the *Bill* getting a second reading surprised everyone'. If that is a legitimate grammatical construction, the subject of the sentence, which cannot be *Bill* by itself, or *getting* by itself, must be a fusion of the two. Hence the name 'fused participle'.

This is not in itself a matter of any great interest or importance. But it is notable as having been the occasion of a battle of the giants, Fowler and Jespersen. Fowler condemned the 'fused participle' as a construction 'grammatically indefensible' that he said was 'rapidly corrupting modern English style'. Jespersen defended it against both these charges. Those best competent to judge seem to have awarded Jespersen a win on points.

What is certain is that sometimes we feel one construction to be the more idiomatic, and sometimes the other, and, in particular, that proper names and personal pronouns seem to demand the gerund. Nobody would prefer 'He coming (or Smith coming) surprised me' to 'His coming (or Smith's coming) surprised me'. That is sure ground.

For the rest, it is always possible, and generally wise, to be on the safe side by turning the sentence round, and writing neither 'the Bill getting, etc.' (which offends some purists) nor 'the Bill's getting, etc.' (which sounds odd to some ears) but 'everyone was surprised that the Bill got a second reading'.

(2) Subjunctive

The subjunctive is the mood of imagination or command. Apart from the verb *to be*, it has no form separate from the indicative, except in the third person singular of the present tense, where the subjunctive form is the same as the indicative plural (*he have*, not *he has*; *she go*, not *she goes*). Generally therefore, in sentences in which the subjunctive might be fitting, neither the writer nor the reader need know or care whether the subjunctive is being used or not.

But the verb *to be* spoils this simple picture. The whole of the present tense is different, for the subjunctive mood is *be* throughout—*I be*, *he be*, *we be*, *you be* and *they be*. The singular (but not the plural) of the past tense is also different—*I were* and *he were* instead of *I was* and *he was*. In the subjunctive mood what looks like the past tense does not denote pastness, it denotes a greater call on the imagination. Thus:

> 'If she is here' implies that it is as likely as not that she is.
>
> 'If she be here' is an archaic way of saying 'if she is here'.
>
> 'If she were here' implies that she is not.

The only remaining regular uses of the subjunctive are:

(*a*) In certain stock phrases: *be it so, God bless you, come what may, if need be* and others.

(*b*) In legal or formal language: the subjunctive is often used in a phrase such as 'I move that so-and-so be appointed secretary'. In America this usage is not confined to formal language, but is usual in such sentences as 'I ask that he be sent for', 'It is important that she be there', and even in the negative form, 'He insisted that the statement not be placed on record', in which the custom in this country has been to insert a *should* ('It is important that she should be there'). With our present propensity to imitate American ways, we may follow suit, as here: 'There have been many suggestions ... that the river be made the basis of a large-scale irrigation scheme' (*The Times*).

(*c*) In conditional sentences where the hypothesis is not a fact:

Were this true, it would be a serious matter.

If he were here, I would tell him what I think of him.

(*d*) With *as if* and *as though*, if the hypothesis is not accepted as true, thus:

He spoke of his proposal as if it were a complete solution of the difficulty.

Other correct uses of the subjunctive may be found in contemporary writings, but it is probably true of all of them that the indicative would have been equally correct, and certainly true of many of them that the subjunctive has a formal, even pedantic, air.

Note. Gowers supplied an example of a subjunctive that he thought sounded particularly archaic, a stock phrase he associated with 'academic front doors': 'Please do not ring unless an answer be required'. (The pretension of this formula had already been comprehensively squashed by John Gray, a friend of Oscar Wilde, who in 1926 capped it in verse with '—protects the villa uninspired, desirable and undesired'.) Yet Gowers's bald conclusion, 'the subjunctive is dying', was quite wrong. The English have not lost (what he also noted) their propensity to imitate American ways, and the subjunctive, far from being dead, or even idling largely out of view, is now here, there and everywhere. Recent copies of *The Times* contain numerous examples: 'the independent adjudication panel did not follow the GMC's own recommendation that he be struck off'; 'it is essential that you be able to support your claims about matters of fact'; 'The commission is proposing that they be forced to ring-fence their retail arms from their other operations', etc. ~

(3) Misuse of the passive
Grammarians condemn such constructions as the following, which indeed condemn themselves by their contorted ugliness:

> The report that is proposed to be made.
>
> Several amendments were endeavoured to be inserted.
>
> A question was threatened to be put on the paper.
>
> A sensational atmosphere is attempted to be created.

Anyone who has written a sentence like this should recast it, e.g. 'the proposed report', 'attempts were made to insert several amendments', 'a threat was made to put a question on the paper', 'an attempt is being made to create a sensational atmosphere'.

Hope should not be used in the passive except in the impersonal phrase *it is hoped*. We may correctly say 'It is hoped that payment will be made next week', or 'payment is expected to be made next week', but not 'payment is hoped to be made next week'. The phrasal verb *hope for*, being transitive, can of course be used in the passive.

(4) Omission of verb

Where a verb is used with more than one auxiliary (e.g. 'he must and shall go') make sure that the main verb is repeated unless, as in this example, its form is the same. It is easy to slip into a sentence such as this:

> The steps which those responsible can and are at present taking to remedy this state of affairs are unlikely to work.

Can taking makes no sense. The proper construction is shown in:

> The board must take, and are in fact taking, all possible steps to maintain production.

Note. Constructions such as 'can and are at present taking' remain commonplace, but this does nothing to dispel their air of illiteracy. A journalist and recent winner of the Orwell Prize defended himself against accusations of plagiarism by saying 'I did not and never have taken words from another context and twisted them to mean something different'. This ought (if true) to have read, 'I did not take and never have taken ...'. Likewise, but with yet more resolve, an official at the White House, called upon to say whether American spies had intercepted the private messages of the British Prime Minister, replied: 'I can confirm that his communications have not, are not and will not be monitored by the US'. To say *have not be* and *are not be* makes no sense either. What the official meant to confirm was that the messages 'have not been, are not being and will not be' monitored. ~

(5) *Shall* and *will*

Twenty pages devoted to this subject in *The King's English* begin with the following introduction:

> It is unfortunate that the idiomatic use, while it comes by nature to southern Englishmen (who will find most of this

section superfluous), is so complicated that those who are not to the manner born can hardly acquire it; and for them the section is in danger of being useless. In apology for the length of these remarks it must be said that the short and simple directions often given are worse than useless. The observant reader soon loses faith in them from their constant failure to take him right; and the unobservant is the victim of false security.

The Fowler view in short amounts to this: that those brought up among speakers who use the right idiom have no need of instruction, but those who lack this advantage are incapable of being instructed, because any guidance that is short and clear will mislead them, and any that is full and accurate will be incomprehensible to them.

Every English textbook will be found to begin by explaining that to express the 'plain' future, *shall* is used in the first person and *will* in the second and third:

> I shall go
> You will go
> He will go

and that if it is a matter not of plain future but of volition, permission or obligation, it is the other way round:

> I will go (I am determined to go or I intend to go)
> You shall go (You must go, or you are permitted to go)
> He shall go (He must go or he is permitted to go).

But the idiom of the Celts is different. They have never recognised *I shall go*. For them *I will go* is the plain future. The story is a very old one of the drowning Scot who was misunderstood by English onlookers and left to his fate because he cried, 'I will drown and nobody shall save me'.

Note. Most English speakers are without a doubt now Celts in saying 'I will'. Even when Gowers was writing he found it judicious to end, 'we can no longer say dogmatically that *I will go* for the plain future is wrong'. He cautioned English officials to stick to 'textbook orthodoxy' in their own writing, but as that orthodoxy no longer holds, anyone these days who finds *shall* too old fashioned to be useful is at liberty to dispense with the shades of meaning that Gowers was here attempting to explain.

If there are those who seek to know more, but find Gowers's short and simple directions here 'worse than useless', as the Fowler view has it, they do at least have Gowers's own writing in this book as a model for the distinction between *shall* and *will* ('I shall have more to say about pedantry when we consider grammar . . .'), as also for the distinct uses of *should* and *would* discussed below ('It is an arbitrary and pointless rule . . . but for the present its observance is expected from those who would write correctly'). Contrary to what is sometimes said, this style of writing, speaking and indeed thinking is not altogether lost in modern English. ~

(6) *Should* and *would*

The various shades of meaning of *should* and *would* derive in the main from the primary ideas of obligation in *shall* and of resolve in *will*: ideas illustrated in their simplest form by 'he should go' (he ought to go) and 'he would go' (he was determined to go, or he made a habit of going).

As colourless auxiliaries, merely indicating the subjunctive mood, the textbook rule is that *should* is used in the first person and *would* in the second and third. *Should,* which is colourless in the first person, resumes its tinge of *ought* in the others: in 'if you tried you should succeed' it has a nuance not present in 'if I tried I should succeed'. But the rule requiring *should* in the first person is now largely ignored (compare *shall* and *will*): *would* and *should* are used indifferently.

In the stock formula 'In reply to your letter of ... I would inform you ...', *would* is not a mere auxiliary expressing the conditional mood, it retains the now archaic meaning of 'I should like to'. In Chapter III I deprecated the use of similar expressions on the ground of their stiffness, and here too it is almost as though one were to say, 'I would have you know'.

Because *would* has this meaning, grammarians condemn such phrases as 'I would like to', 'I would be glad if', 'I would be obliged if' and so on. *Should*, they say, ought always to be used: to say *would* is tantamount to saying 'I should like to like to', 'I should like to be glad if', 'I should like to be obliged if' and so on. This too is a losing battle. But 'It would appear' and 'I should think' remain less dogmatic (and therefore more polite) ways of saying 'it appears' and 'I think'.

(7) Split infinitive

The well-known rule against splitting an infinitive means that nothing must come between *to* and the verb ('to wantonly split the infinitive' splits the infinitive). It is a bad name, as was pointed out by Jespersen, a grammarian as broadminded as he was erudite:

> This name is bad because we have many infinitives without *to*, as 'I made him go'. *To* therefore is no more an essential part of an infinitive than the definite article is an essential part of a nominative, and no one would think of calling 'the good man' a split nominative. (*Growth and Structure of the English Language*, 1905)

It is also a bad rule: it makes for ambiguity by inducing writers to place adverbs in unnatural and even misleading positions. Consider the following:

He decided gradually to kill himself.

The hailstones failed completely to melt.

She chose properly to rewrite the letter.

Was the decision to commit suicide a gradual one, or was the suicide itself particularly slow? Did the hailstones melt almost completely, or melt not at all? Was it proper to choose to rewrite the letter, or was the rewriting of it to be done properly?

The split infinitive taboo, leading as it does to the putting of adverbs in awkward places, is so potent that it produces an impulse to place adverbs awkwardly even when there is no infinitive to split. I have myself been taken to task by a correspondent for splitting an infinitive because I wrote 'I gratefully record'. My critic was, no doubt, under the influence of the taboo to an exceptional extent. But sufferers from the same malady in a milder form can be found on every hand. We cannot doubt that the writer of the sentence 'they appeared completely to have adjusted themselves to it' put the adverb in that uncomfortable position from a misplaced fear that to write 'to have completely adjusted' would be to split an infinitive. The same fear, probably subconscious, may also be presumed to account for the unnatural placing of the adverb in 'so tangled is the web that I cannot pretend for a moment that we have succeeded entirely in unweaving it'. In this there was no possibility of splitting an infinitive because there is no infinitive.

The split infinitive bogy is having such a devastating effect that some people feel it must be wrong to put an adverb between any auxiliary and any part of a verb, or between a preposition and any part of a verb; but the infinitive can be split only by inserting a word or words between *to* and the word that, with *to*, forms the infinitive of the verb. 'To fully understand' is a split infinitive. 'To have fully understood' is not.

Rebels against the taboo will find themselves in good company. George Bernard Shaw was emphatically on their side. In a letter of 1892 to the *Chronicle*, he rounded on a 'fatuous specialist' who had attacked the split infinitive, calling him 'an ignoramus, an idiot' and 'a self-advertising duffer'. In a similar letter of 1907, Shaw wrote to *The Times*:

> There is a busybody on your staff who devotes a lot of time to chasing split infinitives. Every good literary craftsman splits his infinitives when the sense demands it. I call for the immediate dismissal of this pedant. It is of no consequence whether he decides to go quickly, or quickly to go, or to quickly go. The important thing is that he should go at once.

But the most vigorous rebel could hardly condone splitting so resolute as the crescendo of this lease:

The tenant hereby agrees:

    (i)   to pay the said rent;
   (ii) to properly clean all the windows;
  (iii) to at all times properly empty all closets;
  (iv) to immediately any litter or disorder shall have been made by him or for his purpose on the staircase or landings or any other part of the said building or garden remove the same.

Note. In the quotation above, Shaw writes, 'It is of no consequence whether he decides to go quickly, or quickly to go, or to quickly go'. But it is of *some* consequence, as the fatuous, self-advertising duffer might wish to protest. 'He decides quickly to go' may mean his decision is made quickly (his decision to go in a year, perhaps). 'He decides to go quickly' means he decides not only to go, but to go without delay. As for the third version, 'to quickly go', there is neither further sense to be gleaned nor lyrical advantage to be gained from this splitting of an infinitive. And the same could be said of Gowers's examples above—about gradual suicide, melting hailstones and a properly rewritten letter: though in all three sentences the adverb needs to be moved to make the intended meaning clear, there is no need in any of them to split the infinitive in order to accomplish this.

A standard example of a split infinitive that cannot be avoided—except by rewriting the sentence to eliminate the infinitive itself—is one on this pattern: 'She managed to more than triple her output'. If 'more than' is put anywhere else in this sentence, the meaning ceases to be watertight, or changes to something else. Either the subject is credited with achieving more and other than a tripling of output: 'She managed more than to triple her output' (she also quadrupled her list of clients), or the subject triples more than her output alone: 'She managed to triple more than her output' (she also tripled her orders).

Gowers wrote that the rule against the split infinitive was an 'arbitrary fetish', yet he advised officials to stick to the rule on the ground that 'readers will almost certainly attribute departures from it to ignorance of it'. He later admitted that this 'safety-first' approach, which he followed in his own writing, had caused a friend to accuse him of being 'little better than a coward'.

Not until the end of the twentieth century would the Civil Service choose to demonstrate in the most prominent way possible that it had the courage of Gowers's convictions, though he himself never did. The Queen's Speech of November 1999 was naturally dominated by infinitives, but for the first time in history the Queen was caused to split one of them. From a golden throne, she read out the words 'to racially discriminate'. In the subsequent debate on the Speech in the House of Lords, objection was raised to the fact that such a monstrous utterance had been put into the Queen's mouth. The response to this was misleading in more ways than one: 'My Lords, what is good enough for Sir Ernest Gowers is good enough for the Sovereign'.

Though the highest grammatical authorities, aided by innumerable ordinary English speakers, have for decades attempted to demolish the prejudice against the split infinitive, there is great resistance to these efforts, and the taboo remains enormously popular. It follows that even today if you ignore Gowers's cowardly example and, as the Queen did, split an infinitive, you leave yourself open to being thought ignorant. It follows with equal force, however, that you have no great authority for judging others ignorant when they split theirs. ~

X
PUNCTUATION

... that learned men are well known to disagree on this matter of punctuation is in itself a proof, that the knowledge of it, in theory and practice, is of some importance. I myself have learned by experience, that, if ideas that are difficult to understand are properly separated, they become clearer; and that, on the other hand, through defective punctuation, many passages are confused and distorted to such a degree, that sometimes they can with difficulty be understood, or even cannot be understood at all.

ALDUS MANUTIUS, *Interpungendi Ratio*, 1566
(trans. T. F. and M. F. A. Husband, 1905)

This is a large subject. Whole books have been written about it, and it is still true, as it apparently was some five hundred years ago, that no two authorities completely agree. Taste and common sense are more important than any rules. You put in punctuation marks or 'stops' to help your reader to understand you, not to please grammarians; but you should try to write so that your reader will understood you with a minimum of help of that sort. The Fowlers, in *The King's English*, say:

it is a sound principle that as few stops should be used as will do the work ... Every one should make up his mind not to depend on his stops. They are to be regarded as devices, not for saving

him the trouble of putting his words into the order that naturally gives the required meaning, but for saving his reader the
moment or two that would sometimes, without them, be necessarily spent on reading the sentence twice over, once to catch the
general arrangement, and again for the details. It may almost be
said that what reads wrongly if the stops are removed is radically
bad; stops are not to alter meaning, but merely to show it up.
Those who are learning to write should make a practice of putting down all they want to say without stops first. What then, on
reading over, naturally arranges itself contrary to the intention
should be not punctuated, but altered; and the stops should be as
few as possible, consistently with the recognized rules.

The symbols we shall have to consider in this chapter are the
apostrophe, colon, comma, dash, full stop, hyphen, inverted commas, question mark, semicolon. It will also be a suitable place to
say something about capital letters, paragraphs, parentheses and
sentences.

APOSTROPHE

The only uses of the apostrophe that call for notice are (1) its use
to denote the possessive of names ending in *s*, and of pronouns;
(2) its use before a final *s* to show that the *s* is forming the plural of
a word or symbol not ordinarily admitting of a plural; and (3) its
use with a defining plural.

(1) There is no universally accepted code that governs how one
forms the possessive case of names ending in *s*, but the most desirable practice (especially with monosyllables) seems to be not just to
put an apostrophe at the end of the word, as one does with an ordinary plural (strangers' gallery), but to add a second *s*—Mr Jones's
room, St James's Street, not Mr Jones' room, St James' Street.

As to pronouns, all these except the pronoun *one* dispense with an apostrophe in their possessive cases—*hers*, *yours*, *theirs*, *ours* and *its*, but *one's* not *ones* (and *someone's*, *anybody's*, *everyone's*, *nobody's* etc.). *It's* is not the possessive of *it* but a contraction of 'it is': the apostrophe is performing its duty of showing that a letter has been omitted.

(2) Whether an apostrophe should be used to denote the plural of a word or symbol that does not ordinarily make a plural depends on whether the plural is readily recognisable as such. Unless readers are really likely to need help, it should not be thrust upon them. This practice is clearly justified with single letters: 'there are two o's in woolly'; 'mind your p's and q's'. Otherwise it is rarely called for. It should not be used with contractions (e.g. MPs), or merely because what is put into the plural is not a noun. Editors of Shakespeare do without an apostrophe in the line from *Richard III*, 'Talk'st thou to me of "ifs"'. And Rudyard Kipling did not think it necessary when he wrote, in the *Just So Stories*:

> One million Hows, two million Wheres,
> And seven million Whys!

(3) Whether one should use an apostrophe in such expressions as 'thirty years imprisonment' is a disputed and not very important point. The answer seems to be that if *thirty years* is regarded as a descriptive genitive or 'possessive', as *busman's* is in *busman's holiday*, we must write *thirty years' imprisonment*. But if 'thirty years' is taken to be an adjectival phrase (equivalent here to 'three-decades-long'), there must be no apostrophe but the words must be hyphenated: *thirty-years imprisonment*.* The singular form ('a year's imprisonment') can only be a descriptive genitive, but in such phrases as 'games master' and 'customs examination', the words *games* and *customs* are clearly adjectival, and need no apostrophe.

---

* On hyphens see also pp. 255–7.

CAPITALS

Several correspondents have asked me to write about the use of capital letters. The difficulty is to know what to say. No one needs telling that capitals are used for the first letter in every sentence, for proper names and the names of the months and days, and for the titles of books and newspapers. The only difficulty is with words that are sometimes written with capitals and sometimes not. Here there can be no general rule; we are free to do what we think most fitting. But two pieces of advice may perhaps be given:

(1) Use a capital for a particular and a small letter for the general. Thus:

> It is a street leading out of Oxford Street.

> I have said something about this in Chapter I; I shall have more to say in later chapters.

> In this case the Judge went beyond a judge's proper functions.

> Many parliaments have been modelled on our Parliament.

(2) Whatever practice you adopt, be consistent throughout any document you are writing.

Colon

About the use of the colon there is even less agreement among the authorities than about the use of other stops. All agree that its systematic use as one of a series of different pause-values has almost died out with the decay of the formal 'period': the single sentence that contains a number of well-balanced clauses. One person will hold that the colon is still useful as something less than a full stop and more than a semicolon; another will deny it. We need not enter into this. It will be enough to note that the following uses are generally regarded as legitimate:

(1) To mark more sharply than a semicolon would the antithesis between two sentences:

> In peace time the Civil Service is a target of frequent criticism: in war time the criticism is very greatly increased.

> In some cases the executive carries out most of the functions: in others the delegation is much less extensive.

(2) To precede an explanation or particularisation or to produce a list or series: in the words of Fowler, to deliver 'the goods that have been invoiced in the preceding words':

> The design of the school was an important part of the scheme: Post Office counters with all the necessary stores were available and maps and framed specimens of the various documents in use were exhibited on the walls of light and cheery classrooms.

> News reaches a national paper from two sources: the news agencies and its own correspondents.

For the second purpose the dash is the colon's weaker relative.

COMMA

The use of commas cannot be learned by rule. Not only does conventional practice vary from one period to another, but good writers of the same period differ among themselves. Moreover, stops have two kinds of duty. One is to show the construction of sentences—the 'grammatical' duty. The other is to introduce nuances into the meaning—the 'rhetorical' duty. 'I went to his house and I found him there' is a colourless statement. 'I went to his house, and I found him there' hints that it was not quite a matter of course that he should have been found there. 'I went to his house. And I found him there' indicates that to find him there was surprising. Similarly you can give a different nuance to what you write by encasing adverbs or adverbial phrases in commas. 'He was, apparently, willing to support you' throws a shade of doubt on his bona fides that is not present in 'He was apparently willing to support you'.

The correct use of the comma—if there is such a thing as 'correct' use—can only be acquired by common sense, observation and taste. Present practice is markedly different from that of the past in using commas much less freely. The sixteenth-century passage that heads this chapter, translated to keep its original punctuation intact, is peppered with them with a liberality not approved by modern practice.

I shall attempt no more than to point out some traps that commas set for the unwary. First I shall deal with some uses of the comma that are generally regarded as incorrect, and then I shall consider various uses which, though they may not be incorrect, need special care in the handing, or are questionable.

A. Incorrect uses of commas

(1) The use of a comma between two independent sentences not linked by a conjunction. The usual practice is to use a heavier stop in this position:

> The Department cannot guarantee that a license will be issued, you should therefore not arrange for any shipment.

> You may not be aware that a Youth Employment Service is operating throughout the country, in some areas it is under the control of the Ministry of Labour and National Service and in others of the Education Authorities.

> I regret the delay in replying to your letter but Mr X who was dealing with it is on leave, however, I have gone into the matter . . .

On the principle that in workaday writing of this kind, sentences should be short and should have unity of thought, it would be better to put a full stop after *issued* in the first quotation, *country* in the second and *leave* in the third. (See also the entry below on the semicolon, pp. 264–5).

(2) The use of one comma instead of either a pair or none. This very common blunder is more easily illustrated than explained. It is almost like using one only of a pair of brackets. Words that are parenthetical may be able to do without any commas, but if there is a comma at one end of them there must be one at the other end too:

> Against all this must be set considerations which, in our submission are overwhelming. (Omit the comma.)

> The first is the acute shortage that so frequently exists, of suitable premises where people can come together. (Omit the comma.)

> We should be glad if you would inform us for our record purposes, of any agency agreement finally reached. (Either omit the comma or insert one after *us*.)

> It will be noted that for the development areas, Treasury-financed projects are to be grouped together. (Either omit the comma or insert one after *that*.)

> The principal purpose is to provide for the division between the minister and the governing body concerned, of premises and property held partly for hospital purposes and partly for other purposes. (Omit the comma.)

(3) The use of commas with 'defining' relative clauses. Relative clauses fall into two main classes. Grammarians give them different labels, but 'defining' and 'commenting' are the most convenient and descriptive. If you say 'the man who was here this

morning told me everything', the relative clause *who was here this morning* is a defining one: it completes the subject *the man*, which conveys no definite meaning without it. But if you say 'Jones, who was here this morning, told me everything', the relative clause is commenting: the subject *Jones* is already complete, and the relative clause merely adds a bit of information about him (it may or may not be important, but is not essential to the definition of the subject). A commenting clause should be within commas. A defining clause should not. This is not an arbitrary rule; it is a utilitarian one. If you do not observe it, you may fail to make your meaning clear, or you may even say something different from what you intended. For instance:

> A particular need of the moment is provision for young women, who owing to war conditions have been deprived of normal opportunities of learning homecraft . . .

Here the comma announces that the relative clause is a commenting one, designed to imply that the mass of young women had this need, with war conditions as the explanation. Without the comma the clause would be read as a defining one, limiting the need to the particular young women who had in fact been deprived of these opportunities ('those young women who owing to war conditions have been deprived . . .').

The commas are definitely wrong in:

> Any expenditure incurred on major awards to students, who are not recognised for assistance from the Ministry, will rank for grant . . .

The relative clause must be a defining one, but the commas suggest that it is a commenting one, and imply that no students are recognised for assistance from the Ministry.

In the next quotation too the relative clause is a defining one:

I have made enquiries, and find that the clerk, who dealt with
your query, recorded the name of the firm correctly.

The comma turns the relative clause into a commenting one and
implies that the writer has only one clerk. The truth is that one
of several is being singled out, and this is made clear if the commas after *clerk* and *query* are omitted.

The same mistake is made in:

> The Ministry issues permits to employing authorities to enable
> foreigners to land in this country for the purpose of taking up
> employment, for which British subjects are not available.

The grammatical implication of this is that employment in general is not a thing for which British subjects are available.

An instruction book called 'Pre-aircrew English', supplied
during the war to airmen in training in Canada, contained
an encouragement to its readers to 'smarten up their English',
adding:

> Pilots, whose minds are dull, do not usually live long.

The commas convert a truism into an insult.

(4) The insertion of a meaningless comma into an 'absolute
phrase'. An absolute phrase* always has parenthetic commas
around it, e.g. 'then, the work being finished, we went home'. But
there is no sense in the comma that so often carelessly appears
inside it. For instance:

> The House of Commons, having passed the third reading by a
> large majority after an animated debate, the Bill was sent to
> the Lords.

* See also p. 222.

The first comma leaves the House of Commons in the air waiting for a verb that never comes.

(5) The use of commas in an endeavour to clarify faultily constructed sentences. It is instructive to compare the following extracts from two documents issued by the same department:

> It should be noted that the officer who ceased to pay insurance contributions before the date of commencement of his emergency service, remained uninsured for a period, varying between eighteen months and two-and-a-half years, from the date of his last contribution and would, therefore, be compulsorily insured if his emergency service commenced during that period.

> Officers appointed to emergency commissions direct from civil life who were not insured for health or pensions purposes at the commencement of emergency service are not compulsorily insured during service.

Why should the first of these extracts be full of commas and the second have none? The answer can only be that, whereas the second sentence is reasonably short and clear, the first is long and obscure. The writer tried to help the reader by putting in five commas, but all this achieved was to give the reader five jolts. The only place where there might properly have been a comma is after *contribution*, and there the writer has omitted to put one.

Another example of the abuse of a comma is:

> Moreover, directions and consents at the national level are essential prerequisites in a planned economy, whereas they were only necessary for the establishment of standards for grant-aid and borrowing purposes, in the comparatively free system of yesterday.

The proper place for *in the comparatively free system of yesterday* is after *whereas*, and it is a poor second best to try to throw it back there by putting a comma in front of it.

(6) The use of a comma to mark the end of the subject of a verb, or the beginning of the object. It cannot be said to be always wrong to use a comma to mark the end of a composite subject, because good writers sometimes do it deliberately. For instance, one might write:

> The question whether it is legitimate to use a comma to mark the end of the subject, is an arguable one.

But the comma is unnecessary. The reader does not need its help. To use commas in this way is a dangerous habit; it encourages writers to shirk the trouble of arranging each sentence so as to make its meaning plain without punctuation.

> I am however to draw your attention to the fact that goods subject to import licensing which are despatched to this country without the necessary license having first been obtained, are on arrival liable to seizure.

If the subject is so long that it seems to need a boundary post at the end, it would be better not to use the slovenly device of a comma but to rewrite the sentence in conditional form:

> ... if goods subject to import license are despatched ... they are on arrival ...

And in the following sentence, the comma merely interrupts the flow:

> I am now in a position to say that all the numerous delegates who have replied, heartily endorse the recommendation.

Postponement of the object may get the writer into the same trouble:

> In the case of both whole-time and part-time officers, the general duties undertaken by them include the duty of treating

without any additional remuneration and without any right to
recover private fees, patients in their charge who are occupying
Section 5 accommodation under the proviso to Section 5 (I) of
the Act.

This unlovely sentence obviously needs recasting. One way of
doing this would be:

The general duties undertaken by both whole-time and part-
time officers include the treating of patients in their charge
who are occupying Section 5 accommodation under the
proviso to Section 5 (I) of the Act, and they are not entitled to
receive additional remuneration for it or to recover private
fees.

(7) The use of commas before a clause beginning with *that*.
A comma was at one time always used in this position:

It is a just though trite observation, that victorious Rome was
herself subdued by the arts of Greece.   (Gibbon, 1776)

the true meaning is so uncertain and remote, that it is never
sought, because it cannot be known when it is found.
(Dr Johnson, 1781)

It is a truth universally acknowledged, that a single man in
possession of a good fortune, must be in want of a wife.
(Jane Austen, 1813)

We are more sparing of commas nowadays, and this practice
has gone out of fashion. In his book of 1939, *Mind the Stop*,
Mr G. V. Carey goes so far as to write, 'it is probably true to
say that immediately before the conjunction "that" a comma
will be admissible more rarely than before any other conjunction'.

248

B. Uses of commas that need special care

If we turn from uses of the comma generally regarded as incorrect to those generally regarded as legitimate, we find one or two that need special care.

(1) The use of commas with adverbs and adverbial phrases.

(*a*) *At the beginning of sentences.*

> In their absence, it will be desirable ...
>
> Nevertheless, there is need for special care ...
>
> In practice, it has been found advisable ...

Some writers put a comma here as a matter of course. But others do it only if a comma is needed to emphasise a contrast or to prevent a reader from going off on a wrong scent, as in:

> A few days after, the Minister of Labour promised that a dossier of the strike would be published.
>
> Two miles on, the road is worse.

On the principle that stops should not be used unless they are needed, this discrimination is to be commended.

(*b*) *Within sentences.*   To enclose an adverb in commas is, as we have seen, a legitimate and useful way of emphasising it. 'All these things may, eventually, come to pass' is another way of saying 'All these things may come to pass—eventually'. Or it may serve to emphasise the subject of the sentence: 'He, perhaps, thought differently'. The commas underline *he*. But certain common adverbs such as *therefore*, *however*, *perhaps*, *of course*, present difficulties because of a convention that they should always be enclosed in commas, whether emphasised or not. This is dangerous. The only safe course is to treat the question as one not of rule but of common sense, and to judge each case on its merits. Lord Dunsany, in his *Donnellan Lectures*, blames printers for this convention:

The writer puts down 'I am going to Dublin perhaps, with Murphy'. Or he writes 'I am going to Dublin, perhaps with Murphy'. But in either case these pestilent commas swoop down, not from his pen, but from the darker parts of the cornices where they were bred in the printer's office, and will alight on either side of the word *perhaps*, making it impossible for the reader to know the writer's meaning, making it impossible to see whether the doubt implied by the word *perhaps* affected Dublin or Murphy. I will quote an actual case I saw in a newspaper. A naval officer was giving evidence before a court, and said, 'I decided on an alteration of course'. But since the words 'of course' must always be surrounded by commas, the printer's commas came down on them ... and the sentence read, 'I decided upon an alteration, of course'!

The adverb *however* is especially likely to stand in need of clarifying commas. For instance, Burke, in 1791, wrote:

> The author is compelled, however reluctantly, to receive the sentence pronounced upon him in the House of Commons as that of the party.

The meaning of this sentence would be different if the comma after 'reluctantly' were omitted, and one inserted after 'however':

> The author is compelled, however, reluctantly to receive the sentence pronounced upon him ...

(2) The 'throwback' comma.   A common use of the comma as a clarifier is to show that what follows it refers not to what immediately precedes it but to something further back. William Cobbett, in the grammar that he wrote for his young son, pointed out that 'you will be rich if you be industrious, in a few years' did not mean the same as 'you will be rich, if you be industrious in a few years'. He added:

The first sentence means, that you will, *in a few years' time*, be rich, if you be industrious *now*. The second means, that you will be rich, *some time or other*, if you be industrious *in a few years from this time*.

In the first sentence the comma that precedes the adverbial phrase 'in a few years' is a clumsy device. The proper way of writing this sentence is 'you will be rich in a few years if you be industrious'. If words are arranged in the right order these artificial aids will rarely be necessary.*

(3) Commas in series.

(*a*) *Nouns and phrases*.   Below is a list of nouns:

The company included ambassadors, ministers, bishops and judges.

In a sentence such as this one commas are always put after each item in the series up to the last but one, but practice varies about putting a comma between the last but one, and the *and* introducing the last: 'ministers, bishops, and judges'. Those who favour a comma there (a minority, but gaining ground) argue that, as a comma may sometimes be necessary to prevent ambiguity, there had better be one there always. Suppose the sentence were this:

The company included the bishops of Winchester, Salisbury, Bristol, and Bath and Wells.

The reader unversed in the English ecclesiastical hierarchy needs the comma after 'Bristol' in order to sort out the last two bishops. Without it they might be, grammatically and geographically, either (i) Bristol and Bath and (ii) Wells, or (i) Bristol and (ii) Bath and Wells. Ambiguity cannot be justified by saying that

---

* See also pp. 214–5 for the dangers of the throwback comma combined with *which*.

those who are interested will know what is meant and those who are not will not care.

(*b*) *Adjectives.* Where the series is of adjectives preceding a noun, it is a matter of taste whether there are commas between them or not. Both of these are correct:

A silly verbose pompous letter.

A silly, verbose, pompous letter.

The commas merely give a little emphasis to the adjectives. Where the final adjective is one that describes the species of the noun, it is regarded as part of the noun, and is not preceded by a comma. Thus:

A silly, verbose, pompous official letter.

DASH

The dash is seductive, tempting writers to use it as a punctuation-maid-of-all-work that saves them the trouble of choosing the right stop. We all know letter-writers who carry this habit to the length of relying on one punctuation mark only—a nondescript symbol that might be a dash or might be something else. Moreover the dash lends itself easily to rhetorical uses that may be out of place in humdrum prose. Perhaps that is why I have been tempted to go to Sir Winston Churchill's war speeches for examples of its recognised uses.

(1) In pairs for parenthesis:

no future generation of English-speaking folks—for that is the tribunal to which we appeal—will doubt that, even at a great cost to ourselves in technical preparation, we were guiltless of the bloodshed, terror and misery which have engulfed so many lands ...

(2) To introduce an explanation, amplification, paraphrase, particularisation or correction of what immediately precedes it:

> They were surely among the most noble and benevolent instincts of the human heart—the love of peace, the toil for peace, the strife for peace, the pursuit of peace, even at great peril ...
>
> overhead the far-ranging Catalina air-boats soared—vigilant, protecting eagles in the sky.
>
> the end of our financial resources was in sight—nay, had actually been reached.

(3) To indicate that the construction of the sentence, as begun, will be left unfinished (grammarians call this *anacoluthon*):

> But when you go to other countries—oddly enough I saw a message from the authorities who are most concerned with our Arab problem at present, urging that we should be careful not to indulge in too gloomy forecasts.

(4) To gather up the subject of a sentence when it is a very long one; after the long loose canter of the subject you need to collect your horse for the jump to the verb:

> The formidable power of Nazi Germany, the vast mass of destructive munitions that they have made or captured, the courage, skill and audacity of their striking forces, the ruthlessness of their centralised war-direction, the prostrate condition of so many great peoples under their yoke, the resources of so many lands which may to some extent become available to them—all these restrain rejoicing and forbid the slightest relaxation.

Similarly with the jump from the verb:

> I would say generally that we must regard all these victims of the Nazi executioners in so many lands, who are labelled

Communists and Jews—we must regard them just as if they were brave soldiers who die for their country on the field of battle.

(5) To introduce a paradoxical, humorous or whimsical ending to a sentence:

He makes mistakes, as I do, though not so many or so serious— he has not the same opportunities.

FULL STOP

The full stop is an exception to the rule that 'as few stops should be used as will do the work'. I have no advice to give about it except to say that it should be plentifully used: in other words, to repeat the advice I have already given that sentences should be short. I am not, of course, suggesting that good prose never contains long ones. On the contrary, the best prose is a judicious admixture of the long with the short. Mark Twain, in 1890, after advising the young author to write short sentences as a rule, added:

At times he may indulge himself with a long one, but he will make sure that there are no folds in it, no vaguenesses, no par- enthetical interruptions of its view as a whole; when he is done with it, it won't be a sea-serpent, with half its arches under the water, it will be a torchlight procession.

If you can write long sentences that you are satisfied really merit that description, by all means surprise and delight your readers with one occasionally. But the shorter ones are safer.*

---

* The *Guardian* supplies a splendid example of the species of parenthetical, half-submerged 'sea-serpent' sentence that Mark Twain attempted to warn

Always use a full stop to separate into two sentences statements between which there is no true continuity of thought. For example, *and* is too close a link in these sentences:

> There are 630 boys in the school and the term will end on April 1st.

> As regards Mr Smith's case a report was made on papers AB 340 and I understand he is now dead.

HYPHEN

In *Modern English Usage* Fowler makes an elaborate study of the hyphen. He begins engagingly by pointing out that 'a superfluous hair-remover' can only mean a hair-remover that nobody wants, and he proceeds to work out a code of rules for the proper use of the hyphen. He admits that the result of following his rules 'will often differ from current usage'. But, he adds, 'that usage is so variable as to be better named caprice'. In a style book of 1937 produced for the Oxford University Press, *Manuscript & Proof*, John Benbow strikes a similar note when he writes of a 'great twilight zone' in the use of hyphens, and says, 'If you take hyphens seriously you will surely go mad'.

I have no intention of taking hyphens seriously. Those who wish to do so I leave to Fowler's eleven columns. If I attempted to lay down any rules I should certainly go astray, and give advice

---

against: 'In a highly political family, daughter Rachel also worked for Brown at No. 10 while her older brother Stephen—born in 1970, a few months before his father, only child of a mining family from the closely knit Welsh valleys, became an MP—carved out a post-Cambridge career with the British Council'. This sentence may be boggling in many ways, but it is undoubtedly most boggling for its momentary suggestion of a son born some months before his own father. ~

not seemly to be followed. I will attempt no more than to give a few elementary warnings.

(1) Do not use hyphens unnecessarily. If, for instance, you must use *overall* as an adjective (though this is not recommended) write it like that, and not *over-all*. You need a hyphen to avoid puzzling your reader whether *coop* is something to put a hen in, or a profit-sharing association (*co-op*); but the word *cooperative* can be understood without, and is often written this way. Where you do split a word with a hyphen, make sure you split it at the main break.

(2) To prevent ambiguity a hyphen should be used in a compound adjective (e.g. *first-class*, *six-inch*, *copper-coloured*). The omission of a hyphen between 'government' and 'financed' in the following sentence throws the reader on to a false scent:

> When government financed projects in the development areas
> have been grouped . . .

But remember that words forming parts of compound adjectives when they precede a noun may stand on their own feet when they follow it, and then they need not be hyphenated. A 'second-hand car' needs a hyphen, but 'the car was second hand' does not. There must be hyphens in 'the balance-of-payment difficulties' but not in 'the difficulties are over the balance of payments'.

Note. Gowers's advice here is not wrong, but nowadays many writers will do without the hyphen in a compound adjective before a noun if the resulting sentence remains unambiguous ('When I went to the station to buy a first class ticket there was a tin pot dictator managing the queue'). If this is your habit, you must stay alert to the possibility of a misunderstanding. The idea was recently mooted that when universities weighed up applicants for places, pupils from 'low-performing schools' should be given an advantage over pupils from better schools. For want of a hyphen, one newspaper produced the following absurd account of the proposal: 'Exam board suggested awarding bonus points to low-performing school students who get top grades'.

NB when adverbs that end in *ly* are used in descriptive compounds, they do not need a hyphen ('a strongly worded complaint'; 'a densely argued report'). ~

(3) Avoid as far as possible the practice of separating a pair of hyphenated words, leaving a hyphen in mid-air. To do this is to misuse the hyphen (whose proper function is to link a word with its immediate neighbour) and it has a slovenly look. The saving of one word cannot justify writing 'where chaplains (whole- or part-time) have been appointed'. This should be, 'where chaplains have been appointed, whole-time or part-time'.

INVERTED COMMAS

I have read nothing more sensible about inverted commas than this:

> It is remarkable in an age peculiarly contemptuous of punctuation marks that we have not yet had the courage to abolish inverted commas ... After all, they are a modern invention. The Bible is plain enough without them; and so is the literature of the eighteenth century. Bernard Shaw scorns them. However, since they are with us, we must do our best with them, always trying to reduce them to a minimum. (H. A. Treble and G. H. Vallins, *An ABC of English Usage*)

I have only two other things to say on this vexatious topic.

The first question is whether punctuation marks (including question and exclamation marks) should come before or after the inverted commas that close a quotation. This has been much argued, with no conclusive result. It does not seem to me of great practical importance, but I feel bound to refer to it, if only because a correspondent criticised me for giving no guidance on the matter in an earlier edition of this book, and accused me of being manifestly shaky about it myself. The truth is that there is no settled practice governing this most complicated subject. Pages were written about it by the Fowlers in *The King's English*, but their conclusions are by no means universally accepted.

Most books on English advise that stops should be put in their logical positions. But what does that mean? There are two schools of thought. The first is exemplified, perhaps shakily, in this book, and is summarized below. Let us take this as our quotation:

> I guarantee that the parcel will be delivered, and on time.

If this is quoted as a free-standing sentence, its own stops remain inside the inverted commas:

> 'I guarantee', he wrote, 'that the parcel will be delivered,' adding emphatically, 'and on time.'

But if it is quoted as part of a longer sentence that embraces it, and the two end together with the same stop, the stop goes outside:

> He wrote: 'I guarantee that the parcel will be delivered, and on time'.

This applies even to a question mark:

> How could he possibly write afterwards, 'Why did you believe my guarantee'?

But if the two stops are different, a question mark trumps a full stop:

> How could he possibly write afterwards, 'I meant every word of it'?

> He dared to write afterwards, 'Why did you believe my guarantee?'

The second school of thought will not have this. Its adherents, including many publishers, dislike the look of stops outside inverted commas if they can possibly be put inside. But we need not concern ourselves here with questions of taste in printing. The drafter of official letters and memoranda is advised to stick to the principle of placing the punctuation marks according to the sense.*

The second thing I have to say on this topic is a repeat of my warning from the start of the book against over-indulgence in the trick of encasing words or phrases in inverted commas to indicate that they are being used in a slang or technical or facetious or some other unusual sense. This is a useful occasional device; instances may be found in this book. But it is a dangerous habit.

Note. Many people would no doubt still agree with Gowers that inverted commas can be taken to indicate a facetious or an unusual sense. But anyone in this camp is at risk of being disconcerted by the numerous other people who now use inverted commas merely for emphasis. The danger is illustrated by an article on 'the metrics of recruiting':

> With the role of human resources shifting from service and administration to strategic planning partner, we need to take on more accountability for how we impact the success of the business. The biggest impact we can make is on the 'human' resources the organization employs to maintain the business.

The phrase *human resources* is used here first to refer to the specialists who manage an entire workforce, and second, to the workers themselves. In the second instance, in an attempt to

---

* Gowers's preferred system of punctuation has largely fallen out of fashion, though it is still used here and there, for instance in the *Times Literary Supplement*. ~

emphasise that the resources to be 'impacted' are of the living, breathing kind, the word *human* has been put in inverted commas. Yet the effect on those who read inverted commas to mean 'please note that I am using this word facetiously' will be the reverse of the one intended: to them it must seem that the workers are being dismissed—in an offensively conspiratorial manner—as somehow *less* than human. (Either way, the meaning of the second sentence appears to amount to little more than 'In order to do our job we should do our job'.) ~

PARAGRAPHS

Letters, reports, memoranda and other documents would be unreadable if they were not divided into paragraphs, and much has been written on the art of paragraphing. But little of it helps the ordinary writer; the subject does not admit of precise guidance. The chief thing to remember is that, although paragraphing loses all point if the paragraphs are excessively long, the paragraph is essentially a unit of thought, not of length. For the sake of clarity, every paragraph should be homogeneous in subject matter, and sequential in treatment of it. If a single sequence of treatment of a single subject goes on so long as to make an unreasonably long paragraph, it may be divided into more than one. But you should not do the opposite, and combine into a single paragraph passages that have not this unity, even though each by itself may be below the average length of a paragraph.

PARENTHESIS

The purpose of a parenthesis is ordinarily to insert an illustration, explanation, definition, or additional piece of information of any sort, into a sentence that is logically and grammatically complete without it. A parenthesis may be marked off by commas, dashes or brackets. The degree of interruption of the main sentence will vary. Explanatory words that parallel the subject can be almost imperceptible:

> Mr Smith, the secretary, read the minutes.

But the interruption may be the violent one of a separate sentence complete in itself:

> A memorandum (six copies of this memorandum are enclosed for the information of the board) has been issued to management committees.

Parentheses should be used sparingly. Their very convenience is a reason for fighting shy of them. They enable writers to dodge the trouble of arranging their thoughts properly. But a writer's thoughts are left badly arranged at the expense of the reader, especially if the thought that has been spatchcocked into the sentence forms an abrupt break in it, or a lengthy one, or both. The second of the two examples just given shows an illegitimate use of the parenthesis. The writer had no business to keep the reader waiting for the verb by throwing in a parenthesis that would have been put better as a separate sentence. The following examples are even worse:

> to regard day nurseries and daily guardians as supplements to meet the special needs (where these exist and cannot be met within the hours, age, range and organisation of nursery schools and nursery classes) of children whose mothers are constrained by individual circumstances to go out to work ...

> If duties are however declined in this way, it will be necessary for the Board to consider whether it should agree to a modified contract in the particular case, or whether—because the required service can be provided only by the acceptance of the rejected obligations (e.g. by a whole-time radiologist to

perform radiological examinations of paying patients in Section 5 beds in a hospital where the radiologists are all whole-time officers)—the Board should seek the services of another practitioner ...

These are intolerable abuses of the parenthesis, the first with its interposition of twenty-one words in the middle of the phrase 'needs of children', and the second with its double parenthesis, more than forty words long, like two snakes eating each other. There was no need for either of these monstrosities. In both examples the main sentence should be allowed to finish without interruption, and what is now in the parenthesis, so far as it is worth saying, should be added at the end:

to regard day nurseries and daily guardians as supplements to meet the special needs of children whose mothers are constrained ...and whose needs cannot be met ...

or whether the Board should seek the services of another practitioner, as they will have to do if the required service can be provided only ...

Here is a parenthesis that keeps the reader waiting so long for the verb that the subject is easily forgotten:

Close affiliation with University research in haematology— and it may be desirable that ultimately each Regional Transfusion Officer should have an honorary appointment in the department of pathology in the medical school—will help to attract into the service medical men of good professional standing.

In former days, when long and involved sentences were fashionable, it was customary after a lengthy parenthesis to put the reader on the road again by repeating the subject with the words 'I say'. Thus the last example would run:

Close affiliation with University research in haematology—and it may be desirable that ultimately each Regional Transfusion Officer should have an honorary appointment in the department of pathology in the medical school—close affiliation with University research in haematology, I say, will help to attract into the service medical men . . .

Now that this handy device has fallen into disuse,* there is all the more need not to keep the reader waiting. There was no necessity to do so here. What is said as a parenthesis might just as well have been said as an independent sentence following the main one.

It is not only the reader but also the writer who sometimes forgets where the sentence was when the parenthesis started, as in the letter quoted in Chapter III:

> owing to a shortage of a spare pair of wires to the underground cable (a pair of wires leading from the point near your house right back to the local exchange and thus a pair of wires essential for the provision of service for you) is lacking . . .

The writer imagined that the parenthesis started after the words 'owing to *the fact that* a spare pair of wires to the underground cable', and continued conformably afterwards.

QUESTION MARKS

Only direct questions need question marks. Indirect ones do not. There must be one at the end of 'Have you completed your tax

---

* George Eliot uses the 'I say' device in *Middlemarch*: 'Brother Jonah, for example (there are such unpleasant people in most families; perhaps even in the highest aristocracy there are Brobdingnag specimens, gigantically in debt and bloated at greater expense)—Brother Jonah, I say, having come down in the world . . .' But in modern writing this use of 'I say' would be likely to invite what Gowers calls elsewhere 'the prick of ridicule'. ~

return?' but not at the end of 'I am writing to ask whether you have completed your tax return'.

It is usual to put question marks at the end of requests cast into question form for the sake of politeness. 'Will you please let me know whether you have completed your tax return?'

SEMICOLON

Do not be afraid of the semicolon; it can be most useful. It marks a longer pause, a more definite break in the sense, than the comma; at the same time it says 'Here is a clause or sentence too closely related to what has gone before to be cut off by a full stop'.

The semicolon is useful for avoiding the rather dreary trailing participles with which writers often end their sentences:

> The postgraduate teaching hospitals are essentially national in their outlook, their geographical situation being merely incidental.

> An attempt to devise permanent machinery for consultation was unsuccessful, the initial lukewarm response having soon disappeared.

There is nothing faulty in the grammar or syntax of these sentences, and the meaning of each is unambiguous. But they have a tired look. They can be wonderfully freshened by using the semicolon, and rewriting them:

> The postgraduate teaching hospitals are essentially national in their outlook; their geographical situation is merely incidental.

> An attempt to devise permanent machinery for consultation was unsuccessful; the initial lukewarm response soon disappeared.

Note. Gowers was a great advocate of the semicolon and used it liberally in his writing. But it is no longer popular, and many writers now do without it altogether. His first sentence above ('Do not be afraid of the semicolon; it can be most useful') would by most writers today probably be given in one of the following ways:

> Do not be afraid of the semicolon. It can be most useful.
> Do not be afraid of the semicolon as it can be most useful.
> Do not be afraid of the semicolon: it can be most useful.

If it is really fear that is leading to the semicolon's neglect, then this is fear at the expense of subtlety. In an address that Gowers gave in 1957, 'H. W. Fowler: The Man and his Teaching', he demonstrated a use of semicolons that cannot be bettered by any other style of punctuation. Gowers wished to tell the story of how Fowler lost his job as a schoolmaster. Fowler, who was not a professing Christian, had refused to prepare the boys in his charge for Confirmation, and as a result was overlooked for a housemastership when a post fell vacant. This is Gowers's summary of what happened next:

> He protested; the headmaster was firm; and Fowler resigned.

Here the semicolons quietly suggest that these episodes in Fowler's life succeeded one another like toppling dominoes. ~

SENTENCES

A sentence is not easy to define. Many learned grammarians have tried, and their definitions have been torn to pieces by other learned grammarians. But what most of us understand by a sentence is what the *OED* calls the 'popular' definition: 'such a portion of a composition or utterance as extends from one full stop to another'. That definition is good enough for our present purposes, so the question we have to consider is the general guidance that can be given about what to put between one full stop and the next.

The two main things to be remembered about sentences if you want to make your meaning plain is that they should be short and should have unity of thought. Here is a series of eighty-six words between one full stop and another that violates all the canons of a good sentence. In fact this example might be said to explode the definition, for it would be flattering to call it a 'sentence'. A friend who was good enough to look through this book in proof called it instead 'gibberish'.

> Forms are only sent to applicants whose requirements exceed one ton, and in future, as from tomorrow, forms will only be sent to firms whose requirements exceed five tons, and as you have not indicated what your requirements are, I am not sending you forms at the moment because it is just possible that your requirements may be well within these quantities quoted, in which case you may apply direct to the usual suppliers, of which there are several, with a view to obtaining your requirements.

If we prune this of its verbiage, and split it into three short sentences, a meaning will begin to emerge:

> Only firms whose requirements exceed five tons now need forms. Others can apply direct to the suppliers. As you do not say what your requirements are I will not send you a form unless I hear that you need one.

The following is an even worse example of a meandering stream of words masquerading as a sentence:

> Further to your letter of the above date and reference in connection with an allocation of . . ., as already pointed out to you all the allocations for this period have been closed, and I there-

fore regret that it is not possible to add to the existing allocation which has been made to you and which covers *in toto* your requirements for this period when originally received, by virtue of the work on which you are engaged, a rather higher percentage has been given to you, namely 100 per cent of the original requirements and at this stage I am afraid it is not practicable for you to increase the requirement for the reasons already given.

The fault here is more one of excessive verbiage than of combining into a single sentence what ought to have been given in several. Indeed the thought is simple. It can be conveyed simply thus:

Your original application was granted in full because of the importance of your work. I regret that the amount cannot now be increased, as allocation for this period has been closed.

XI
EPILOGUE

> He that wyll wryte well in any tongue, muste folowe thys
> councel of Aristotle, to speake as the comon people do, to
> thinke as wise men do : and so shoulde euery man vnderstande
> hym, and the iudgement of wyse men alowe hym.
>
> ROGER ASCHAM, *Toxophilus*, 1545

A book designed as a guide to officials in the use of English
runs the risk of giving a false impression. It cannot help being
concerned mainly with faults to be corrected, and so may make
the picture look blacker than it is. The true justification for such
a book is not so much that official English is especially bad, as
that it is especially important for it to be good. The efficiency of
government, central and local, depends to an ever-increasing
extent on the ability of a large number of officials to express
themselves clearly. At present there is a popular idea that
most of them cannot—or will not—do so. The term *officialese* has
been invented for what is supposed to be their ineffective way of
trying.

I do not know exactly what the word means, and for once the
Oxford English Dictionary is not illuminating. It defines *officialese*
unhelpfully as 'the language characteristic of officials or official

documents'.* Even with the illustrations the *OED* cites we are left in some doubt about the true characteristics of this language. But that *officialese* is not ordinarily used as a term of praise is certain.

I should be sorry to be thought to support the popular notion that officials write a language of their own of a uniquely deplorable kind. Undoubtedly they have their peculiar faults of style. So have journalists theirs. It is reasonable to attribute those of officials in the main to the peculiar difficulties with which they have to contend. Much of their energy has to be devoted to the task of translating the language of the law into terms that are simple and yet free from ambiguity, a Herculean undertaking when the original has been made obscure precisely in order that it should be unambiguous. Moreover our system of government imposes on officials the need always of being cautious and often of avoiding a precision of statement that might be politically dangerous. And officials do not easily shake off the idea that dignity of position demands dignity of diction. But it is certainly wrong to imagine that official writing, as an instrument for conveying thought, is generally inferior to the lamentably low standard now prevalent except among professional writers. It is not only officials who yield to the lure of the pompous or meretricious word, and overwork it; it is not they alone who sometimes fail to think clearly what meaning they want to convey by what they are about to write, or to revise and prune what they have written so as to make sure that they have conveyed it. From some common faults the official is comparatively free. Most write grammatically correct English. Their style is untainted by the silly jargon of commercialese, the catchpenny tricks of the worst sort

---

* Since Gowers wrote this, the *OED* has gone further, describing *officialese* as 'formal and typically verbose' and 'turgid or pedantic'. ~

of journalism, the more nebulous nebulosities of politicians, or the recondite abstractions of Greek or Latin origin in which men of science, philosophers and economists often wrap up their thoughts.* Sometimes their writing is very good, but then no one notices it. Occasionally it is excellent.

The fact is not that officials do uniquely badly, but that they are uniquely vulnerable. Making fun of them has always been one of the diversions of the British public. The fun sometimes has a touch of malice in it, but the habit springs from qualities in the British character that no one would like to see atrophied. The field for its exercise and the temptation to indulge in it are constantly growing. *De facto* executive power, which during the seventeenth and eighteenth centuries moved from monarchs to ministers, is being diffused lower still by the growth of social legislation. Tennyson's 'fierce light which beats upon a throne, And blackens every blot' is no longer focused on the apex, but shines on the whole pyramid. So many people have to read so many official instructions. These offer a bigger target for possible criticism than any other class of writing except journalism, and are more likely to get it than any other class, because our critical faculties as readers are sharpened by being told—as we all so often have to be nowadays—that we cannot do something we want to, or must do something we do not want to, or that we can only do something we want to by going through a lot of tiresome formalities.

So it is natural enough that official writing, undeniably inclined towards certain idiosyncrasies of style, should have been worked up into a stock joke. The professional humorist, in print or on the stage or on the air, by quoting or inventing bits of it can always be sure of a laugh. It is a way of getting one's own back,

* But see pp. 141–2. ~

and is pleasantly flattering to the critics' sense of superiority. Walter Bagehot once pictured the public of his day as saying to themselves with unction:

> Thank God, *I* am not as that man; *I* did not send green coffee to the Crimea; *I* did not send patent cartridge to the common guns, and common cartridge to the breech loaders. *I* make money; that miserable public functionary only wastes money. (*The English Constitution*, 1867)

So may we imagine the critic of today saying: 'Thank God, *I* am not as the official; when *I* write I make my meaning plain; those miserable public functionaries only obscure theirs, if indeed they ever had any'. The critic may even be right—about the miserable functionary.

Though the spirit that still moves us to mock our officials may be healthy, the amusement can be overdone. One or two recent critics of so-called 'officialese' have indulged in it to excess, deriding without discrimination, putting in their pillory good as well as bad, sometimes even mistaking the inventions of other scoffers for monstrosities actually committed. That is regrettable. It is a curious fact that attempts to teach 'good English' often meet with resistance. Probably the explanation is that an exaggerated importance was for a long time given to things that do not greatly matter. The conviction still lingers that instruction in good English means having to learn highbrow rules of no practical usefulness. It will be no easy task to put the truth across that 'good English' consists less in observing grammatical pedantries than in a capacity to express oneself simply and neatly. Unfair criticism arouses reasonable resentment, and increases the difficulty of creating an atmosphere receptive of the new ideas. Even the notion that *officialese* in its derogatory sense is encouraged by authority has not wholly disappeared. The truth is, on the contrary, that great pains are now taken to train staffs to write clear and straightforward English. This may not always show in the results, but that is another thing.

It does not seem to me to be true to say that the language itself is in decay. Its grammatical and syntactical usages are carefully preserved, perhaps too carefully; but it is constantly being invited to assimilate new words, and seems capable of digesting many of them without any great harm, many indeed with profit. Some of the changes that have taken place in the meaning of words have weakened the language, but others have strengthened it, and on the whole there is no great cause for disquiet here. The language remains as fine and flexible an instrument as it was when used by Shakespeare and Bacon; in some respects it has been enriched. There are those alive today, and those recently dead, whose exact and delicate English would bear comparison with the outstanding writers of any generation. What is wrong is not the instrument itself but the way we use it. That should encourage us to hope that we may do better. When we are tempted to say that we have fallen away from the high standard of those who came before us, we must not forget the vast increase in the part played by the written word in our affairs. With such an increase in quantity it would be surprising if there were not some deterioration in quality. The field in which these faults are most readily noticed—the writings of officials for the guidance of the public—is relatively new. We cannot say whether the crop that grows there is better or worse than it was a hundred or more years ago, for no crop then grew there.

However unfair it may be that official English should have been singled out for derision, the fact has a significance that the official must not forget. Readers are on the lookout for tricks of style that they have been taught to expect from official writing. Shortcomings are magnified, and the difficulties that all writers have in affecting the reader precisely as they wish are for officials wantonly increased. So much the greater is the official's duty to try to convert *officialese* into a term of praise by cultivating unre-mittingly the clarity of thought and simplicity of expression that have always been preached by those who have studied the art of writing. Thus may we learn, after the centuries-old advice that heads this chapter, how, by speaking as plain people do, and think-ing as the wise, to make ourselves understood by all.

APPENDIX

Legal English cannot be pretty if it is to serve its purpose

A choice does sometimes have to be made between the simplicity that conveys a ready meaning and the elaboration necessary to a precise one. In Parliamentary Bills, Statutory Orders and other legal documents the choice is likely to be unavoidable. Those who are to be held irrevocably to meaning what they say must be very careful to say what they mean.

Eric Partridge slips into confusing what is unavoidable inelegance in legal English with the faults of the ordinary official, when, in *Usage and Abusage*, under the heading 'Officialese', he quotes from an article in a newspaper making fun of this extract from the Shops (Sunday Trading Restriction) Act, 1936:

> the following provisions of this Act shall extend only to shops, that is to say, those provisions of section six and section eight which relate to the approval by occupiers of shops of orders made under those sections, the provisions of paragraph (*e*) of subsection (1) of section seven and the provisions of paragraph (*e*) of section twelve.

If example were needed to show that legal language is not always elegant or luminous, these few lines would serve well enough. But that needs no proof; everyone knows it.*

Moreover with the whole Act before you (and you cannot expect to understand excerpts from it otherwise), the meaning conveyed by the quotation above is precise: it says unambiguously that certain provisions

---

* If all the commas are left out, as they are in *Usage and Abusage*, this passage is made to look even harder to understand than it really is.

of the Act apply to trading only in shops, and that all the others apply to trading not only in shops, but also in any place that is not a shop.

A real difficulty did arise over this Act, but not because of any obscurity in the words quoted by Partridge. The trouble was with the penumbra of meaning round the word *place* used in another section, to which this one refers. The court held that this penumbra was not as large as had been supposed. The person who drafted the Act had naturally assumed that, as it covered both sales in shops and sales in places that are not shops, its provisions were complete. But what of the stop-me-and-buy-one man? The Court held that the ice-cream vendor's tricycle is neither a shop nor a place, and that the bit of ground on which it happens to be standing is not a place either. Sales of ice cream from a tricycle were therefore outside both categories, and the seller escaped the meshes of the Act. This curious instance of the waywardness of words shows how hard it is for the drafters of Acts to foresee every possible path down which their choice of expression may lead the judicial mind. It also provides an illustration of the truth that legal ambiguities are caused more often by diction being over-simple than over-elaborate.

To illustrate the difference between ordinary phraseology that makes its meaning plain and legal phraseology that makes its meaning certain, let us take an example at random. I open the volume of Statutory Rules and Orders for 1945, and, turning over the pages until I find a short one, alight on the 'Rags (Wiping Rags) (Maximum Charges) (Amendment) Order'. In the summer of 1945, it appears, the President of the Board of Trade, moved perhaps by compassion for those who follow what must be a spiritually unsatisfying occupation, decided to increase the profit allowed for washing wiping rags. The Order effecting this (if we omit the common-form provisions about the Interpretation Act and the Short Title) runs as follows:

> The Rags (Wiping Rags) (Maximum Charges) Order 1943 (as amended) shall have effect as if in Article 1 thereof for the figure '8' where it occurs in the last line there were substituted the figure '11½'.

This by itself conveys no meaning at all to anybody. Because the same is true of so many Orders, instructions have been given to all departments that every Order submitted to Parliament must be accompanied by an explanatory memorandum. In this case the explanatory memorandum was:

> This Order permits launderers of wiping rages to add 11½ per cent to the charges they were making during the week beginning the 31st August, 1942, for such work.

That statement is immediately intelligible. Why was it not possible for the Order itself to be equally lucid? Because, although the explanatory memorandum is probably enough to tell most people all that they want to know, it is not precise enough to give unmistakable guidance in doubtful cases, or to support a prosecution for its breach. What is a 'wiping rag', and what are 'charges'? Both need definition, and both are elaborately defined in the original Order:

> (i) basic charge means in relation to services to which this Order applies,
> (*a*) the charge for such services in the ordinary course of the business in the course of which those services were being performed during the week beginning 31st August, 1942, in accordance with the method of charge then in being in relation to that business for performing such services; or
> (*b*) the charge made for such services in the ordinary course of a substantially similar business during the said week, in accordance with the method of charge then in being in relation to that business for performing such services;
> Provided that in any case in which a person who performs such services proves that such services were being performed in the course of his own business during the said week, 'basic charge' shall only have the meaning specified in sub-paragraph (*a*) of this paragraph.

'Rags' means any worn-out, disused, discarded or waste fabric or material made wholly or mainly from wool, cotton, silk, rayon or flax or from any mixture thereof.

'Wiping rags' means rags each one of which is not less than 144 square inches in size and has been trimmed and washed and is suitable for use as a wiping rag.

Why then, it may be asked, did the amending Order not repeat these definitions, and so make all clear? Because the definitions are so complicated that simply giving them again as amended (re-enactment of the Order) would have been far from making the meaning of the Order immediately clear. Research would have been necessary to find out what was old and what was new. If the whole of the old Order had been reprinted with the substitution of 11½ for 8, not only would there have been a waste of paper, but everyone would have had to look through both old and new Orders with minute attention, merely to discover in the end that the only change was in the figure. Moreover, the two volumes of Statutory Rules and Orders for 1945 already contain no fewer than 3,000 pages. No one would ask for more.

The reader may be provoked into thinking that the washing of wiping rags can hardly be worth even the lavishness of words that it already receives. But that is beside the point. The point is that the law, whatever it is about, must be certain; and if it is necessary for the law to concern itself with washing wiping rags, it must be no less certain here than anywhere else.

A well-meant attempt was made by the minister in charge of the Bill that became the Workmen's Compensation Act 1906 to make perfectly clear to ordinary people what sort of accidents gave rise to a right to compensation. He insisted on using the simple words 'arising out of and in the course of' the employment. But simplicity proved to have been bought at such a cost in precision that those words must have caused more litigation than any other eight words on the Statute Book. Halsbury's *Laws of England* takes more than thirty-eight pages to explain the phrase and cite the cases on it. One of them concerns a worker who suffered burns as a result of 'petrol used for cleaning greasy hands near stove': though the injury took place at work, how definitely could it be said to have arisen, in the simple words of the Act, 'out of and in the course of employment'?

Note. After Gowers had come under fire for this defence of inelegant legal English, he decided in a revision of his work, 'by way of redressing the balance a little', to cite a 1943 article from the *Spectator* that gave what he called a 'remarkable' example of the reaction that legal drafting could provoke in a reader:

> My attention has been called (I have just invented this service-able phrase) to Statutory Rules and Orders 1943 No. 1216, issued by the Ministry of Supply. You can buy it from the Stationery Office for a penny. Its operative clause runs thus:
>
> 1. The Control of Tins Cans Kegs Drums and Packaging Pails (No. 5) Order, 1942(*a*), as varied by the Control of Tins Cans Kegs Drums and Packaging Pails (No. 6) Order, 1942(*b*), the Control of Tins Cans Kegs Drums and Packaging Pails (No. 7) Order, 1942(*c*), the Control of Tin Cans Kegs Drums and Packaging Pails (No. 8) Order, 1942(*d*), and the Control of Tins Cans Kegs Drums and Packaging Pails (No. 9) Order, 1942(*e*), is hereby further varied in the Third Schedule thereto (which is printed at p. 2 of the printed (No. 6) Order), in 'Part II. Commodities other than Food', by substituting for the reference '2A' therein, the reference '2A(1)'; and by deleting therefrom the reference '2B'.
>
> This is excellent news, that will gladden the heart of every public-spirited citizen. Why the Ministry of Supply could not leave it at that is unimaginable. Jettisoning gratuitously the sound and time-honoured principle that a Government Department never explains, it adds—quite incredibly—an Explanatory Note, which reads:

The above Order enables tinplate to be used for tobacco and snuff tins other than cutter-lid tobacco tins.

What is to be said of this unwarrantable insult to the national intelligence? What kind of people do they think we are? Do they suppose we can't read plain English? ~

INDEX

Note.—Words discussed are shown in *italic*, and subjects, in roman type.